Irish Servicewomen in the Great War

Irish Servicewomen in the Great War

From Western Front to Roaring Twenties

Barbara Walsh

PEN & SWORD
HISTORY

First published in Great Britain in 2020 by
Pen & Sword History
An imprint of
Pen & Sword Books Ltd
Yorkshire – Philadelphia

Copyright © History Ireland, 2020

ISBN 978 1 52676 794 3

A CIP catalogue record for this book is
available from the British Library.

Printed and bound in the UK by TJ International Ltd,
Padstow, Cornwall.

Pen & Sword Books Limited incorporates the imprints of Atlas,
Archaeology, Aviation, Discovery, Family History, Fiction, History,
Maritime, Military, Military Classics, Politics, Select, Transport,
True Crime, Air World, Frontline Publishing, Leo Cooper, Remember
When, Seaforth Publishing, The Praetorian Press, Wharncliffe
Local History, Wharncliffe Transport, Wharncliffe True Crime
and White Owl.

For a complete list of Pen & Sword titles please contact

PEN & SWORD BOOKS LIMITED
47 Church Street, Barnsley, South Yorkshire, S70 2AS, England
E-mail: enquiries@pen-and-sword.co.uk
Website: www.pen-and-sword.co.uk

Or

PEN AND SWORD BOOKS
1950 Lawrence Rd, Havertown, PA 19083, USA
E-mail: Uspen-and-sword@casematepublishers.com
Website: www.penandswordbooks.com

Contents

List of Plates

Plate 1: A typical mixed draft of WAACs ready to embark for France.

Plate 2: The Signals telephonists at work on the Western Front from 1917 onwards included a number of Irishwomen. Note their special brassards/armbands worn by all male and female members of a Royal Engineers' Signal unit in France.

Plate 3: One of the many different recruitment posters.

Plate 4: WAAC clerical workers on duty in an ordnance office.

Plate 5: A camp's catering and cleaning workers line up for that day's orders, supervised by a forewoman.

Plate 6: Inspection parade by Chief Controller of the QMAAC, held in Dublin, 1918.

Plate 7: Faded images from the past. Matilda (Tillie) Nevin (second from left) and lifelong friend Marjorie Simmons with army pals in France.

Plate 8: The camp at Moore Park, Fermoy, County Cork, in 1917.

Plate 9: WAAC/QMAAC forewomen are lined up by an administrator.

Plate 10: The staff of the Rouen Signal office mustered for an inspection 1 September 1917 included several from Ireland with more to follow.

Plate 11: Attempts to make things homely included the creation of many similar WAAC camp gardens in army bases and depots.

Plate 12: The dormitory-style sleeping quarters in the huts were basic.

Plate 13: WAAC administrators from landed families in rural Ireland could always find a horse to ride on off-duty days.

Plate 14: No socializing rules broken: Signaller Mollie Crook (on the right) seen here with two pals from the Rouen Signals office, 1918.

Plate 15: A quayside in Rouen, home to the 3rd Echelon of GHQ.

List of Abbreviations

AA	Assistant Administrator
AC	Area Controller
AEF	American Expeditionary Forces
AG	Adjutant-General
A.G.11	Adjutant-General Department 11 (or XI)
ATS	Army Territorial Service
BEF	British Expeditionary Force
CC	Chief Controller
DAG	Deputy Adjutant-General
GHQ	General Headquarters British Army in France
GPO	General Post Office
IRA	Irish Republican Army
L of C	Lines of Communication
NHI	National Health Insurance
NCO	Non-Commissioned Officer
OC	Officer Commanding
OCA	(QMAAC) Old Comrades' Association
P&TCA	Postal and Telegraphs Clerks' Association (1914–1919)
QMAAC	Queen Mary's Army Auxiliary Corps
RE	Royal Engineers
RMS	Royal Mail Steamer
R of P	Restriction or Removal of Privileges
SOSBW	Society for the Oversea Settlement of British Women
UA	Unit Administrator
VAD	Voluntary Aid Detachment
WAAC	Woman's Army Auxiliary Corps
WRAF	Women's Royal Air Force
WRNS	Women's Royal Naval Service
WO	War Office

Acknowledgements

I must first convey my grateful thanks for wonderful advice and assistance provided by staff members and facilities at BT Heritage and Archives, the UK National Archives, National Army Museum and the Imperial War Museum. In addition, sincere appreciation is extended to the WRAC Association, Winchester, for permission to use extracts from their archived Old Comrades' Association gazettes. Acknowledgement for help is due also to the National Library of Ireland and the Kildare County Council Library and Arts Service in addition to the BBC Written Archive Centre, Reading, the Cupar Library Duncan Institute and the Royal Signals Museum, Dartford, the Library archives of Alexandra College, Dublin, State Library of Victoria, Melbourne, and the many other organizations providing heritage and local history information such as Geoff Allan, at the Isle of Wight Family History Society, and Jo White and Bev Hanson, from Eaglehawk Local Heritage Society, Australia, who responded to my request for help when this study commenced. To these must be added all the individuals and family descendants who have generously supplied life-stories and family histories that have been used. They include Jack and Douglas Flett, Bill Hanna, Betty Tyzzer and 'Genevieve', Ian Hart, Mary Hart, Simon Carter, Stephen Cockbill, Tim Dale, Peter Green, Genny Norris and David Oakley, and not forgetting many other descendants of WAAC members who kindly offered information and even photographs during the early stages of the research; it is a great pity that I cannot include all the wonderful accounts of their own individual family memories of grandmothers and grand-aunts, godmothers and cousins and I extend apologies to anyone who has been inadvertently omitted. I am extremely grateful to so many others, too, who were unfortunately unable to help but kindly responded to enquiries. Finally, the unstinted encouragement and help offered by my own extended family and many good friends from far and near has been much appreciated. To all this I can now add my sincere thanks and appreciation for the support, hard work and encouragement of Claire Hopkins, Laura Hirst, Chris Cocks and the team at Pen and Sword, who put great effort and enthusiasm into bringing this piece of history to light.

Barbara Walsh, 2020
www.barbarawalsh.com

Introduction

One hundred years ago, thousands of Irishwomen were returning home from serving in the Great War to discover that the contribution they had made to help end that conflict was being looked upon in much same way as the returning army servicemen, who were being by then reviled with contempt and even branded as traitorous.

Within two decades hostilities had returned. The Great War came to be known as the First World War and in recent years those negative viewpoints of the men who served have been fulsomely and graciously corrected. Likewise, the heroic Irish nurses and young women who joined the Red Cross and Voluntary Aid Detachments (VAD) in 1914–1918 to undertake the care of the wounded, often at great risk to themselves in war zones, have become generously acknowledged and written about, too. However, a similar level of well-publicized recognition for the hundreds of other Irishwomen who were equally brave and enterprising as enrolled members of the Women's Auxiliary Army Corps (WAAC) is long overdue within the historical record of twentieth-century Irishwomen.

Although later renamed in 1918 as Queen Mary's Army Auxiliary Corps (QMAAC), the acronym WAAC remained in popular use and the study will give it preference. Both forms will be used and, when it is felt appropriate for clarity, WAAC/QMAAC are combined. Two later established branches of the Corps, the Women's Royal Naval Service (WRNS) and the Women's Royal Air Force (WRAF), founded in 1918, are each worthy of a separate investigation into their Irish membership and, consequently, these two sectors will not be covered in the narrative, apart from an occasional passing reference.

The approach for this study will be to fill some gaping voids in the broader historiography of women's lives during the definitive final years of the First World War and early 1920s by placing a closer focus on the story of the Irish girls, drawn from every class, creed and ability who volunteered to enrol as members of the WAAC/QMAAC. By far, the largest majority worked as rank and file cooks, catering staff and cleaners, but there were also a great many office workers, such as clerks and typists and in high-tech telecommunication services. There were also onerous responsibilities as supervisory administrators – the WAAC version of commissioned officers – and all these tasks at every level of rank were carried out in army barracks, depots and camps across Ireland as well as in Scotland, England and Wales, in addition to serving in France. The period covered by the input of the WAAC/QMAAC spanned from 1917 until their official disbandment in late September 1921. For all members of the Corps those service years 1917–1919 were to create long-lasting friendships with former army colleagues from every region of these islands. The study widens its sphere of interest when the narrative moves on to greet the arrival of the following decade's 'Roaring Twenties'. The variety of experiences that their postwar lives introduced included greater assertiveness, new careers, and migration to discover new lifestyles as settlers in Canada, Australia and elsewhere.

In presenting this story of the Irish membership of the WAAC and their postwar lives, it is hoped to set the focus more closely on the voices of the often-up-to-now silent rank and file members, so that they be allowed to emerge from the deep shadows of long neglect to take their rightful place beside all other female volunteers of the First World War. In addition, the narrative will aim to broaden the platform for further investigative work. Well over 400 army service records for Irish recruits have been scrutinized – the majority of which being Irish-born recruits – although a significant number of young women from England, Scotland and Wales have been also included in this story in order to display the heterogeneous structure of the Corps and to provide useful compare/ contrast viewpoints. There will be gaps left that still need to be filled, more questions to be asked and more satisfying answers to be found.

Particular attention will be drawn to the Irish members of one rather special, if small sector of the WAAC whose work within telecommunications was carried out side by side with male army colleagues in Signal units. Their responsibilities entailed keeping the crucial military lines of communication operational and secure on the Western Front – a key factor which contributed to the final successful outcome of the war. Afterwards, largely air-brushed out of the official historical narrative and thus forgotten, these skilled women telegraphists and telephonists, trained in Morse and technically adept in what was then fast-changing 'modern' technology, were all employees of the General Post Office. Each girl had volunteered to be seconded to the Royal Engineers in 1917 and their ranks included young women who had worked in GPO exchanges in every corner of Ireland.

No hard 'be-all and end-all' final conclusions can be aimed at in this study. Instead, it is hoped that the narrative will encourage others to dig deeper into local history and family archives to widen the picture. With more accessible digitized archives and online sources which can be shared by researchers and scholars, there will be opportunities to expand and refine the findings as a fruitful field of study. By doing so, it is hoped progress might be made to broaden our understanding of the era that bridged the end of the First World War and early years of the next decade. There are alternative viewpoints to uncover and discuss and, if a fresh balance of knowledge can be achieved, it will be of some use to create greater understanding of those turbulent times.

Full-scale demobilization of all servicemen and servicewomen had commenced in 1919 and the first four chapters look back to the events in Ireland and elsewhere from 1917–1918. The organization of a woman's auxiliary army, recruiting campaigns, rules and regulations, camp life and cheerful camaraderie of the Irish, English Scottish and Welsh girls were not without hardship and dangers for those serving in France. The following two chapters then move on to reveal the story of hitherto neglected essential work of the 'Signallers' in army bases near the front line. The difficult negotiations over that sector's pay and conditions which led to background wrangles and subsequent dismay over the ranking status given to their senior personnel members were all matters that had relevance for employees of Irish post offices who were now in uniform. The chapters to follow cover events up to and beyond the Armistice to describe both lighter and darker moments until the dispersals from army life commenced.

From that time on elements of disappointment make an appearance. Rights for women in the workplace are being raised. There is a lack of work, and branches of the Women's Corps' own 'Old Comrades' Association' are founded both at home and overseas to help provide support for their former members. Interesting emigration opportunities are opening up such as the schemes for assisted free passages to Canada and Australia, while at home in Ireland, political events begin to accelerate the changes taking place within society for those returning war veterans. In one chapter, the narrative compares and contrasts the lives of four women who married ex-servicemen: two couples who migrated to Australia as settlers and two who remained as homemakers in their own country. The final chapter describes how Irish ex-WAAC friends marked Armistice Remembrance Days in Dublin in the decades leading up to the outbreak of the Second World War. For women in Ireland conflict in the wider world was destined to once more bring significant changes to many lives.

It is hoped this study will open up opportunities for further research so that a greater appreciation of the women of those bygone days can be rightly celebrated.

Chapter 1

A British Army Corps of Women in Ireland?

'The story of the WAAC is a perfect paradigm of the prejudices, preconceptions, and preoccupations which rise to the surface when there is any question of integrating women into some particular aspect of a man's world.'

Marwick[1]

In October 1919, an important letter from London was delivered to the Dublin-based headquarters of the Queen Mary's Army Auxiliary Corps (QMAAC), founded just two years earlier as the British Army's Women's Army Auxiliary Corps (WAAC).[2] The contents of the letter confirmed that the discharge – aka demobilization – of sixty-two more Irish members of the Corps attached to the Irish Command who were awaiting the termination of their engagement had been approved.[3] The girls on the list included office clerks, hostel forewomen, cooks and catering workers whose agreed length of service in a number of army garrisons and barracks around Ireland had ended.

Who were these young women? What was this army corps doing in Dublin and why had so many Irishwomen been keen to come forward to serve 'for the duration of the war' or longer? More familiarly always called the 'WAAC' in preference to their later, more formalized title, these girls were drawn from families of every class, creed and background across all thirty-two counties of Ireland, and had shared a wide spectrum of skills and talents. What had driven them to volunteer?

The answer lies in the ravages the terrible conflict the First World War had inflicted upon the thousands upon thousands of families who had lost sons, brothers, husbands and other relatives on the Western Front in France, Flanders and elsewhere. By 1917, many hundreds more of the country's young men were still being killed or injured on the battlefields and there is plenty of evidence to show how members of their families –

their sisters, cousins and, on occasion, their wives – came forward in their droves to join this new women's army corps with the aim of helping to bring an end to the campaign's horrific sacrifice of lives cut short before their time.

To what extent were the girls in uniform allocated to army garrisons, barracks and camps across the whole of Ireland? Surviving records reveal that not only were female army auxiliary recruits posted to fill several different categories of work within military installations in almost every location where there was an army presence in Ireland – but that they were also sent off to serve in a variety of locations in England as well as being posted to sensitive security sectors of the British Expeditionary Force (BEF) bases on the Western Front. All in all, Irishwomen's overall involvement in the push to end the war was not at all inconsequential.

The largest deployments of WAAC/QMAAC women were those who were sent to serve in Dublin and Cork, but their presence is very evident in a number of the other locations such as Ballyshannon, Belfast, Cahir, Cork, Fermoy, Kilkenny, Tipperary and Templemore. By the end of 1918, the city of Dublin itself held by far the greatest concentration spread across a number of Irish Command's barracks and depots which soon prompted one newspaper reporter writing on women's dress codes to comment favourably on these army women's 'khaki uniforms and hats [which were] now familiar sights in Dublin', adding the quip that 'few will dispute the becomingness of this official apparel'.[4]

Yet, within a few years, the historical memory of the activities of the WAAC/QMAAC in Ireland from 1917–1919 was destined to fade into oblivion, due to the political and social impact of the new Free State which understandably took precedence in how history was recorded and cherished. Only in recent times is it being acknowledged that the contribution of the men and women from Ireland who served with the British Army in the Great War was both brave and generous.

It was to be several months after the Armistice of November 1918 before the demobilization of all army service personnel began to gather greater momentum. By then the task of winding down activities at women's corps' Dublin HQ had become an integral part of a slow and carefully structured reduction of its membership which aimed to hold onto only those whose work was still needed for a range of supportive services. For a great many girls, their contribution would not finish until the very end of 1919 or early in January 1920, for there was plenty of work which remained to be done. The army had a mountain of paperwork which still awaited those who had served as the army's backroom clerks, office workers and record-keepers and the recruitment of newcomers was to continue right up to the very end.

In France, the military firmly held on to their WAAC telecommunication girls who were attached to the Royal Engineers (RE) Signal units at all main bases and general headquarters (GHQ) for as long as they could after the war. The role of these women had been key to the efficient movement of troops and equipment and the main bulk of that sector of the WAAC, who became known informally as the 'Signallers', would not leave their posts in Europe until October 1919. A few small sectors of the WAAC remained for other duties up to September 1921.

The winding-down of the corps was well underway by 21 August 1919. On that day, the War Office (WO) in London issued a press release, published in *The Times* newspaper, which announced that '20,000 members of the WAAC have been demobilized since the Armistice and between 300 and 400 are being released every week'. There was a very necessary caveat to be added to that statement, however, because 'Those who are still retained in France are fully engaged in the work of clearing up, and some time must necessarily elapse before all of them can be set free'. At that time it was thought that the total strength of the Corps by the end of the war had numbered about 41,000 women but this is a very much underestimated figure. Later calculations put the number of WAAC/QMAAC to have been as high as 57,000 members, of which, perhaps, up to 9,000 served in France and Flanders from 1917 onwards.[5]

A month later, another War Office press release announcing further demobilizations took care to add what sounded like a reassuring statement: 'Any woman who has definite work awaiting her is released at once.' It should be borne in mind, nonetheless, that secure postwar work for women everywhere was not going to be easy to find, especially for those former members of the Corps who returned home to Ireland.

A British army corps for women?[6]
Two years earlier, the introduction of the first Irish-based units of the WAAC in mid-summer 1917 had come at a time of great change within military circles. By the end of 1916, a serious setback for those in charge

of the BEF campaign in France and Flanders had emerged over the now-dangerous shortage of men on the Western Front. As the war dragged on into a third year, it was becoming more of a problem that thousands of fit, well-trained soldiers were being held back from active service not only to undertake catering and cleaning duties at camps and base depots, but to engage in routine desk work such as essential clerical record-keeping activity and storekeeping. By the autumn of 1916 it was clear something would have to be done to free up combat-ready troops for the final push to end the war.

One of the most crucial areas where help was needed had come about because of the army's increasing reliance on the use of telecommunication technology for conveying tactical orders and controls. By 1916, the bases behind the lines were handling huge volumes of wire-borne traffic and a serious shortage of experienced personnel capable of operating upgraded military telephone and telegram exchanges had arisen.

VADs and others from Ireland helped to lead the way

Since the start of the war in 1914, there had been a huge amount of women's entirely voluntary charitable help already supplying essential support. Known as Voluntary Aid Detachment (VAD) groups, Irishwomen had come forward as willingly as their sisters in England, Scotland and Wales to provide the army with hospital nursing care, ambulance services and canteen facilities for troops at home and abroad. These VADs – whose work should not be confused with that of the 1917-founded WAAC – were led by upper-class and professional women who had recruited members from the Women's Legion, former suffragette organizations and similar bodies. There was a simultaneous reliance being placed on women workers in the industrial cities of England who were being urged to fill the gaps left by the departure of the male workforce in factories and public transport services. Their contribution undoubtedly provided welcome assistance – but it was recognized that all these efforts were working independently, and questions were being raised within military and governmental circles as to what additional, more coordinated war-work might willing women be safely asked to undertake.

One of the first scholarly studies to be carried out by a historian, Arthur Marwick, many years later, which aimed to put focus on the war work of women, took care to point out that attitudes were being profoundly affected by a change of government in London at that time. In December 1916, Lloyd George had taken over the leadership of the parliamentary coalition and, as Marwick observes, the new government's influence 'marked a definitive stage towards direct State control of all aspects of the war effort'.[7]

Within military circles, it was being increasingly, if reluctantly, accepted that while the supportive work of the VADs in caring for wounded troops was useful and important, what the War Office really needed to set up was their own strictly controllable signed-up Woman's Auxiliary Army Corps (WAAC), with a separate command structure, whose rank and file could be ordered to undertake a diversity of necessary supportive tasks.

There was, nonetheless, a disturbing drawback to all this planning. Everyone was aware of a proliferation of women's quasi-militaristic organizations in recent years, most of which shared the disturbing common aim of 'taking up arms' in defence of their homeland.[8] For many onlookers, the sight of uniformed women in khaki, marching, saluting each other and behaving as soldiers was received with huge disapproval.[9] Could any of these pseudo-military organizations be safely absorbed into this proposed women's army? Public opinion in England was largely negative and it was a situation that was even more acutely sensitive in Ireland, which had witnessed the foundations of two determinedly paramilitary groups, the Republican women's Cumann na mBan and the Ulster Women's Rifle Corps, which was loosely attached to the Ulster Women's Unionist Council (UWUC).[10] The impact being made by all these clearly determined women on the deeply entrenched mindset of military men conjured up the need to be very, very wary.

Very soon the scene was set. The War Office and army chiefs of staff invited the leaders of these women's groups to join forces with a few well-connected professional ladies who were well known to them, if not already closely related by kinship tie to military families. Might they be trusted to take charge of a new women's corps under the direction of the Army Council? To implement this decision, the War Office set up a new section of the Adjutant-General's department called A.G.11 to work closely with the WAAC on all matters.[11] It was agreed that thousands of young women could be put to good use under their command as uniformed

WAACs to replace men as cooks, waitresses and domestic staff in army bases and depots on the Western Front. There were also assignments that could be filled if the army enrolled more girls with experience as office workers, typists and storekeepers for the increasing volumes of routine military record-keeping and filing. A number of well-trained women clerks who had secured much valued positions as dedicated civil servants in government-run offices were already being usefully deployed to help with clerical tasks in London and, in addition, it was thought that many more young women from more privileged family backgrounds who had learned how to drive a motor vehicle – or had dabbled in early aviation as a hobby – could be further encouraged to sign up as either motorbike despatch riders, aircraft maintenance mechanics, or drivers for senior officers' staff cars. As might be expected, a number of Irishwomen did come forward to work in these capacities, as shall be shown.

Finally, in a move that was of crucial importance in the midst of all this activity, an even more innovative suggestion was being mooted. Could a unique contingent of women be engaged 'on loan' from the General Post Office (GPO) and given the responsibility of helping to ensure the efficient functioning of military telegraph and telephone Signal units being run by the Royal Engineers' Lines of Communication (L of C)? It was a daring idea. On a day-to-day basis as enrolled members of the WAAC, these GPO women would be sharing duty rosters and responsibilities with similarly skilled male army colleagues. They would be given the capacity to hear the private discussions and secret messages that passed between army commanders and their duties included the constant monitoring of the military orders 'coming down the wire' from the front by telegraphed Morse code. A rare privilege. Although army campaign strategies had been slow to modernize at first, the fast-changing techniques of that era's warfare was facing increasingly huge reliance on these often still-experimental L of C telecommunications networks. It was clear to the more forward-looking military minds that here lay a key to the British Army's eventual success or failure. As for the personnel working in Signal units, military research has shown 'it was beyond doubt that official recognition of the Signal Service and established Communications was an indispensable element of Command and Control'.[12]

By the end of 1916 the problem of finding enough personnel for the use of the L of C had become crucial. Since 1914 the British Post Office had already called on thousands of its male employees – including many Irishmen – to volunteer for service with the Signal units in France and Flanders. The nature of their work at the front was often dangerous and the consequent loss of these skilled workers in the trenches and other frontline sectors had been high.

With casualties still rising, it was increasingly difficult for the army to find enough competent staff capable of handling all the telegraph and telephone traffic in the base exchanges further back behind the lines. After two years of warfare, the Post Office was itself bereft of suitably qualified men they could release for military use.

A letter sent by the Director of Signals, the then Brigadier-General John Sharman Fowler, to the Postmaster General had been unequivocal. He had studied the situation and repeated the message being received from France which confirmed that for those responsible for the security and efficiency of the L of C., an untenable crisis was looming unless they took drastic action. Christmas 1916 was fast approaching. There was need for urgent action and he wanted to discover if any arrangement to allow some of the GPO's best female operators to be sent over to France might be tried out?[13] The suggestion was soon being investigated.

By April, approval had been received for the Royal Engineers to have a tiny, but important new section of WAAC attached to the Signal units. Their work would be undertaken under particularly stringent conditions.

The call for girls who were technically adept Post Office telephone operators and telegraphists received an eager response from young women in many different exchanges. Recruits had come forward from all over England, Scotland and Wales as well as from Ireland.

Before the scheme could begin, an amount of upgrading to improve the equipment they would use was needed and careful billeting arrangements were required, too, as it was extremely important these volunteers were kept largely apart from other WAAC members for the reason that the work included 'high security' elements.

Their former rigorous GPO training had, of course, given those Post Office employees enormous astuteness and understanding of that era's telecommunication systems far beyond the ken of anyone – either male or female – who had never previously worked in this fast-changing techno-driven sector. Consequently, these selected members of the Corps would be allowed the privilege of wearing uniforms which shared exactly the same identifiable blue and white armbands (military brassards) as those being worn by the Royal Engineers male colleagues who were serving beside them in army 'Signals'. The concession implied they enjoyed a more uniquely egalitarian status not found in other army units which is a factor many historians have since later failed to recognize as bearing implications far beyond its time and place. That specially separated existence was to become one that was to be well regarded by the highest-ranking officers of the Corps and there will be more to say about the 'Signallers' in later chapters.

It may be added here that the Director of the Army Signal Service, the soon-to-be-promoted to major-general John Fowler, was an Irishman from a family in Rahinstown, near Summerhill, Meath, and an extremely talented engineer with a distinguished army career in India. John Fowler also held a veterinary qualification and certificates from the School of Musketry; his well-know and well-respected family continued to live in Rahinstown for many decades to come.

The publicity drive to recruit women

Publicity for the broader recruiting drive for the Women's Army Auxiliary Corps commenced on 28 February 1917. On that day, a column in the London *Times* newspaper carried the headline: 'Women's War Work in France: Posts to be filled'. Elsewhere, there were similar newspaper announcements. A distribution of recruitment posters was received enthusiastically. Applications came pouring in and within a month the first fourteen WAAC to go 'overseas' had been assigned to work as cooks and waitresses for the officers' mess at the Abbeville base in France. Wider interest soon gathered and evidence reveals that enquiries started to be received from Irish girls from every walk of life, education and ability as early as March and April.

It was soon being seriously considered by the War Office that the WAAC need not be confined to working in bases in France and Flanders, but could be also usefully employed in catering and clerical posts in many of the army depots and camps across the UK, too. It was arranged for a

WAAC Controller to be appointed to each of the British Army's home commands in addition to 'where necessary, a deputy controller to each area'.[14]

Only one sector of WAAC employment had been slow to implement their recruitment plans because, by contrast to catering and clerical work, quite an amount of preliminary investigation and preparation was needed before an intake of technically trained Post Office women could be negotiated.

Ruled by Army Council instructions

To formally set out the first official conditions under which recruits would serve, Army Council Instruction No. 537 of 1917 was issued on 28 March 1917. Assuming the women would only be needed to work in the BEF bases, the document set out just six separate sectors for tasks women could undertake:

- 'A' Clerical. Typists, shorthand typists
- 'B' Cooks, waitresses and domestic staff
- 'C' Motor transport staff
- 'D' Storehouse women, checkers and unskilled labour
- 'E' Telephone and Postal Services
- 'F' Miscellaneous services which do not fall within any of the above
- An additional category was added by 1 June 1918: 'G' Technical Employment (Mechanical Section)

There was also another section engaged in top-secret cryptanalysis who were attached to Army Intelligence. They became known as the 'Hush-WAACs' who were rarely spoken of publicly until decades later. (See Table 1 in Appendix I)

By mid-July 1917 as a result of WAAC activities showing signs of being widened far beyond their original arena of support, the Ministry of Labour was soon involved in the recruiting drive, which meant the direct engagement of local employment exchanges throughout England, Scotland, Wales and Ireland.

Pay and conditions

In due course, an increasing number of alterations to the terms and conditions and pay rates for 'home service' and other sections were felt to be desirable and throughout the rest of 1917 a number of changes were made and at least five versions were issued as a new 'Regulation' by the Army Council.[15] Eventually, on 1 June 1918, by then well over a year following their foundation, the final, definitive Army Council Instruction No. 652 of 1 June 1918 was issued to replace all those earlier versions and added appendices. It constituted a formidable document of clauses and sub-clauses which set out the finer details of how the Corps was to be run.[16]

The slow process to devolve a structure which could deal adequately with the remuneration of personnel within the women's Corps had not been an easy task and it must be said that some of the decisions en route did not bode well for a frictionless future. A legacy of contentious issues was about to emerge.

Throughout 1917 – much to the army's displeasure – the pay and conditions being offered to young women began to receive increasing scrutiny by several UK employees' unions.[17] As fears arose within military circles it was soon known that 'the Adjutant-General Sir Neville Mcready was most anxious that women could be treated exactly as soldiers in order to make sure there was no trade union influence over them.[18] It was to be a frustrating aspiration. The chiefs of staff, powerful as they were, could not always gain success and it was not long, for instance, before the National Union of Printing and Paper Workers began to instigate arguments over pay scales for their trained women printers who were being sought to volunteer for work in the army. The outcome of that particular dispute was that 'the War Office was compelled to offer competitive wages'.[19]

Notably, British Post Office officials were by that time also embroiled in a series of long, drawn-out wrangles over the pay scales and hours of work for their telegraphists and telephonists who were to be seconded to the Royal Engineers for work in France These negotiations and other contentious issues in relation to the ranking status of senior Post Office women within the hierarchy of the Corps will be addressed more fully in chapters 5 and 6 of this study.

Ranks and titles

One point to note is that when initiating the concept of an army corps made up entirely of women, the War Office had insisted that no military titles were to be given to any member of this new women's auxiliary army service, although eventually by 1918, according to historian Charles Messenger, between themselves the women had begun 'to being referred to by their ranks, rather than by Miss or Mrs', adding, 'and saluting became commonplace'.[20]

Nonetheless, in setting out the protocols of ranking divisions there was a clear intent to keep that era's divisions of social class intact. The girls who enrolled as 'Workers and Forewomen' all received the Corps' military-style army numbers in exactly the same way as soldiers enlisting as privates or NCOs in a British regiment. By contrast, the other young women who were chosen to supervise them as WAAC 'Officials' were not given army numbers, but merely kept their individual civilian social titles, e.g. 'Miss', 'Mrs', 'Honourable' and so on and the creation of a clear social divide between the 'Officials' and lower ranks would seem to have been the primary aim of this protocol. These 'Officials' aka 'Officers' held titles and privileges which created defined levels of command, respect and responsibility. The top post was designated as a Chief Controller (CC) whose rank was equivalent that that of a military major-general.[21] She was assisted by a Deputy or Assistant Controller, although the structure of that arrangement was soon destined to be doubled by creating two Controllers, one with responsibilities for London and the UK, and the other for WAAC activities in France. Staff who served under them with equivalent levels of status as army officers held posts as Area Controllers which roughly equalled the rank of colonel, supported by a number of Unit Administrators and Assistant Administrators, all of whom operated as subordinate commissioned officers. However, it has to be said that the refusal of the Army Council to allow these ranks to use the same male military titles and badges as their male colleagues had been deeply disappointing and difficult for the new Corps' leadership to accept.[22]

How many Irishwomen served? Uncovering the evidence

One of the most serious drawbacks faced by all who aim to gather knowledge is that archives holding most of higher-ranking WAAC records were destroyed in a German bombing raid on London in the Second World War. There are only around 7,000 surviving army service files – 12.3 per cent of the 57,000 who served – but the existence of the WW1 Service Medal and Award Rolls 1914–1920 is useful for identifying those who served in France. There are additional accurate sources, too, such as the information to be found in the circulation of newsletters for members of the Corps' own Old Comrades' Association which contain references to members' postings and backgrounds. Similar information can be gathered from Post Office (now British Telecom) archives and old in-house employee publications which often provide missing details for hitherto unidentifiable WAAC members. A comprehensive outline of the Old Comrades' Association', its foundation and work is provided within Samantha Philo-Gill's quite recent work. (See bibliography)

When applications began to be accepted in March 1917, Irish girls were among the first to come forward and those deployed in France from an early date included two Irish-born shorthand typists.[23] Catering and domestic workers of all kinds were taken on for work in the BEF bases as well as ledger and records clerks, and others willing to take responsible supervisory roles. Distinct patterns emerge which leave a strong impression that the proportion of workers and specific skills they brought matched up well to the number of enrolments that were taking place in other regions with similar population sizes – such as Scotland or Wales or Northern England. Table 2 in Appendix I provides an analysis of 411 members of the WAAC who have been identified as Irish-born and whose category of work and postings are known.

The calculations show that 65.8 per cent were 'B' workers recruited to prepare, cook and serve army mess food, and to carry out laundry work and other domestic tasks. The next largest category at 24.8 per cent consists of the WAAC classified as 'A' who were clerical workers, typists, shorthand typists and telephone clerks. The signallers, who were all GPO women restricted to serving only 'overseas', i.e. in BEF Royal Engineers' Signal units, accounts for 5.8 per cent – and they present a small but significant portion of the Irishwomen who can be distinctly identified as having worked in France. The remaining balance is made up of forewomen or administrators, whose postings are less easy to identify because so few of these higher graded women's army service files have survived. At least twelve more administrators are known to have been drawn from Ireland, but the location of their army postings – whether in the 'home service' or 'overseas' remains a mystery.

The WAAC offered a choice of where to serve

Every entrant on enrolment was asked if she would agree to work on the basis of serving 'at home and overseas', but there was also the option of choosing to remain posted solely 'at home' – and it would seem that Irish recruits mostly preferred the latter option, although it might be reminded that this term included locations in England and Wales, too.

Girl who opted to serve solely 'at home' could be deemed 'mobile' (in other words they could be sent off to work in any army installation where they might be needed), or they could chose to remain 'immobile', i.e. employed only close to their homes. In the case of the latter they might also be allowed to remain living at home. There was one important exception to this rule – which was applied to any of the young women recruited or promoted to positions within the Corps' higher status as an 'Official' (a commissioned officer rank). Before being accepted for an induction training course to be appointed as an 'Administrator', these women had to be prepared to agree to serve in all locations, wherever needed and could not refuse to be sent 'overseas' to France.

Non-denominational and non-political

From the start, the professional women who founded the Corps had adopted a non-denominational and non-political stance in line with military protocols. So whether recruits came from England, Scotland, Wales or Ireland, one of the first lessons these young women had to learn was how to get along with army colleagues from a wide variety of different home, regional and cultural environments and, in this respect, some of the most fortunate recruits were the professional telecommunication employees of the Post Office segregated into the 'E' category, who, in their civilian lives, were already accustomed to functioning under the same aegis as their work colleagues, no matter from which region of these islands they hailed from.

When recruiting got underway the very first enrolments for their higher-ranking officers were all processed by the WAAC in London. Receiving and distribution depots were swiftly put in place for rank and file and everything was run on the same lines as established army traditions.

The logistics of organizing a fast-growing army of women needed skilful planning and smooth-running routines. By mid-summer in that first year of their existence most WAAC units attached to the army's regional commands were operational. They sent regular reports back to the Corps' London HQ, but otherwise undertook the selection and deployment of staff, with the assistance and direct involvement of the employment exchanges in their assigned areas. The English Northern Command was based in York, the Western Command in Chester, the Southern Command in Salisbury, and the city of Edinburgh was home to the Scottish Command, and so on.[24] There was also a training centre at the large army camp in Aldershot, a section of which had been taken over by the WAAC to be run as the 'Aldershot Dispersal Depot'. The Irish Reception and Dispersal Depots, albeit rather slower to get going, as will be shown, ran affairs for the whole of Ireland from their Dublin HQ.

A fit person to be trusted?
The young women wishing to enrol had to give the names of at least two, and sometimes three, reputable people from whom character references could be supplied and this process for application was soon being handled by local labour exchanges who then passed on the documentation to the various regional WAAC recruitment units so that medical examinations and other formalities could be completed. For girls who were offering to work as 'clerks, typists, or like occupations', referees were required to answer one particularly important question under clause four: 'Is the applicant to your knowledge a fit person to be trusted with access to document of a confidential nature?' It was a salient point for anyone being asked to confirm the reliability of a recruit from Ireland where the struggle to define the political path ahead was still in flux. It is an issue that will be returned to.

The only exceptions to the procedure of filtering new entrants through the labour exchanges were for the young women who were drawn from the Post Office or directly transferred to the army from one of the other government-run Civil Service departments. These recruits needed no independent references having been already constrained as civilians by an oath of allegiance under the Official Secrets legislation. All these women were considered to be 'on loan' to the army and their initial selection had been dealt with within their own organizations by their individual department manager or postmaster who had the responsibility of confirming approval for the volunteers who came forward. In making those selections, a great deal of care was taken to pick candidates who were felt were most suitable. The criteria imposed on Post Office staff members who offered to serve required them to be not only extremely experienced and reliable employees but it was desirable that they had a knowledge of the French language. It is very noticeable that young women from several of the largest Irish post offices in Ireland feature among some of earliest drafts of WAAC 'Signallers' aka telecommunication workers to be despatched 'overseas' to the Royal Engineers L of C in Signal units on the Western Front.

When dealing with recruits for all the other tasks for which 'workers' were needed, newcomers who opted for serving only 'at home' were held for a while under the watchful eye of their hostel forewomen and local administrator to assess their abilities, before being despatched to work in garrisons and barracks all over Ireland. Apart from cooks, or waitresses and other catering staff including cleaners, large numbers of WAACs who could undertake office work were needed. Those who were allocated work as 'Filing' and 'Ledger' clerks or as 'Shorthand Typists' were distributed across a number of Irish locations in addition to being posted to army installations in England where they would fill similar rolls. Candidates who showed potential or who already had experience in senior positions often gained positions or later promotion to act as hostel forewomen, either in Ireland or in one of the other regional commands. There was a process, too, which allowed for even higher promotion – a full commission to the rank of an 'official' which could be gained following a recommendation and a short training course. An appropriate supervisory job equal to that of a junior officer in the army would follow. The bases in France each had their own area and unit administrators aided by a staff of assistant administrators. Soon up and running efficiently, the Corps thus formed a tightly structured, self-governed organization, under the rigorous command of its own hierarchy. In the background, however, it was the War Office, the Army Council and the military generals who had the final say in most of the decisions being made.

Joining up

An application to join the Corps was a careful process for candidates at every level of rank, and the procedure was the very same for Irishwomen as for the recruits from elsewhere. In those first few weeks and months before the Irish units had come into being in Dublin, applicants with Irish addresses were enrolled in a number of English – or even sometimes Scottish – depots. There were many instances of young women applying for the more senior positions relying on a recommendation by word of mouth through an army family connection or from one of the existing voluntary women's organizations already engaged in war work. If deemed suitable and subsequently called-up to attend a reception depot, it was usually arranged that each new applicant would be first instructed in what would be expected of her before she formally signed up. Further assessments might be made before she was allowed to commit herself as a member of the Corps. For many, the step they were taking was to be a life-changing occasion.

Many freedoms had to be sacrificed. There would be stringent army rules and regulations to abide by, accompanied by an enforced daily regime and discipline. In due course, the formal enrolment ceremony and protocol of that occasion would have emphasized the seriousness of the commitment each girl was taking. Once enrolled, there would be no turning back.

One of these ceremonial occasions was later described by a young woman who had been recruited as a records clerk for Army GHQ in France and her account provides a most evocative picture of the seriousness attached to these young women's commitment – and their consequent genuine apprehension over the step they were taking, writing that

A grave faced Colonel came one day and conducted the ceremony of our formal enrolment. He sat at a small table [with] our Unit Administrator sitting beside him, and one by one we passed before them as our names were called. It was a rather a solemn business, this complete surrender of our personal liberty, and even the most frivolous of us felt momentarily awed. We had to sign our undertaking to submit to army discipline no matter what might be required of us, and before the document was finally blotted and put away, the question was put to each recruit: 'Would you like to make any change in what you have just signed?' A few took this opportunity of backing out again, but not many. The faint-hearted ones slunk away with averted eyes, to rejoin their comfortable homes the next day.[25]

Recruitment numbers dropped back in 1918 – except in Ireland
By the start of 1918 in England, Wales and Scotland, the overall recruitment volumes were to subsequently ebb to a far more uneven response and by that time a sense of greater urgency must have gathered in Dublin. The initial setting-up of recruitment facilities for Ireland had been slow. Would-be Irish recruits had often made their own way to other depots in England or Scotland to enrol or, if already working there, had signed up at their local labour exchanges in, say, Manchester, Doncaster or London and it was at that precise point that recruitment started to be stepped up considerably in Ireland.

Chapter 2

Setting Up Under the Irish Command

There's to be a family wedding,
But I guess I won't be there,
For I've gone and joined the Army,
And I might be anywhere.

I. Grindlay[1]

Publicity for the establishment of the Corps in Dublin was launched by a piece in *The Irish Times* on 26 July 1917, which announced that 'Local Labour Exchanges will register recruits', accompanied by the news of the arrival of a senior WAAC controller, who had been sent over to help seek out suitable buildings to use for depots and hostels:

> Miss [Hilda] Horniblow, Deputy Controller of the Corps has been recently inspecting buildings with a view to the establishment of hostels if suitable accommodation can be obtained. A selection committee will be established by the War Office, and it will be their duty to interview candidates and adjudge their fitness.

Four days later, a leader writer in *The Irish Times* newspaper expanded on the topic by announcing that '5,000 women were already in khaki' in England and that a large hostel was to be opened in Dublin for the training of women for service at home and in France. Clearly enthusiastic, he endorsed the concept of a training depot as one that 'will be welcome to many Irishwomen who have looked for the opportunity of "doing something for the war"'. The piece goes on to extol the idea by suggesting that joining the Corps provided the means of 'obtaining a useful occupation' but that that 'physical fitness was imperative and a good character essential'. Suitable training was promised, the scale of pay was adequate – even liberal – when the provision of quarters and rations were taken into account. 'Women who have taken up this work speak in glowing terms of their experience' and, as if to hammer home the positivity of the message, the editor sums up the appeal as being 'national work of the most necessary and honourable kind'.

A week earlier a report had been issued in London which claimed that '574 Irishwoman had enrolled with the WAAC, making up 2.4 per cent of enrolments by that date'.[2] That number was to rise substantially. The Controller for Ireland was soon to have a dedicated recruiting unit. It was charged with the task of supplying personnel for all the army garrisons and barracks in Ireland as well as additional and much-needed office and catering staff who could be sent to several army locations in England and to BEF bases in France and Flanders.

As elsewhere, recruitment of rank and file from Ireland aimed to coordinate the processing of new applications through a number of selected local employment exchanges in each of the provinces. If a girl's references and subsequent interview fulfilled requirements, she would be then called up so that she could be given army medical checks. Those found fit enough were then to go to the main 'Receiving Depot' in Belfast to be signed in, supplied with uniforms and some rudimentary training before being despatched to wherever they were needed.

The WAAC HQ in London must have felt that it was a great advantage to have the services of a 39-year-old Dublin woman, St. Clair Frances Swanzy, whose home address was in Coolock.[3] She had been one of the first Irishwomen to come forward to enrol in London for a clerical position 'at home'. Her offer to help had come in to them within a few weeks of their foundation in March and by mid-May, Miss Swanzy had travelled to London. Promotion within the Corps came swiftly.

The daughter of a Dublin ophthalmic surgeon, Sir Henry Rosborough, St. Clair was the elder sister of the now renowned modernist artist, Mary Swanzy, and the family was well known within the social circuit of London life. With such impeccable references the Corps almost immediately decided to take St. Claire on as an assistant controller of the London Clerical Section. Within a month, following the subsequent announcement that recruitments were to be handled by the Ministry of Labour via local labour exchanges, Miss Swanzy's posting was swiftly upgraded to that of the Assistant Controller of Recruitment in Ireland.

A unit was to be set up back in Dublin. She was soon transferred to their HQ there, where she was joined in this work by two assistants – one a girl from a Church of Ireland family in Greystones, Enid Morphy, and another young woman, Sylvia Sheridan, the daughter of a Roman Catholic senior civil servant – Chief Clerk in the Estate Branch of the Irish Congested Board, whose home was in the salubrious Pembroke Road in Ballsbridge, Dublin. Both girls were signed on as commissioned officials and started off as Assistant Administrators (AAs) within the Dublin recruitment unit.

One of their first priorities was to seek out and persuade others to enrol as 'Administrators' like themselves, who – to use Swanzy's own words – were required to be 'girls of good education, especially those who have any experience of managing other women'. Anyone with 'special qualifications' was welcome, even if they were 'only willing to start by joining up as one of the lower-ranking Hostel-forewomen or Forewomen cooks with a view to gaining higher promotion'.[4]

Swanzy was probably instrumental in motivating two Irish woman doctors to join the WAAC as medical officers: the recently qualified Elizabeth Budd from Maryborough (now Portlaoise) who, as a women member of the Royal Army Medical Corps (RMAC), became attached to the Irish recruiting unit. Dr Budd served until the Corps was disbanded in 1921. When she left the army she moved to Dartmouth Square in Dublin and became a 'demonstrator of anatomy' at the Royal College of Surgeons in Ireland.[5] A second Irish medical doctor, Marjorie McMullen who, as a member of the Royal Army Medical Corps was also attached to the WAAC, served in France as a medical officer. There was also one other unusually talented woman who came forward. This was Aleen Cust, from Tipperary town, who was to become Ireland's very first veterinary surgeon in 1922, following her membership of the Corps. In 1915 Miss Cust had volunteered to join the Veterinary Corps to 'aid in the care and treatment of warhorses'. She would serve six months in France in 1918 as a member of the QMAAC, by which time she may have been working in an army bacteriological laboratory.[6]

It would be very wrong to leave the impression that Irish membership of the WAAC had only initially attracted the attention of a certain class of educated professional women, however. When offers to join began accelerating in 1918, records from that time reveal it to be manifestly true that the Corps offered opportunities for all classes and all nationalities, single or married.

Hold-ups lay ahead

However, despite the continued glowing enthusiasm of several sections of the press who were supportive, events moved slowly enough in 1917. Suitable hostels and office accommodation for the Corps were hard to find. By the third week of September that year, The *Irish Times* had observed ruefully: 'No campaign for securing women for the Corps has yet to be launched,' adding that the reason for the delay was because 'Hostel accommodation has yet to be completed'. In the meantime, better progress was being been made in Belfast. By 9 October the same newspaper announced that the Grand Central Hotel in Belfast had been 'taken over by the Government' for the use of the WAAC.

What had caused the delay? Although there were plenty of suitable applications trickling into their office, WAAC officials may have decided that there was some need to tread warily in Dublin. It was not that there was no support for the war from many citizens, especially from Home Rule voters, but Nationalist and Sinn Féin feelings were running high and the Corps had still not found a suitable, more permanent 'home' for their HQ other than the use of a spare office in Kilmainham Barracks, which they must have known was not entirely suitable. By mid-November, little had changed. An *Irish Times* journalist writes that although no hostels for recruits were as yet set up, the Irish Controller and her recruitment officer 'Miss Swanzy' had commenced work at the military headquarters in Kilmainham – which at that time was being used to the full for the Commander-in-Chief of British crown forces in Ireland. In due course, more convenient accommodation was found for WAAC administration staff in Jury's Hotel in Dame Street, which was conveniently located not far from the army in Dublin Castle's Lower Yard where a section of the buildings here had also been made available for their use.

It might be noted that despite a rather sluggish official start, a significant number of women who wished to enrol were already coming forward, even though the Irish recruitment programme had yet to gather momentum. Several young women had not waited to use the local labour exchanges but took more imaginative courses. For example, one Dublin applicant, a 31-year-old shorthand typist called Florence Lowe who lived in Cabra, instead of going to London, had decided to make contact with the women's section of Glasgow's National Service Department. By April 1917, Glasgow had arranged for the necessary references to be vetted and her enrolment went ahead without further delay. By the end of May, Florence was on her way to join one of the first batches of office clerks to be sent to St. Omer, one of GHQ's forward bases in France which lay extremely close to the front. She was later attached as the 'only shorthand typist' allocated to the colonel in charge of the Heavy Repair Shop in Rouen – who would acknowledge his utter reliance on her competence when she sought demobilization.[7] Florence was to serve with the BEF for almost two and a half years from mid-May1917 right up to mid-October 1919.

Other early arrivals posted 'overseas' to a base in France were two Post Office telephone operators sent from the Belfast Exchange – both fluent French speakers – whose formal applications dated from May 1917.[8]

Under the special procedures for the selected Irish Post Office staff members who were sent to serve at the front, these and the others to follow had no direct input from the local employment exchanges as the permissions and arrangement were always in the remit of their individual postmasters. If approved, instructions were then issued for them to go directly to England by boat and rail, very often to report into the Folkestone Receiving Depot. It was here that those first two young women from the Belfast Exchange underwent their enrolment ceremony and basic army training, as has been described earlier. By mid-June Jean Henry was off to France in a draft of over thirty young telephonists drawn from a number of exchanges across England and Scotland. Her companion, Kathleen Welch (who had an additional good knowledge of German) did not reach France to be formally signed in there until the following day.[9] She may have been taken ill with sea-sickness en route or delayed for some other reason, as could sometime happen to members of a draft. She and Jean Henry were attached to the Royal Engineers in the Boulogne Signal unit and an issue of the GPO staff journal soon afterwards wrote of the pride their colleagues at home felt for their courage 'amid hopes they will both be spared to return safe and sound'.[10]

Within the next few weeks many more young women drawn from Irish post offices and exchanges across the whole of Ireland were despatched to various other Signal units in France. Post Office girls often volunteered in pairs – sometimes friends from work – but sometimes sisters, too. For example, in Jean Henry's group the Liverpool, Birmingham, Bristol and Sheffield GPO exchanges had each provided two volunteers who were former workmates, as had the three main cities in Scotland: Edinburgh, Glasgow and Aberdeen. The rest of the girls in their draft came from homes elsewhere in England, with the greatest number all drawn from the GPO in London.

The depot at Folkestone

By the end of that first summer of 1917, similar consignments of volunteer telegraphists and telephonists were sometimes supplemented by the inclusion of ten or more office clerks and shorthand typists to make up a draft of thirty to forty women, which was the preferred size for each group on the move. For those being sent across the English Channel to France, a recruitment and distribution depot was established in Folkestone in the large former hotel – the Metropole – which had been commandeered early on in the war for use as a hospital for Belgian troops. By 1917 all these patients were gone and the building lay unused, so it was reallocated to the WAAC and there were often as many as 600 girls – including most of the Irish – being accommodated here while waiting to be moved to postings in France.[11] For some, the waiting here could become tedious to the extreme. One late recruit in June 1918 recalled: 'Days dragged like lead and the aim of every girl was to see her name on the bi-weekly list of those due to embark for the front.'[12] The same reminiscences commented wryly of the tedious daily routine of 'Drill twice a day' and chaffed at the restrictions imposed: 'No-one was allowed out of their quarters in the Depot after five o'clock in the evening, except on Saturdays when the time limit was 6 pm'.

By contrast to later delays, the first large-scale movement of 'B' drafts for France had been able to get away to France quite swiftly. There was, for instance, a 21-year-old girl from Bangor, County Down, who had signed up as a WAAC 'army cook' in London in July 1917. Within a month the girl was a member of a catering team at the BEF base in Rouen. She would serve there for over the next two years until dispersals commenced on September 1919.[13]

In Belfast, Dublin and elsewhere, newly recruited Irishwomen were undergoing exactly the same routines in their local despatching depots. This would be the life that lay ahead. The conditions of service had been an anomaly from the start, as shall be made evident. On the one hand, the military – whose spokesmen in dealing with the new women's Corps was the Army Council – were adamant that women would be only accorded the status of 'civilians' – but on the other hand, they insisted that the women should be subject to similar army protocols and rules which placed constraints on the discipline of private soldiers and their officers. Girls therefore had to get used to the imposition of army-style curtailment of their freedom, which was accompanied by rigid timekeeping, roll calls, army food and quarters for the next two years or more. Punishments were rigidly imposed for any breach of the rules, and fines and 'Restriction or Removal of Privileges' (R of P) meted out. Life was equally strict for girls working in Irish camps and barracks as they were in England or in France. Fines of 2s 6d, almost a whole day's pay, were quite commonly imposed.

In Kilkenny Barracks, one young woman was fined for being late for an evening roll call; another had the same fine for a 'breach of discipline' in Victoria Barracks, Cork.[14] All were subjected to similar rules no matter in which region they were serving. One incorrigible Clare woman from Sixmilebridge who was sent in June 1918 to work as a mess waitress at an army base in Etaples, a coastal town sixteen miles south of Boulogne, was frequently reprimanded and fined the standard 2s 6d for repeated misdemeanours which included being 'late', 'absent for duty', 'improperly dressed', 'wearing incorrect uniform' or 'absent from camp without a pass'. She had clearly found the discipline hard to bear. At one stage, her bad behaviour resulted in seven days' R of P plus the postponement of leave.[15] Yet there was never any question of her being dismissed from the force for these relatively minor offences. She was later transferred to Abbeville and served here until the final dispersal in October 1919.

By 1918, the Folkestone Depot was always full to capacity with a throughput of as many as 600 women being handled at any one time. A waitress from Castletown Geoghegan in Westmeath who had joined up in London was another who had been processed through that depot in July 1917. She, too, had been sent straight off to the Etaples base for over twelve months before being transferred back to the Dublin HQ having been upgraded to working as a general clerk until her discharge in 1919.[16] Opportunities to gain promotion or an upgrading of skills for women was undoubtedly one of the advantages that joining the Corps might offer in addition to the pay scales which women from many parts of Ireland would have found advantageous by comparison to what they could earn at home.

In addition to all the girls being processed through Folkestone, several Irish recruits would be likewise prepared for enrolment and drafting in the former married quarters of the army camp at Aldershot and regular supplies of personnel sent from Ireland to the Western Front were to continue for another twelve months, well into the autumn of 1918; the majority of these later recruits served until the end of 1919.

From the Post Office authorities' particular viewpoint, the number of telephone and telegraph operators that could be spared for Signal units had to be limited and evenly spread over every exchange in the organization's whole network. By the end of August 1917 most of the original estimated numbers needed had been placed in France and, although more were to follow over the following year only a few new recruits from Irish exchanges could be spared to go out as personnel or replacements. (See Table 3 in Appendix I) There will be a great deal more to discuss about the role they were to play in France.

Meanwhile, in Ireland, networking and word-of-mouth contacts were still working hard to encourage others to make their own way to one of the English commands and thereby entirely bypassing the Dublin HQ. One example of this process may be found in Sligo-born Elizabeth Katherine Fowler who had already been serving as a civilian as an 'organising secretary and treasurer in Military Hospitals in Egypt'.[17] She had returned to London earlier that year and joined up as a hostel forewoman but was soon upgraded to an assistant administrator.

Winter had arrived by the time the Irish Controller and her staff had settled into their Dublin HQ. Their most urgent task was to organize an active recruitment campaign, which they planned to start in the spring – but even as they started to make these plans a serious setback had to be faced. A rumour was gathering momentum which claimed the military proposed to impose conscription on young men in Ireland. The news soon raised widespread outrage. Up to that time, British army service had been entirely voluntary for these boys – hence the long-standing support of Irish nurses and VADs, sisters, fiancées and wives anxious to help. From the WAAC point of view such a change in public opinion was a considerable setback.

A successful Irish anti-conscription campaign was soon launched; passions ran high, the political connotations were significant and the climate of public opinion wavered between loyalty towards their boys who had bravely volunteered to fight in France and what they felt was 'justifiably right' under previous agreements over the case for Home Rule. The arguments grew so bitter that the anti-conscription campaign was ultimately a tremendous success. No forced army enlistments were ever imposed in Ireland.

That very vocal and well-supported public protest had been a disaster for the plans of the Dublin-based WAAC, however. Hopes of organizing meetings and parades to encourage women to come forward on a voluntary basis in the spring had to be temporarily suspended and it would be mid-summer before they could feel confident enough to start conducting a series of fresh exhortations to rally female support for the men who were already serving in the trenches.

By the summer, while progress might have dragged along slowly enough in organizing rallies, the depot in Belfast was already acting as an important reception and dispersal centre. Upcoming recruitments were reliant on a close liaison between all the local labour exchanges and the WAAC recruiting team who were cooperating with depots in Dublin, Waterford, Limerick, Cork and elsewhere. If accepted, a girl who had applied to enrol would eventually receive a call to report in for final signing-on. She was asked to agree to serve for an open-ended length of time which was by then being described as for 'the duration of the war'. She was then sent a free railway travel warrant to Belfast, where she would receive some rudimentary training before being kitted out in her uniform and sent onwards to postings in the UK or France or, alternatively, despatched to garrison towns, camps and depots somewhere in Ireland.

Their period of induction was the same routine that was carried out in all the other command regions. The girls first underwent a couple of weeks or so of instructions in the rules and regulations of army life and, for the majority of the Irish recruits, these inductions took place in the Belfast Depot. Things to be learned included implicit instructions as to the correct way to behave as army personnel from that time onwards. Correct protocols of rank had to be observed at all times and the training included many practical lessons such as how to 'form fours' and march in an orderly column like regular soldiers. The army provided quarters in billets or camps and they received army rations just like any enlisted man. There were also rules regarding the various forms of transport they could – and could not – use and they were warned that, outside of working hours, encounters of male and female military personnel were to be strictly restricted and controlled. It proved to be a difficult rule to impose.

Even despite the anti-conscription agitation campaigns, a growing number of women had started to pass through the Belfast Depot and the administrators there were soon very busy with the task of processing all new recruits following their enrolment at the Dublin HQ and elsewhere in the provinces. Records show that a large number of the Irish recruits were put to work at home in the army camps and depots across the whole of Ireland, having been transported by train to the nearest railway station. On August 12 1918, for example, the *Irish Independent* newspaper reported that:

> Ninety members of the Queen Mary's Army Auxiliary Corps marched through Dublin on Saturday on their arrival from Belfast. At Kingsbridge they were inspected by Major General Fry before proceeding to the South of Ireland.

Kingsbridge (now Heuston) Station was the major rail hub to Limerick or Cork.

Recruitment rallies 1918
War Office statistics for April 1918 – cited in Fionnuala Walsh's thesis – record that the Irish Command's contingent of women at that time was

composed of 'sixteen units in Ireland staffed with WAAC personnel but it was anticipated that this would eventually rise to thirty to thirty-five units'. There were two Administrators, seven Deputy Administrators, fifteen Assistant Administrators and one Quarter-mistress in place by that time. Within the next few months the recruitment push was accelerated and what is noticeable are the number of promotions from the ranks that began to be given to young women who had originally enrolled as hostel forewoman. By later summer 1918 the Irish Command's use of WAAC/QMAAC workers and administrators was obviously growing much larger and would continue to do so into 1919.

Not surprisingly, the recruitment rallies were to generate a mixture of results and some indications as to how these meetings went may be gleaned from some of the contemporary provincial newspaper reports for later on that summer. Accounts of parades and meetings held in Ballina, Ballymoney, Londonderry and Portrush reveal they received a predictably good reception. By that time another ex-pupil of Alexandra College and university graduate, Norah Stack, MA, who had been in charge of recruitment in the English Northern Command in 1917, was helping in the Dublin unit, assisted by Swanzy and Morphy.[18]

A recruiting meeting in Monaghan was described by the *Anglo-Celt* newspaper on 12 October 1918 as having held a parade of the Women's Army Auxiliary Corps attended by the band of the Somerset Light Infantry. A concert programme had been arranged; the band played a selection of airs and there was an exhibition of physical drill by the WAAC. The report noted that there were 'openings for cooks and waitresses and clerks and anyone joining would learn something'. Those attending applauded one speaker's observations that 'the war was almost won' but that 'women should join up at once' so it could be said 'they had done their part'.

Local journalists and newspaper editors understandably put their own slant on the publicity being generated. There was a concerted effort to appeal to women readers and the correspondents covering these rallies took care to pitch their pieces to suit their own specific readership support. When covering an event in Portrush on 31 August 1918, for example, one *Belfast News Letter* correspondent hit the right note: 'A gratifying amount of recruits joined up.'

By contrast, when the QMAAC was allowed make use of the hall in Maryborough for a similar recruiting meeting on 12 October 1918, the editorial staff of the *Nationalist and Leinster Times* regarded the event as a controversial issue by citing the difficulties encountered by other local groups who wished to use the hall. They pointed out that when the Gaelic League had sent in a similar request for access 'it was not as readily available for them'.

Later, on 2 November 1918, yet another local newspaper, the *Sligo Champion* reported on events in the town which reveals a local atmosphere that was similarly hostile:

> After a concert given by members of the Women's Army Auxiliary Corps in Ballina on Monday night of last week, disorder was rife in the town for some hours, with the result that there were several baton charges. During the progress of the concert a crowd of about 200 collected outside the hall and indulged in all sorts of horseplay carried by shouting and cheering and the singing of Sinn Féin songs. The police dispersed the demonstrators once or twice but each time they reassembled and started afresh to groan and shout. The concert being over, the police escorted the WAACs to the hotel and while they were passing through the town the booing and shouting continued. It was not until the party got onto Knox Street that some stones were flung at the police and one of the officers of the WAACs was struck with a stone but luckily was not injured.

Recruits of all ages and backgrounds welcomed

While efficient clerical workers were much in demand by the Dublin HQ to assist with the copious amounts of paperwork which the recruitment campaigns generated, the other category of enrolments who eagerly responded to the recruiting drive were the 'B' uniformed 'workers' who were needed for domestic and catering work. Women who had the right experience for supervision, for example, were accepted up to the age of 40 – and they did not necessarily have to be single, as many had husbands already serving with the forces. One had a husband with the army in Egypt. In December 1917, having failed to be enrolled in Dublin, she left her two boys in the care of her parents in the Dublin suburb of Rathgar and travelled to Manchester to try again, thinking that her education by Dominicans in Louvain and fluency in French in addition to an 'understanding of German' would see her sent to France as a clerk without delay.[19] It did not happen; by the end of May she had been sent instead to Park Hall Camp at Oswestry in Shropshire and was discharged from here three months later. Not everyone succeeded, no matter how keen they were. Behind the scenes reports were written, behaviour and performance assessed.

The acceptance of married women's enrolments would seem prone to producing other curious outcomes. On 29 September 1917 a report covering a local council meeting was published in the *Meath Chronicle*. It carried the story of another anxious married Irishwoman who was determined to join up:

> A houseless member of the Women's Army Auxiliary Corps, Mrs Margaret McGuinness, [who] had got an appointment with the Women's Army Auxiliary Corps has made an approach to the local Council asking them to adopt her six children.

The report, unfortunately, does not explain how the problem was eventually resolved, but merely records that the meeting of the councillors – who were not only probably taken aback by this strange request but may have been, in addition, quite disapproving of the idea that women should serve in an army corps – had advised Mrs McGuinness to 'try and get a house in Navan and take out her children [from the orphanage]'. So was that woman's dilemma satisfactorily solved or not? It remains an unanswered question which some local historian might find interesting to tease out.

The rates of pay

Wage rates for the lowest ranking Irish recruits who were not 'mobile' would have appeared attractive, even in Dublin. In June 1918, Unit Administrator Swanzy, the Irish Command's recruiting official, was reportedly offering £24 a year for 'unskilled domestics' and £26 a year for waitresses to work as members of the Corps.[20] These rates compared well with £18 per annum being earned by one typical recruit, a 20-year-old housemaid in Dublin, and it may be taken that wages in the capital city, moreover, would have rated considerably better than most other places in those days.[21]

A revised set of regulations for pay issued June 1918 reveals the remuneration for other categories of WAAC workers such as clerks and typists was considerably greater than the rates for army catering or domestic tasks, especially for supervising forewomen who would be eventually earning over £2 a week within twelve months. For the many hostel forewomen who gained promotion to join the ranks of the 'Administrators', the pay was even more attractive. Nonetheless, those higher earnings, expectation of overtime and the hours worked in each week were destined to become contentious issues in certain sectors of army employment.

The pay being offered for forewomen in different categories of 'workers' had depended on which sector they had been assigned to, with hostel forewomen receiving slightly more at £45 per annum than the forewomen cooks and waitresses who only received £40. In the meantime, the structure of payments for the 'officials' who were commissioned administrators fell into an entirely different league. When recruitment began to be sought from Ireland in November 1917, *The Irish Times* had announced the rates of payment for an administrator to be £150–£175 per annum. All these wages were to be increased by 1918. Some of the larger hostels and receiving depots also required the additional services of a dedicated quartermistress (the WAAC equivalent of a quartermaster in charge of all supplies and equipment), who received £150, while the lower entry rank of assistant administrator was paid an annual wage of £120. Accommodation or 'lodgings' were provided for these officials, but a weekly deduction of 15s 6d was made to cover the cost of their board. (A slightly lower scale of 14s applied to the 'A' clerical workers and those serving in the 'B' mobile category were 'entitled to free board and lodging service and washing'.)[22]

As has been already indicated, the rates of pay and conditions for the Post Office 'Signals' women in France required separate negotiations to be conducted with the Army Council; the long, wrangling problems and implications this situation provoked will be an issue more closely examined in a later chapter.

Much higher-ranking colleagues such as the area controllers, recruiting controllers and senior staff in headquarters received considerably higher rates than were traditionally entirely consistent with regular army practice. Earnings for 'Officers' ranged from a hefty £500 a year down to a more modest £200. The provision of quarters was not always guaranteed, nonetheless. Following enrolment each new recruit was issued with her uniform which was signed for on an official form called 'Articles of Uniform to be Held on Charge'. For the lower-ranking 'Workers' and 'Forewomen', the full kit consisted of a khaki gabardine coat dress to be worn with a hem that measured no more than twelve inches from the ground, one pair of shoes, two pairs of stockings, one pair of gaiters, one greatcoat, two pairs of overalls, three loose collars made of poplin (white for forewomen and chocolate brown for workers). Greatcoats and belted mackintoshes were also issued; and for girls recruited by the Post Office they also received a pair of shoulder badges and the special signallers' blue and white brassard or armband.

All the girls received a round-brimmed felt hat which sported a decorative metal badge. Although not officially listed because they were supposed to supply their own underclothing, some basic underwear was available which included 'a pair of knickers, made with a sizeable pocket on the thigh for pay book and other things'.[23] Rules were strict. From then on, no outer civilian clothes were to be worn, although a later concession permitted the additional wearing of a grey or tawny fur collar with their greatcoats during the winter months.[24] These fur collars can often be seen featured in formal portrait photographs some of the girls had taken when on leave.

Higher-ranking recruits – the 'Officials' – wore a rather more sophisticated uniform consisting of a tailored jacket and skirt accompanied by a shirt and tie, but before being accepted or promoted to act as one of those junior commissioned officers, applicants had to first undertake an intensive training course in Bostall Heath, near Woolwich. It was a process which will be revisited in more detail later.

A slow start for some applicants

Although there is marked evidence that many applications were being received from Ireland throughout 1917–1919, the outcome for such offers to sign up was often very slow to be activated and it seems likely that a large number of keen applicants were not followed up on until the early months of 1918.

For instance, a girl from Woodenbridge in Avoca, County Wicklow, Bridget Kelly, who applied on 12 October 1917 via the Kingstown (Dun Laoghaire) employment exchange was not finally posted by the Irish Command to the School of Musketry in Dollymount as a domestic worker until July 1918. Likewise, an application in December 1917 from another farmer's daughter, Annie Kelly, who lived beside the camp on the Curragh in Kildare, was only signed on for similar work in Dublin by March 1918. Both girls subsequently served in uniform for twelve months until discharged in 1919. Similar examples are frequent. Several reasons for such delays might be suggested.

In Dublin itself, it was likely to have been the amount of time it took to acquire the use of enough suitable hostel accommodation. Apart from being the base for the Irish Command's WAAC/QMAAC administration HQ, the city would have held the greatest number of WAACs spread across a substantial number of barracks and depots. Belfast became a very busy distribution depot and an increasing number of recruits were despatched from here by train and boat to locations in Ireland, England and from here onwards into France. As already mentioned, there was a large depot at Folkestone for those who crossed the Channel but Southampton was also being used.

It possible to posit that, in addition to making sure adequate quarters – which the WAAC called 'hutments' – were prepared in time to accommodate women assigned to camps and garrisons in Ireland, some of the long waiting times could have been caused by the necessity to check the references which had to accompany each enrolment application. It is also equally possible that because of the good wages being offered there was no shortage of girls seeking work in the 'B' category as cooks, waitresses and other household workers.

By late spring 1918, despite all the hold-ups, Miss Lace Pritchard's staff unit in Dublin had nonetheless expedited a spread of WAAC 'Workers' far beyond those attached to the city's army barracks and camps.

Assignments all over Ireland

In Dublin City itself, rank and file girls had been widely dispersed for a variety of work in the Royal (Collins) Barracks, Richmond (Keogh)

Barracks, Marlborough (McKee) Barracks, Portobello (Cathal Brugha) Barracks and Wellington (Griffiths) Barracks and the School of Musketry in Dollymount. In addition, the WAAC also took on responsibility for the catering arrangements for the Officers' Training Corps at Trinity College throughout the time they were encamped there. As a consequence, when the two senior WAACs who had been in charge of that unit in Trinity came to be demobilized in 1919, they would continue to be employed by the college to run the administration of the canteen catering and college shop for many long years after the war.[25]

In Kildare, there is plenty of evidence of WAACs engaged in the Beresford Barracks at the Curragh Camp. The garrison office at Newbridge employed the WAACs as typists, registration and index filing clerks, as well as members of the Corps categorized as 'B' workers who were termed 'General Domestics', a term that covered an enormous range of abilities from army cooks to kitchen helpers and waitresses. All military installations had increased in size during the Great War and it is now recognized that the Curragh Camp had evolved 'into the largest military station in Ireland and it continued to be an important training centre for the British Army until 1922'.[26] For the army men in charge of its operation the pressure of keeping on top of all the clerical office work, military record-keeping and flow of correspondence that was necessary to ensure everything ran smoothly, the introduction of some extra personnel who were experienced WAAC 'A' clerical workers and typists must have come as a great relief.

Likewise, accurate and indisputable evidence exists to show that, by early 1918, many more newly recruited WAAC staff were taken on as office staff or given promotion to more senior status as 'Officials' to help with the operation of other expanding army installations. Reminiscing on her service days, one former administrator, Honor Connelly, the Wicklow-born daughter of a Church of Ireland curate, whose brother served in France, later enthusiastically recalled her trips to Fermoy. She remembered how the women's camp in Moore Park was 'one of the prettiest camps the WAAC ever had', having been 'always so well run that it required very little inspection'.[27] The comment nonetheless makes it clear she must never have seen the possibly less spartan, if necessarily sandbagged and more air-raid-proofed camps that were prepared for the intake of the WAAC in France and Flanders, where flowerbeds and vegetable gardens almost always enhanced the surroundings for its occupants.

Similar drafts of the Corps were sent off to military installations elsewhere: Finner Camp in Ballyshannon, County Donegal, Ebrington Barracks in Derry, Ballykinlar in County Down – also known as Abercorn Barracks. The Royal Munster Fusiliers' large training centre in the old Richmond Barracks at Templemore – referred to by the WAACs as the 'Bombing School' – had housed a School of Instruction for officers and NCOs.

The WAAC were also posted to the Randalstown Munitions Store in County Antrim to work for the Royal Enniskillen Fusiliers and 14th Royal Irish Rifles for a variety of tasks which included clerical work by at least one young woman from Roscommon who had previous experience of similar army deskwork attached to weapons and ammunition in Dublin. She was later sent briefly to HQ No 3 Command Depot in Ripon, North Yorkshire, and from here retuned to Ireland to assist in the garrison office, at the Curragh Camp as an index and filing clerk. Having gained experience in such specialized work, she was going to find it difficult to find gainful employment in 1920 following demobilization.[28]

The category 'B' recruits who worked mainly as cooks or waitresses were well spread across all the army installations such as Ebrington Barracks, Londonderry, the army barracks in Kilkenny, and for the South Irish Horse, a special reserve cavalry regiment which was based in Cahir, County Tipperary, and so on. Each location would have had supervising hostel forewomen and an administrator for their unit.

One of the most noticeable features to be revealed by an examination of the spread of these army women across Ireland is how often those who had signed up to be 'mobile' were sent to locations which were some considerable distance from a girl's home area. Recruits from Kerry, Roscommon and Belfast were despatched to work in the Curragh Camp in Kildare; others with family roots in Monaghan and Antrim lived and worked in Cork's Ballyvonare Camp with new service friends from Clare. The Irishwomen who were despatched to army establishments in England might end up in London – or in Warwick, or Salisbury, Manchester or Bristol. Was it just coincidental; perhaps a process driven by the sequential dates of their enrolments? Or might it have been a deliberate policy to ensure that groups of former buddies from any one local region or town did not form themselves into segregated cliques that might have an adverse consequences? The concept of WAAC 'togetherness', which aimed to nurture mutual help and support, was based on shared new experiences. There was no desire to put any focus on inherited geographical backgrounds or ethnic, political or denominational deep-seated prejudices that existed.

Mixed drafts of WAACs drawn from Down or Tyrone were sent to Ballyvonare Camp in Buttevant, in those days occupied by the 10th Royal Munster Fusiliers or Cameron Highlanders. Similar batches from Ulster were dispatched to serve in the Victoria (Collins) Barracks in Montenotte, Cork. There were, of course, a few instances of an exception to these rules arising when deemed expedient. By April 1918, however, when a gap in staffing resources in the garrisons at Cork Harbour arose, a different course of action was taken. It will be worth taking a closer look.

WAAC clerks for telephone work in Ireland

By early 1918, the army's severe shortage of office staff in their Cork garrisons had escalated to a crisis point. The situation there was very indicative of the pressures being created by the increasing lack of manpower that spring. With no army personnel available to handle telephone calls and no relief staff on the way, the officer in charge of Cork's military exchanges had arranged for a batch of sixteen WAAC 'General Clerks' to work for him as telephonists.[29]

As already indicated, the use of trained female telecommunication personnel seconded to the Royal Engineers from the government-run Post Office Authority was a complex arrangement that was strictly confined to the 'loan' of these young women for work in security-sensitive sections within BEF bases and HQs on the Western Front. Although, when the war stretched on into 1918, such was the increasing demand for office telephone operators in many of the 'home-based' army camps and depots in England and Ireland, that the WAAC began to seek recruits whose prewar work in more progressive private businesses – such as solicitors' offices, large wholesalers or similar outlets – had given these girls some rudimentary knowledge of how to operate a small telephone switchboard.

These young women were not among those selected to serve in France as WAAC 'E' category in Signal units, which was specialized work for the army strictly confined to the campaign being waged on the Western Front. By contrast, the girls who worked in sector 'A' as 'General Clerks (telephonists)' would therefore have not undergone the rigorous months of technical training as a 'Learner' which all Post Office staff underwent. General clerks might be sometimes acceptably proficient for use in the handling of many mundane telephone duties for 'home service' in army barracks and depots and it was usually arranged that they could be engaged locally as needed. The girls who took up duties as serving WAAC members in Cork's military exchanges thus included several former pupils of the Presentation Convent in that area. After leaving school they had been employed by small local business enterprises in Whitegate and Crosshaven.

Although all were vetted and enrolled via the local labour exchange, it is nonetheless curious to see that clause number four in their reference forms seeking reassurance over their discretion when handling sensitive information had a mixed response from the local residents who had been asked to confirm confidence in the applicant's trustworthiness regarding what was termed as 'access to document of a confidential nature'. Not all their army service files have survived but out of the seventeen references that are contained in ten surviving files, six referees had left that question completely unanswered. Fourteen gave a positive 'yes' or similar, and there were two more cautious responses, 'I believe so' or 'I think so', which sound a mite uncomfortable with the question. It was unlikely that anyone would answer in the negative.[30]

In retrospect, the decision to employ them as signed-up WAACs, who functioned under army rules might not now be seen as having been an altogether wise move. How loyal were all these girls? The army was aware of the persistent rumours that Sinn Féin was still actively operating covert intelligence in the area and having WAAC recruits operating telephone lines might have been seen at the time as ensuring the army's garrison offices were less vulnerable to breaches of security. But was this a sufficient safeguard? In her thesis on the impact of the Great War on women in Ireland, Fionnuala Walsh has examined their sister body, the Women's Royal Navy Service (WRNS) in some detail. It is her contention that this branch of the service may have been far more aware of dangers:

'All women recruited from Ireland were subject to scrutiny by the Irish branch of the Naval Intelligence department, while in England and Scotland only those required for special confidential work underwent the same security.'[31] Her study provides an example citing the Commodore of the Kingstown sub-division, who was 'unwilling to trust confidential papers to girls who might feel themselves bound to pass their knowledge on'. He felt it to be therefore 'inadvisable to recruit through the Labour Exchanges'.

By contrast, the lack of army records in regard to the WAAC on the topic of security presents a drawback. As will be shown when the work of John Ferris on army cryptography is discussed briefly in Chapter 4, it is his contention that: 'Archived records for maintaining Naval security during that period were far superior to that of the Army'.[32]

Chapter 3

Serving 'Overseas'

'Meanwhile, the military tried their best to ensure that no one would ever mistake a member of this new Corps for a "real" soldier.'

Kate Adie[1]

In the latter months of 1917 a regular stream of Irish-born recruits had been making their own separate ways to sign up at the WAAC HQ in London or elsewhere. For girls travelling from Ireland who volunteered to serve 'overseas', two hazardous sea-crossings lay ahead. Many of those who were not already living or working in England were assigned to one of the drafts of young women who were being despatched regularly from the mustering depot in Belfast to postings that ended in one of the army camps in England. The route was by boat and rail.

For those going on to 'overseas' postings, the traffic for rank and file back and forth from France was siphoned through the HQ's Connaught Club in London via either the Folkestone Distribution Centre or an army camp in Aldershot, whence they joined a contingent that was ready to embark from one of the departure ports on the English Channel – Folkestone or Southampton.

The earliest departures from here were often drafts of girls providing quite a mixture of skills. For instance, on 10 July 1917, one large group heading for the BEF army bases near Etaples was made up of twenty-eight signallers (seventeen telephonists and eleven telegraphists), together with fourteen clerks and four household workers.[2] These new recruits were drawn from many different home backgrounds and a diversity of economic circumstances. They would have been led by an 'Assistant Administrator' (AA) – a commissioned WAAC officer whose training had included what was described as 'escorting' work. Each draft was usually made up of thirty to forty young women plus one or two escorts and, as time went on, some of the final batches specifically allocated for new or expanded Signal units in large bases might be entirely made up of thirty or so Post Office staff volunteers travelling together.

The system settled into a more smooth-running routine by late summer 1917. It had become easier to arrange for groups to be made ready for despatch to the same destination depot or unit in France but the contents of these drafts became more varied. Sometimes all the newcomers shared one category of work, e.g. they might be a batch solely consisting of 'E' 'Signallers' or they might be girls classed as 'A' who were needed as clerical staff, or as 'B' recruits for domestic and/or catering work. As time went on, many of these drafts going to and fro across the English Channel together contained mixtures of 'ledger clerks' and 'telegraphists and telephonists', as was the case when four girls from Post Office exchanges in Coleraine, Dublin, Dungannon and Kells who left for France on 17 August 1917, were accompanied by thirteen of their fellow Post Office employees from all over England and Scotland. (See Table 4 Appendix I)

Two of their companions had been sent from Lancashire, two from Scotland and the remaining nine girls were single volunteers from a diversity of regional GPO exchanges ranging from the West Riding of Yorkshire, across the Midlands and down to Essex in the south-east. The remainder of their companions were made up of twelve 'office ledger clerks' who had been recruited from a number of equally scattered locations in England which included one girl born in the Isle of Man.

A week earlier, a group specifically destined for the base at Rouen had been confined to Post Office staff and was made up of a combination of telegraphists and telephonists drawn from every regional province, albeit, in that case, there was only one from Ireland. It may be argued that this process of mixing background cultures and local loyalties became an asset that was much valued by many of the more enterprising of these young women in later life.

Before being formally enrolled all who came forward would have undergone an army medical to ensure they were fit for service life and for those who opted for either home or overseas, a vaccination against smallpox was essential unless they had already undergone this procedure as a child. The procedure entailed having a patch of skin on the upper arm scraped quite deeply by a lancet and a specially prepared small amount of the virus rubbed into the exposed raw surface. The recipients felt unwell for a couple of days afterwards and for those who had been treated it was also a commonplace complaint that the scars from their smallpox inoculations were still raw and uncomfortable when their uniforms were issued, especially if it was during the colder winter months when heavy greatcoats were worn. Moreover, for some girls who unluckily suffered a more severe reaction to vaccination and who had not yet fully recovered, orders received for imminent embarkation proved to be a particularly difficult challenge to face.

On setting off, in addition to the army-issue kit bags they wore slung over one shoulder, each uniformed girl had been ordered to bring any extra personal belongings in a suitcase 'no larger than its owner could carry unassisted' and told to provide themselves 'with warm travelling rugs'.[3] The advice was appreciated as 'a softening touch,' but having to face the sea-crossing of the Channel swiftly reminded them that they were now within an active war arena.

The entrances to all the French ports were being actively patrolled by British minesweepers. When on board a transport ship WAACs had to don uncomfortable life-jackets and they were often held up for hours at sea while waiting for the route to be declared safe. For example, an ordnance clerk from the south of England who was travelling with a draft to an unnamed port was to later write about the rough seas and terrible seasickness their group had endured on their trip and describing how the uncomfortable experience of that voyage was not helped by the sight of a floating mine their ship had just avoided.[4] The dangers of the English Channel were merely the first of many challenges they would have to face.

Perilous sea-crossings

Irish members of the Corps who volunteered to serve as 'mobile' members were just as likely to be sent to anywhere in England as they were to be posted to one of the Irish garrisons or camps. For those who, in addition, offered to undertake 'overseas' duties, the assignment to England or France entailed at least one – but often two – hazardous sea journeys before reaching their destination. Skulking enemy submarines were still active in the English Channel and the threat to shipping on the Irish Sea leg of route had continued to be lethal. Although the tactics of adopting zigzag routes for vessels plying Irish coastal waters to avoid lurking German U-boats had greatly improved safety since the sinking of the RMS *Lusitania* just off Kinsale Head in 1915, the danger of these stealthy attacks still remained high. By the summer of 1918, German U-boats were regularly holding up vessels en route between the ports of Holyhead and Dun Laoghaire (at that time called Kingstown). Passenger traffic was often delayed which made it far more difficult for Irish WAACs to report back to their bases on time when returning from a stint of well-deserved leave which had begun to be rolled out in 1918. When viewed in retrospect, the wartime perils that lay in wait for all who had no choice but to risk their lives travelling those dangerous sea-routes was borne extremely stoically. The 1918 issue of army regulations for women allowed each girl 'a fortnight's leave with pay during each year's service, provided the exigencies of the service will permit'.[5] Everyone was eager for a few days' respite away from the war zone and what may be described as a constant flow of young army women to and fro between family homes and army bases went on for almost two years regardless of the accompanying threat to their lives. It was always borne in mind that Irish members would need up to three days' travelling time because of the extra sea-crossing and they were invariably treated with considerable flexibility. Normally, army rules governing activities of the WAAC carried little tolerance for late returns to duty following an authorized absence. Fines and loss of privileges (L of P) were rigorously imposed for such breaches. However, when two sisters, from the GPO in Dublin became delayed for twelve hours by the threat of torpedo attacks at Holyhead, they took care to write to WAAC HQ London to seek permission for some extra hours' leave of absence when on their way home for their first spell of leave in January 1918.[6] They had been working in the GHQ 3rd Echelon in Rouen since early 1917 and there is evidence of a quite flexible response being applied. Their request was attended to sympathetically at HQ. An extension of leave for twenty-four hours was granted without question by return of post and duly logged in by the Record Office administrator in Rouen. It might be added that such minor incidents in the smooth-running machinery that kept movements of all military personnel under control – whether male or female – makes for just one example of the necessary minutiae of paperwork, handwritten memos and letters, typed formal instructions and telegrams, through which the Women's Auxiliary Army was administered.

Almost ten months after this example, there was increasing talk of a possible ceasefire to bring the conflict to an end. Those two sisters and others who had enjoyed being home the previous Christmas would have been doubtlessly looking forward to another stint of home leave and it was fortunate that leave due for most of the many drafts of girls Ireland had been already fulfilled in the spring or summer months of 1918. Yet, despite all the speculation that yearned to see an end to the war and all seemingly remaining satisfactorily quiet on the shipping routes across the Irish Sea, one solitary U-boat was still on the prowl. The menace had not gone away. Autumn was nearly over when, ten days into the month of October, an Irish Sea captain's luck finally ran out. That morning, shortly after leaving Kingstown (today's Dun Laoghaire), the RMS mail boat *Leinster* was hit by two German torpedoes and the vessel slipped swiftly beneath the waves within only ten to fifteen minutes. It was a disaster. The vessel was carrying over 770 people, made up of civilians, troops and crew members. Over 500 lives were lost. Research into the names of those who drowned or who later died has recently revealed that at least two of the casualties from the attack were servicewomen. One was a recently appointed WAAC assistant administrator, May Westwell, with an address in Warrington in Manchester, who was a 30-year-old former women's fitness instructor, possibly a school sports mistress.[7] May had been spotted as having potential and was transferred from the UK to the Irish Command. She was sent to Belfast to be trained as a QMAAC administrator and, having qualified in July 1918, she was given the task of conducting drafts of girls to camps around Ireland. The other named servicewoman identified as a casualty was a 19-year-old native of Cork, Josephine Carr, a clerk with the Women's Royal Naval Service (WRNS) who was that service's first casualty from enemy action.

These two were not the only Women's Auxiliary members who died as a result of an attack on the high seas. Earlier that summer a party of WAACs were among personnel caught up in a tragic incident that took place in the English Channel in August, 1918. Travelling with them was a prominent member of the Corps, Mrs Violet Long, who was the married sister of the Chief Controller for France, Florence Leach. The latter had appointed Violet as her London-based deputy controller and she had been on board the vessel because she was returning from an inspection of a camp in Bourges where a mixed unit of recently arrived American Army women recruits and experienced WAAC records clerks had commenced a joint undertaking to work for the United States military.[8] There will be more to say about that unit, later. On 2 August, having completed her report, Controller Long was set to return to London. That afternoon she embarked on the hospital ship *Warilda*, which was carrying 600 wounded as well as a draft of QMAAC back to England. It would be another sailing to end in tragedy. Contemporary accounts of the German attack reported that: 'When the ship was torpedoed amidships and sank, one hundred and twenty-three lives were lost'. Of these, WAAC Controller Violet Long was the sole woman casualty. She had been crushed to death against the ship's side while transferring to a lifeboat.

Some early arrivals of Irishwomen in France

Based on records that have survived, a great many drafts of 'overseas' WAAC were disembarked at Boulogne. However, there were occasions when they might be travelling to France on similar hospital ambulance ships via Le Havre, which would then carry on up the River Seine to the port of Rouen, one of the largest and busiest of the bases. Once here, new recruits not allocated to this base would then have to continue their journey separately to their destinations by rail. For those experiencing the final leg up the picturesque river there was sometimes additional excitement. One such girl was Dundalk-born Bertha Castle, a 33-year-old telegraphist who had been working in the London GPO and who was among the first of the army's L of C girls to arrive in France.[9] Her draft crossed the Channel on 23 May 1917 and they travelled up the Seine to Rouen, whence they continued on to an army base in Dieppe by train. Years later, in an account of that first journey to France, she clearly recalled how thrilled she was to have been introduced to 'my first experience of ship's wireless. I had the privilege of entering the wireless cabin and I picked up Morse signals being sent out by Berlin'.[10]

From the start, the transport arrangements for a group of WAACs was always carefully guarded for very necessary security reasons. It was only when their vessel was on the point of docking at one of the French ports, that a sealed 'Top Secret' envelope would be opened by a WAAC 'Official' acting as their group's travel escort, to reveal the name of the base to which they were to proceed.[11] For a few of the very earliest arrivals of women sent to the army from post offices to operate telecommunication systems in France, who may not have been given the benefit of always travelling under the eye of a watchful 'Official', their first encounter with the French railway system was soon reported on with both amusement and exasperation. There is one description of how a small party of girls had travelled for days through the French countryside. They had been left for hours at remote stations and unexpectedly switched from train to train on a number of occasions, even late at night, sometimes having to clamber up into carriages from the tracks below. One of them afterwards made the comment that 'I have never had such journeys in my life!'[12] Worse was to come. When finally reaching what they thought was the army base that was expecting them they were disconcerted to find that: 'On reporting to the Signal Office the first morning, we were informed we should have gone somewhere else and were not wanted there'.

It had not been a great start for that young woman, but the system soon settled into smooth-running routines which despite often disrupted timetables still managed to cope with all the preliminary delays and schedule changes which had to be faced in those first few months of that summer. For example, a scribbled comment in the official QMAAC July 1917 War Diary for the base at Rouen, where many of the Irish girls would serve, noted that an arrival of 'a draft of 17 women' which included fourteen clerks for the 3rd Echelon, were over a month late and the writer described them as 'still due for June 11th programme'.[13] There is no surviving WAAC War Diary for June that year, so it is unlikely that any reason for the delay can be found except that the base here had undergone a substantial building programme to improve facilities for the GPO women who were assigned to Rouen base. Everything needed may not have been in place for them by June. Several new camps were being constructed at this location, too, but a number of subsequent arrivals by the end of the July present more positive evidence of things finally falling into place for the "L" Signals unit here.

The recorded movements of personnel shows it to have been an uneven pattern. The next draft arrived five days later. It consisted of seventeen 'other ranks', described as 'Clerks for OC Signals' and eight 'Household' workers and it may be taken that girls designated as 'Clerks' were actually telegraph or telephone operators from the GPO and not general clerks assigned to the management of records or correspondence at the base.[14] The War Diary's logged entries which covered all comings and goings make it quite clear that the next group of girls who made it there by 30 July benefitted from having no ambiguity attached to what their role was to be. All were undoubtedly former GPO staff women, three of whom came from Ireland. The log notes: 'Arrival of 26 telegraph and telephone clerks – Signals Section,' which is followed by another entry to cover three more 'telephonists' arriving on 9 August and, finally, on 12 August, a draft of thirty girls, who were also ex-GPO staff were signed in to take up their duties.[15] Several who came in already held a much higher ranking and responsible position in their home exchanges as supervisor, and although that rank became described by the army as a 'Forewoman', others would receive the promotion – and the extra pay it carried – within the next two years.[16]

By the end of the month of August, the anticipated full assignment of 175 staff women for the Signal unit at that base had been completed and – as was soon to be proved many times elsewhere – the introduction of WAAC 'Signaller' telegraphists and telephonists here and elsewhere soon became indispensable for the successful operation of all military campaigns from that time onwards.

Malicious talk is deflected

In the months leading up to Christmas 1917, just as the recruitment drive in Ireland was gearing up to make some significant progress, an unforeseen setback almost put the progress thus far achieved into reverse. Dark rumours had been gathering momentum in the UK where a class-driven spate of gossip was spreading tales of rampant immorality among the girls serving with the overseas WAAC units. It was even being alleged that 'prostitutes were infiltrating the WAAC to ply their trade, supplying addresses at base camps where soldiers and officers could seek them out'.[17] The problem has been described by the scholarly work of Lynda Dennant as creating an atmosphere that was becoming quite 'frenzied and consequently the fears on the effect of recruitment were taken seriously', citing as one example how:

> The Wales Division responsible for recruiting WAAC noted in its report for October 1917 that 'Terrible rumours' are pervading South Wales with regard to the behaviour of the soldiers and WAAC girls at Rouen. It has been stated by a man who has just returned from France, that he has heard 'that the men and women are mixing together in the most promiscuous manner' and that the morals are much worse since the arrival of the British girls than even before.

Similar prurient stories were escalating. The wider public's attention was being excited despite contesting theories being put about that 'enemy agents' were behind these terrible rumours.[18] Today, these stories might be labelled as 'fake news' but the effect they were having on the flow of new recruits was causing consternation at WAAC HQ and it was clear that something effective had to be done to put a stop to these malicious allegations. By January 1918 the task of countering such talk was given to the Ministry of Labour and six 'thoroughly representative women' – all with highly reputable credentials – were soon appointed to make an official inspection. Their official brief was

> to investigate the rumours of immorality with a view to 'calming' public opinion. It was also to examine the conditions in which the WAAC were accommodated and worked. The six members of the Commission spent a week in France in March 1918 visiting 29 camps and hostels, and speaking to administrators, base officials, chaplains, medical staff, and YMCA and YWCA, representatives.[19]

The result was reassuring. 'The statistical evidence on their return regarding widespread immorality bore no relation to the horror stories circulating in the country at large.' On their return to London the ladies issued a press statement which effectively silenced the rumours. They had found the Corps activities and behaviour to be worthy of the highest praise, declaring them to be 'a healthy, cheerful, self-respecting body of hard-working women conscious of their position as links in the great chain of the Nation's purpose, and zealous in its service'.[20]

Within a month or so following the publication of that strong rebuttal, prosecutions taken under the Defence of the Realm Act had identified and fined some of the guilty culprits who had spoken out publicly, if unwisely, to voice genuine concern for perceived dangers to the moral welfare of young women. Hefty fines of £40 and £50 respectively were imposed.[21]

Concern over the behaviour of the girls sent to France had raised a great deal of interest in the press nonetheless and, consequently, a number of journalists were officially invited to visit the camps in France. The result was a number of satisfyingly enthusiastic 'positive' reports – aka propaganda – about the well-being of the girls who had joined up in support of the army. In one such article, the *Daily Mail* correspondent gives a glowing description of women's quarters in a Nissen hut, writing that:

> Dainty pink casements flutter at the windows, lockers are covered with material of similar colour, lights gleam through rose-coloured shades, window-boxes are gay, and freshly-cut flowers beautify the hut. … All the huts are alike in that over each girl's bed is her little picture gallery of the home folk, the babies, the khaki boys, the father, the mother and sisters.
>
> Life in camp is greatly preferred to house billets. Camp life arouses the girls' enthusiasm – it is a spot of their very own, something in which to take pride, to beautify.
>
> The conversion of an ugly corner into a rockery, the healthy look of the vegetable plots, the decoration of the new stage, a successful dance – all these are matters of personal interest with the girls. They thoroughly enjoy living, working and playing together.[22]

While the report may have overly puffed up the scene, there is plenty of surviving evidence which confirms that the WAACs did indeed try to make the best fist of what must have been difficult living conditions. They did make gardens. Flowers and vegetables were grown and there were modest efforts to add small decorative touches to their billets.

Life in camp

For some new recruits, the simplicity of arrangements for their accommodation was tolerable enough, bar the lack of sheets on their beds. It might be considered that family sizes were generally much larger at that time. Girls who had grown up in households with several sisters were accustomed to sharing rooms – and often beds, too – so dormitory living and limited shared space was not too much of a drawback, or even a novel experience for many. Recruits drawn from the middle classes may have attended all-girls' boarding schools or convent schools run by religious orders and they, too, would have encountered similar communal sleeping arrangements, austere surroundings and strict routines. Young women from remote Irish rural families who might have been lucky enough to find a job in their local town or the nearest city were used to lodgings or accommodation shared with workmates. Owners of retail outlets often insisted their female employees acceded to their 'live-in' conditions, which housed staff in dormitories with a matron installed to keep an eye on them.

There were occasional genuine grumbles. Canteen mess meals, morning and night-time roll calls, no talking after 'lights out' and insistence that blankets were folded in strict military style on bunks and left undisturbed all day after early morning roll call were all irksome but necessary rules to abide by. Signallers – whose sleep patterns were fractured by shifting rosters – received special permissions. When in camp they were housed 'all in the same hut [because] our hours are more or less irregular – some of us being on night duty and some on day duty'.[23]

Surviving records of their service days at the Rouen base reveal there were certainly great efforts to make the WAACs feel welcomed on arrival. A member of the 30 July batch of signallers – the first batch of twenty-six GPO girls to arrive here – recalled how:

> looking round the camp with its clusters of Nissen huts dotted among the fruit trees, we felt we would soon be at home! … Our first meal in camp was at the sergeants' mess at Remounts. We formed up and we marched the short distance from our compound to that of the men's. Arrived there, we found Colonel Westlake and the adjutant standing on the steps of the office and received a very fatherly greeting from

the colonel before going on to the mess. I can see that room as clearly now – long trestle tables laden with a lovely meal, salmon and salad, new bread and warm cakes waited for us, and, believe me, we did that meal justice. Quite a little army of sergeants waited upon us and they really were pleased to see us … After the meal, I remember so well, [our camp administrator] Miss Laird gave us permission to smoke, and it was a very contented crowd of WAAC who wended their way back to unpack and distribute their belongings. I can truly say that never in my life have I been happier than I was at camp.[24]

Miss Mary Holmes Laird, the administrator who is referred to here, was a remarkable Scottish woman who was an old hand at adapting to army life, having already served in Serbia and Salonika with the French Army prior to joining the WAAC.[25]

In some locations, accommodation in a camp was not always possible and billets in old, partly abandoned buildings had to be arranged. One early arrival of a girl appointed as a forewoman describes how:

The bathing arrangements are too killing. They are on the first floor, which is a big stone room, curtained off in cubicles with a kind of tarpaulin, and behind these are two taps and a drain, and a tin bath … Then in the next room, which is also of stone, are cubicles again in which are wooden tables with tin bowls and jugs on for ordinary cat-licks.[26]

Some appreciation of the stern restrictions imposed on their day-to-day lives raises the point that being deployed in army bases had necessitated not only their curtailed personal freedom but it minimized tiny self-indulgent habits most young girls of their age were accustomed to enjoying. The simplicity of a list of 'personal effects' returned to the mother of one girl following her death from what was known as the 'Spanish flu' in 1918 bears a poignancy that is almost overwhelming.[27] The young telegraphist from Derby had travelled out and served with several GPO colleagues from Dublin, Wicklow and Carlow at a base in France since the end of July 1917. The true nature of the those harshly grim lives these girls endured in the performance of their duties is revealed in the modest amount of extra warm clothing she had been allowed in addition to her regulation WAAC all-year-round uniform kit – the dress, overalls, trench coat, boots and shoes. These items were merely augmented that winter by that girl's own extra underskirt, three pairs of woollen combinations, a woollen bodice and three pairs of woollen knickers. To combat the intensely cold nights, she had been allowed the comfort of her own dressing-gown, pyjamas, bed socks and hot water bottle. Apart from these extras and the ownership of a pair of slippers for off-duty hours, her only other personal belongings merely comprised a suitcase, towel, nightdress case, six handkerchiefs, a small linen bag, case of needles and a book of music. Only the latter two items give some hint as to this girl's leisure time activities. The acceptance of such pared-down simplicity was almost monastic in its absence of worldly possessions, a testimony to the sacrifice they were all making. A postscript to this story points up that bonds of loyal friendship that were nurtured by these young women's shared wartime experiences in France ran deep. Seven years later, a small party of her former colleagues made a short nostalgic return trip to that French town to seek traces of their WAAC days. Their memory of her had not been forgotten. Before they left, they took the tram out to the cemetery to visit her grave. It was a moment of sombre reflection.[28]

Settling in

Settling into the BEF bases on arrival took some adjustment for everyone because army billets varied according to rank. In towns and cities various buildings were requisitioned for the use of more senior members of the Corps such as unit administrators, but for the majority of rank and file 'Workers' and 'Forewomen', the accommodation they were given usually consisted of newly constructed huts in segregated camps for women and it was generally agreed that the convenience and conviviality of camp life was much preferred to that of the often cramped living quarters allocated to 'Officials' elsewhere in a base. Acute overcrowding for the latter was common. When the father of one Birmingham girl, junior to a newly arrived higher-ranking colleague, heard that because space was so limited in one of these old buildings her bed had been moved out to an adjoining curtained-off section of a landing, his outraged moral fury when writing to the Chief Controller of the Corps was palpable: '… the thought and publicity of my own daughter, brought up with the greatest care, of sleeping on a landing is more than a shock!'[29] The girl herself had been stoic over the move but the deputy controller still ordered her area controller to set up an enquiry which revealed there had been no protests over the arrangement as she often worked night duties and the landing was quieter than alternative, larger rooms that were in use during the day. There must have been many others who decided it was sometimes better not to let those at home know the full story of what the ups and downs of army life were really like.

When newly recruited drafts arrived at a camp they were divided up into groups of eight girls per Nissen hut. Each hut was furnished with army-issue iron bedsteads and hard 'biscuit' mattress. There were plenty of blankets – but no sheets – a pillow for each girl and a couple of coarse pillowslips and huckaback towels. Everyone was allocated a small shelf for their personal belongings and the hut was equipped with a partition at one end to contain: 'Two rough cubicles, one for the Forewoman in charge, the other fitted up with a tap and sink and two large zinc washing bowls.'[30] Meals were taken in the camp's mess hall.

For the first arrivals it was soon the general consensus that food served in an army mess hall was plentiful – but monotonous. Each girl was entitled to a daily WAAC ration of the following:

½ lb Meat, ½ lb Bread, ½ oz Tea /or 1 oz Coffee or Cocoa, 2 oz Sugar, ¼ oz Salt, 2 oz Bacon, 3 oz Jam, ¼ lb Fresh vegetables, ½ lb Potatoes, 2 oz Rice or oatmeal, 1 oz Margarine, 1/8th pint of Milk, 1/100th oz Pepper, 1/100th oz Mustard and 1 oz Cheese.[31]

Food and beverages were consumed from enamelled tin plates, mugs and jugs – and as one girl was later to recall – when their tea came in a teapot 'it was as good a brew as anyone could wish for', except that the tea had been made in a large army-style metal vessel called a dixie that had recently been used to 'boil our breakfast ham'. The tea 'tasted like nothing on earth' and there were grouses all round, albeit followed by stoic sighs of 'what a blessing to get coffee instead'.

So while the food was wholesome, the WAACs soon learned to adapt to the restrictions of a dull menu with as much good grace as they could muster. 'Potatoes were boiled in their skins [and] rice figured with detestable frequency; rice and bully-beef, rice and cheese, rice rissoles, rice pudding with jam sauce - and just rice.' The commentator also noted how

Loaves of bread were almost invariably smothered in hairs from the sacks in which they were packed ... and the limited bread ration was a sore trial to most of us at first until we got used to eating our meat without it. Army biscuit could be had for the asking but were incredibly hard and required iron teeth to tackle it.

Indeed, the toughness of the army biscuits became legendary. Many of the girls' records show them to have suffered dental problems during their service days and, in later life often sharply recalled the problems they had coping with the hard biscuits, describing them as 'hard tack' when remembering how essential it was to ensure they were properly soaked in some liquid or other to soften them up before making any attempt to bite into them and there were occasions when teeth were broken or damaged when a girl was impatient or foolish enough to try to eat them dry.[32]

Meals consisted of breakfast: 'Bacon or cold ham, bread, margarine, jam or marmalade, tea or coffee.' Dinner was in the middle of the day, with 'hot meat, two vegetables and gravy', the vegetables being 'mostly potato and carrot or turnip and onion with occasional salads in the summer'. Cabbage was limited because 'the French growers charged such exorbitant prices'. The same applied to fruit. 'Milk pudding and jam sauce or plum-duff (no bread)'[33] was the staple fare for dessert. At teatime, the girls had 'bread, margarine, jam and tea with bully-beef and pickles or cheese-savoury, or pork and beans'. For supper there was 'Biscuit and cheese, cocoa or tea (no bread)'. Girls soon learned to be enterprising and when given a pass to go into town were able to break the monotony of army diet by surreptitiously buying a meal from restaurants that were 'only too happy to supply fried eggs and chipped potatoes or omelettes – at a price'. The food usually had to be 'consumed off the premises' because most local restaurants and cafés were out of bounds.

For the girls from Ireland, the ample but dull army catering was found to be very different from what they were still quite accustomed to at home. They found there was no customary plentiful supply of butter or buttermilk and no brown or white soda bread. Dishes such as boxty, colcannon, and black and white pudding were unheard of and, as has been shown, the ration of potatoes was meagre and supplies of cabbage very scarce. Consequently, unlike colleagues from homes across England and Wales who knew that food restrictions and shortages at home were getting increasingly worse, they must never have found the army meals served up to them remarkably satisfying. Within twelve months it would worsen, but it was probably still better than the increasing restrictions being put on civilians in England where rationing of sugar, milk, butter and meat had been introduced.

In Ireland, the shortages had not been so severe – afterwards prompting one WAAC official from London to comment that her regular inspection visits to camps in Ireland throughout the whole of 1917–1919 as being full of 'pleasant recollections [because] in those days Ireland seemed a land flowing with cream and butter to a Controller used to English rations'.[34]

In 1918, freshly enrolled personnel passing though in the WAAC/QMAAC dispersal base in Folkestone on their way to France also suffered from the increasingly severe UK rationing. Despite being under military control they fared very much less well than all their fellow Corps members who had crossed the Channel ahead of them months earlier. One girl later remembered how 'Food was very limited. On alternate days we had "High Tea" that we found to mean two meals were amalgamated at six o'clock. On the other days we had tea at four and a further meal of soup at night. The tea consisted of one slice of bread and jam and a mug of tea'. Staple food for dinner was 'rabbit and one potato in a dirty skin' and the dreariness of daily servings of rabbit had 'grown tedious'.[35]

Chapter 4

The Diversity of Work 'Overseas'

Yes, we're "just a little bit of home
Come out to lend a hand,"
And we've found a welcome waiting
Here in this foreign land.

John Oxenham, 1917[1]

The attachment of the WAAC to the army's separate regional commands brought about a sudden great need for many more trained women who could supervise and give support to the forewomen (aka NCOs) who were needed to run billets and hostels for ordinary 'workers' enrolled as catering and cleaning staff, office workers and so on. A post as a 'Hostel Forewoman' could often lead to being offered subsequent promotion to a commissioned rank, and examples of young women from Ireland who signed up as hostel forewomen between October and November 1917 can be found. Being early recruits, they may have served first in London or elsewhere the UK, but they were soon to be on their way to becoming WAAC 'Officials' bearing the rank of a 'Unit Administrator' or 'Assistant Administrator'. Having been recommended for that upgrading of status, their first step was to undergo a training course which was usually undertaken in Bostall Heath Camp in the London area. Commissions followed not long afterwards and some then returned to Ireland to be attached to the Irish Command.[2] The surviving records of five such cases reveal that three were from Dublin, one lived in Sligo and one was from Cork.[3]

The one from Cork – an almost-40-year-old women – presents an example of the many volunteers who came back to Ireland or England from a prewar location in the southern hemisphere. In her case she also illustrates how the WAAC controllers and their staff took careful stock of the potential for all young women from Ireland who harboured a driving ambition to succeed.[4] It had not been an easy process for that keen candidate and she underwent several sometimes difficult assignments before finding her feet. As a former teacher and governess, possibly the daughter of a former naval man or businessman who had long connections to South Africa in civilian life, she had already founded a private school prior to leaving for South Africa to seek a different lifestyle several years before the outbreak of the war in 1914. By 1916, however, in the hope of doing 'war work', and maybe with an eye out for also improving her position in life, she had returned to Cork, where she had a number of well-connected friends. When she signed up to join the WAAC in October 1917 she believed herself to be well qualified to become a commissioned officer in this new women's army corps. At that time, WAAC units for the Irish Command had not yet been fully settled into Dublin and elsewhere, so she took the mail boat to Holyhead and went by train as far as Chester to be enrolled by English Western Command and, following a short training and assessment session, was sent straight away 'overseas' as a hostel forewoman at a French base, probably with the idea of being groomed to become an administrator. But things had not gone well there. She was assessed by the area controller as 'not suitable for a post as Administrator overseas' and sent back to London where she was given another chance to prove herself. She passed the administrator's written test and survived a short stint up in Wales, by August 1918 was once more despatched 'overseas' to France where she served for almost twelve months in Wimereux. She was later allowed home to Ireland where, at her own request, demobilization was granted and she was able to return to South Africa in late September 1919 with plans to resume work as a schoolteacher.

Her case might be seen as demonstrating the obverse side to what was soon to become a flow of new emigrations seeking alternative lifestyles outside Ireland. Samples of similar recruits born overseas who returned to serve with the WAAC – often bearing Irish surnames – are not difficult to find.

The responsibilities of serving as an 'Administrator'

Administrators were not drawn from a strictly homogeneous sector of society. The practice of promoting potential candidates from the ranks of catering or clerical workers brought about a gradual change to what may have otherwise become extremely strict class divisions. A great many of the earliest 'Officials' had joined up via the Women's Legion whose members had merged with the new women's army corps at the time of the Corps' foundation. It was essentially a housekeeping role almost aligned to that of an army quartermaster. As Dennant's study puts it, those chosen as desirable candidates were often 'House Mistresses and housekeepers in schools and large institutions, and women trained in welfare work'. She pointed out that, in England, there were already 'Superintendents of Hostels which had been organised by the Ministry of Munitions'. In Ireland, candidates for administration posts were also drawn from sectors that Dennant's work identified as 'University women, and those who have gained experience in Canteens and girls' clubs', adding that 'the qualities chiefly sought in them is that they should have been used to dealing with girls, have helped to organise games and women's work, and above all that they should have tact and strength of character'.[5]

At all times, the supervision and discipline of the workers and forewomen in WAAC camps and billets was an important factor in maintaining a productive level of work from the girls they were responsible for. Before being appointed, each 'Administrator' underwent a special course of training. Carrying the status of a commissioned officer, they were addressed as 'Ma'am' and girls from other ranks were instructed to always stand in their presence, although one account clarifies: 'We were told that should an Administrator chance to enter the Mess room while a meal was in progress, we need not rise to our feet as we did at other times, but we must "leave off eating".'[6]

Although required to display similar deference toward these higher-ranking colleagues, the girls brought in to undertake office duties and similar clerical work were often rather sympathetic towards the administrators and the tasks imposed on them. They appreciated the difficulties of their responsibilities, especially when they had to work out rosters and accommodation problems. As worker Hay put it: 'We liked them all more or less but especially the Unit Administrator whose rank corresponded to that of an Army Colonel. After the first few days she was chained to her office, coping valiantly with tangles of Red Tape which grew more and more complicated as time wore on.'

Obviously under pressure, one of the assistant administrators later spelt out that much of her work entailed two responsibilities: the first was day-to-day household management and the second the maintenance of equipment:

> I have at present two jobs, [one as] AA to the hostel and [another as] acting quarter-mistress. In my first capacity I help to keep an eye on the household management, and I indent for the rations and coal on the appropriate army forms (their name is Legion). Reports are brought to me of leaking pipes, broken bedsteads stopped-up drains, etc., and every week have to go through the complete list of equipment for the Hostel and see that everything from chairs and tables down to the last scrubbing brush and spoon is in place, and to note all breakages. I make out passes and censor letters (a hateful job) and sometimes take roll call.[7]

For many who served as administrators the work might be quite different from their former existence as civilians, although for young women who had formerly worked in schools or colleges there are discernible parallel lines which may have influenced their selection for this type of promotion. For example, anyone with an interest in sporting activities was likely to be put in line for a 'commission' because administrators were expected to encourage the younger WAAC members under their care 'to play hockey, cricket and tennis'.[8] In the early days, any organized events outside of work were aimed at discouraging off-duty relaxations that allowed the mixing of ranking status. Nonetheless, the deliberate policy of isolating the signallers from all other sectors and categories of work within the Corps may have become more relaxed after the Armistice as accounts have turned up which refer to organized hockey matches and sports days which pitted teams of 'clerks, signallers and gardeners' against teams made up of 'orderlies, waitresses, laundresses and cooks'.[9] A recollection of the aim to keep the Post Office signallers at a distance from other WAAC girls in work and play had certainly been ignored in these instances, although it must be kept in mind that those events were very probably organized in 1919, by which time the highest levels of security and imposed class distinction had been slightly relaxed.

Otherwise, it can only be concluded that minor breaches of rules – if carried out under the supervision of an enthusiastic unit administrator – were tolerated at times.

To keep morale high in France enterprises such as concerts and 'amateur theatricals' were also welcomed by the controllers. In Rouen, for example, one UA who had been a musical comedy star in civilian life before the war, needed very little encouragement to allow performances of a Gilbert and Sullivan operetta carrying an apt storyline about social class divisions. It was directed by an RE engineer and while the chorus was entirely made up by female servicewomen who were 'workers', the principal soloists, male and female alike, had apparently not allowed any question of rank to cause a problem. There will be more to be said later about the event.

Looking forward to the postwar era, it is very striking how many of the former administrators continued to be keen on sports and many became engaged in organizing the development of the Girl Guides movement. Since 1911, there had been an Irish branch of Baden-Powell girl guides. It was later re-organized into two bodies when the Government of Ireland Act came into being in 1920, but the links remained over the decades and, by 1999, they once more became an all-Ireland body and, as such, continue to be members of the World Association of Girl Guides and Girl Scouts.

Ranking system keeps personnel strictly apart

From 1917 to 1919, apart from evidence drawn from accounts of surreptitiously organized sporting or entertainment deviations to the norm, the Army Council ruling that no worker or forewoman was allowed to socialize with the higher-ranking 'Officials' was generally scrupulously observed. Their comings and goings were kept separate, which meant that all commissioned ranks were billeted in special quarters. If accommodated in a camp, they had their own separate huts and mess halls. If elsewhere, either in requisitioned quarters or in a section of a barracks, they also remained entirely segregated.

Other ranks who rated as workers or forewomen – which included the clerks and the signallers – were permitted a limited amount of socializing with soldiers and NCOs and despite the rules, devious ploys were undoubtedly used by some of the more persistent young lieutenants and captains who had girlfriends who were from the lower ranks. Strict regimes spawned deception. Rules were broken and army engineers in Signal units became particularly adept at making friendships with the shorthand typists and clerks working in GHQ's back offices. One case, cited as an example, was the story that 'a sergeant who regularly visited one of the clerks in the WAAC headquarters was really an officer, who had borrowed the disguise to pursue his courtship'. It was a tale with a happy ending and 'he survived the war to marry his girl'.[10]

At other times, a rather ludicrous situation might arise when brothers and sisters and other family relatives or close friends served at different levels of rank. When home on leave, or on similar off-duty occasions, borrowed items of clothing were often used to concealed true military status. In one of her poems Grindlay describes how a prewar acquaintance who had become 'a lady brass hat' lent her a uniform and hat as a 'disguise' so that the pair could go out to 'celebrate' their chance meeting in Paris in 1920.[11]

Army work in telegraph offices
Today's lack of knowledge in regard to the Irishwomen who served 'overseas' in "L" Signal units ('E' category) may not only be due to the relatively small number of WAACs who served in this capacity by contrast to the thousands recruited for work in the other six segments of activity, but rests very much with the strictly confidential nature of their work. Similar rules of non-disclosure had been an essential component of their employment as civilian employees of the Post Office and it is not surprising, therefore, that very little of their army work-a-day experiences was ever divulged. Only an occasional glimpse would be revealed in oral interviews or published memoires of rank and file members, decades later.

For example, in a research project conducted in 1995, a description of telegraphists' working conditions was gathered from a surviving WAAC centenarian who explained how 'The girls worked in shifts from three in the afternoon until three in the morning' in a location that was 'deeply underground'.[12] The Duplex system used 'two girls sitting beside one another. One received messages and one transmitted them. The Germans were not able to tap-into this system and the messages were about what the troops were doing, the officers, who they were, where they were, etcetera'.

The ability for girls to read and write Morse code messages had long been a necessary skill to learn in the course of Post Office training and subsequent employment in Irish rural townships. Examination of army records has shown that a number of the women working in these bases were telegraphists. Although, rather more of them were drawn from Dublin, there were several who came from homes in Antrim, Armagh, Kilkenny, Waterford and Westmeath.

It can be appreciated that the maintenance of security was mandatory for anyone working in a Signal unit. An account written by a WAAC who served in the Battalion HQ in Calais reveals how they were forbidden to personally possess 'any bottles of any description, not even iodine or smelling-salts'.[13] It was a ruling which might now strike as inexplicable, but the explanation was straightforward enough: 'We learned afterwards that the puzzling embargo on bottles was designed to prevent our taking out supplies of invisible ink, and possibly writing home indiscretions which could not be deleted by the Censor.'

This writer's well-received reminiscences, published in 1919, reveal her to have been one of a team who had worked in the 'Q' department of the 1st Echelon of GHQ. The officer heading up 'Q' was the BEF's Deputy Assistant Quartermaster-General. The BEF was divided into three echelons of GHQ – although the term was soon dropped for the 2nd Echelon, which was the army's physical HQ. The 3rd Echelon was based in Rouen, a busy port on the Seine which has been described as 'a sprawling busy Army base which supported many diverse sections of operational needs'.[14] Rouen was a centre for the coordination of troop movements and supplies and it also held a large number of military hospitals. There were thousands of clerical workers based here, too. Their task was to look after all the army records for serving rank and file.

For the Signal unit girls attached to GHQ echelons, the handling of top-secret messages coming down the wire was a routine procedure and the constant flow of encrypted telegrams had first to be decoded before being passed on to one of the WAAC clerks so that the contents could be 'laboriously repeated over the telephone to the Units concerned for action'.[15] It was later explained that:

The Code seemed a frivolous affair, on first sight. I remember quite well one telegram which ran: 'Five Puffins and a Periwinkle left Popinjay for Peppercorn on 3rd ult.'. This gave warning of the movements of some troops and transport. ... The code books were locked away in an iron strongbox, along with the Order of Battle and other documents which no-one else in the office was allowed to handle. Certain secret information such as the times and dates of troopship sailings was sent to us in a complicated cipher, the key of which, for added security, was kept in the safe.

When the messages that came down wire had been decoded the key would be locked up and the original cipher destroyed, so that no-one got the chance to compare it with the translation. Code Books became obsolete every few months, and just as we were beginning to memorise the more commonly used words, a new edition would appear.

Even when security constraints did not require such stringent secrecy, their working conditions were by no means ideal:

Basements were utilized whenever possible and, where suitable cellars existed, signal offices were always established downstairs in preference to the better-lighted and more airy rooms on the ground floor.[16]

For the first arrivals who took up duties in May 1917, the complicated twenty-four-hour duty rosters for the former GPO telephonists were later described rather wryly by one young woman as having been 'most peculiar' and, certainly by comparison to their former duties as civilians, it would have taken some time to get used to it.[17] Shifts for different days of a week for each girl might commence at either 8 a.m., 10 a.m. or 11 a.m. Likewise, there were two afternoon shifts, one from 1 p.m. to 5 p.m. and another from 4 p.m. to 8 p.m. The evening shifts covered from 5 or 7 p.m. up to 10 p.m., which were followed by the night duties which all started at 10 p.m. and ran through until 7 or 8 in the morning – albeit on alternate days. Sundays were treated like any other day of the week. The work patterns were demanding but there is evidence that once they had settled into the new routines – which were undoubtedly helped by strict roll calls and the rigorous army rules by which they lived – the system worked smoothly.

Another commentator, one of the higher-ranking WAACs, when writing in October 1917, had observed how the women 'attached to the RE as "signallers" [telegraphists and telephonists] who work seven to eight hours a day, Sundays included', were being praised by 'their [RE] officers [who] all say their work is splendid and already they are releasing many men for further up the line'.[18]

Although of immense use, these tasks were nonetheless carried out in conditions that were far from favourable for the health of girls who toiled for hours working in 'stuffy little back rooms whose only window looked out onto a dingy yard on which the sun never shone. ... Most of us averaged about seventy hours a week on duty, all told'.[19]

Cryptographic security systems and the women known as 'Hush -WAAC'

One branch of important activity that should also never be forgotten was the elite band of bilingual recruits who came to be known as the 'Hush-WAAC' who were quietly set up in September 1917.[20]

Having been kept tucked out of sight far more stringently than the 'Signallers' throughout the war, their work was later briefly acknowledged by Bidwell without revealing very much detail:

A small and select party of six Assistant Administrators, all fluent German speakers, was recruited into Army Intelligence radio intercept service for translation and deciphering duties, where they worked long hours and, until May 1918, without a day off.

Their top-secret activities were thus kept well under wraps – a factor which prompted even the former C-C of the WAAC/QMAAC to recall in her memoires: 'Their activities were confidential and we knew little of them.'

The originally very small group of half a dozen linguists had soon increased considerably in size and importance. Put to work in a top-secret sector of GHQ at St. Omer under the control of Brigadier-

General John Charteris, head of intelligence, this sector's input into the creation of sophisticated encryption techniques for the military is now being viewed as one of the most insightful innovations of the Western Front. Recently issued research work by Jim Beach, University of Northampton, and two colleagues from the History and the Military Intelligence museums have drawn up a list of seventeen administrators and seven non-commissioned supportive clerical workers.[21] One of the named administrators has been confirmed as an Irishwoman from Milford in Donegal, Catherine Hayes Osborne, whose war service in WAAC would have been almost completely forgotten by her local community had Caroline Carr at the Donegal County Museum not restored her place back into local history in 2017. Catherine Osborne's army service file had not survived and very little more is known about her army days except that her enrolment date was 28 September 1917 and that she served in France with the unit until early November 1918. Her 'engagement' as an administrator was terminated on 1 January 1919.[22]

For many years, investigation of the nature of these girls' contribution was understandably thwarted by the unavailability of information for researchers who were interested in military cryptanalysis. It was not until the end of the twentieth century that historian John Ferris and others were able to start throwing more light on the topic.[23] There was to be considerable frustration vented. He pointed out that while 'the navy deliberately preserved archives, … conversely, the army chose to destroy all but a handful of its original intelligence files', adding that although 'Britain had six efficient code-breaking bureaux between 1914 and 1918, … destruction has been particularly marked regarding signals intelligence. Only 25 of the (at least) 3,330 files of the code breakers at GHQ France survive'.

That Irishwomen were involved in this work should not come as a surprise. There is at least one other instance that has come to light only recently – albeit a generation later – which throws up a connection between the next generation of cryptanalysts working at Bletchley Park in the 1940s and a WAAC who had broken the bounds of society's polite convention by 'doing her bit' in 1917.

An obituary, published in The *Irish Times* on 16 July 2016, generously acknowledged the contribution to history made by Irishwoman Leslie

Greer, née Tyrrell, MBE, who worked as a cryptanalyst at Bletchley Park in the Second World War, having been inspired perhaps by her mother's contribution to the First World War in France as a WAAC motorcycle despatch rider who had been attached to the British Army's Royal Flying Corps.[24] One can but comment that her mother remains one of the many other 'lost names' who remain unacknowledged for their courage during the Great War.

Terror from the air

Unlike some of the other bases further to the north, Rouen was well behind the lines and relatively quiet until the spring of 1918. But tension was rising. A new offensive was clearly in the offing. Up to that time, attacking German war planes had only been capable of reaching army depots nearest the front line. They were now able to carry bombs further afield and, on 7 February that year, the GHQ 3rd Echelon reminded military personnel at the base that 'Precautions against air raids must be observed'.[25] Rouen was no longer safe from airborne attacks.

That month, throughout the town and surrounding areas, preparations for what came to be known as a 'Blackout' in World War Two were undertaken in compliance with instructions issued by the Army's Routine Order No 3246:[26]

> From sunset ... the lighting of all houses, buildings (public or private), workshops, stores and all buildings which show a bright light through windows, shop-fronts or glass openings, whether looking out into the street, back-yard or garden shall be screened. The same regulation applies to garret-windows and skylights. ... In places where it is not possible to screen the windows themselves with shutters, blinds, curtains etc., every individual light will be shaded with brown paper or other opaque material in such a way as to prevent any ray of light from being projected through windows or skylights.[27]

Extra precautions were taken in the camps and trenches were dug. The WAACs were issued with tin hats and practised the drill for taking shelter when the approach of 'hostile aircraft' triggered an air raid warning.

Practices that had been already adopted by other bases nearer the front lines were put into action:

> It was by our office telephone that we got the first hint of an impending raid; the bell would ring like mad [to convey] a hurried message re. hostile aircraft bombing such-and-such a place and advancing in so–and–so a direction.[28]

By that time, both sides of the conflict had shifted tactical operations into much greater reliance in another sphere: the war in the air. The past twelve months had witnessed advances in aircraft design which allowed for much greater capability in active combat some distance away from the front lines and, as military historian Priestley has reminded:

> Signal camps and signal offices also began to suffer and casualties to signal personnel in rear areas increased considerably. In the autumn of 1917, the enemy bombing squadrons began to single out Divisional headquarters for special attention and, after considerable damage had been caused, the order was issued that sufficient bomb-proof shelters must be constructed to house all ranks.[29]

Although enemy bombing attacks on Rouen did not commence until July 1918, there had already been a great deal of ferocious targeting of more northern bases up along the coast where WAAC signallers were serving. Throughout the early summer there were air raids on Bordeaux, Wimereux and Abbeville, where 'on the night of 21/22 May a [German] aerial torpedo struck camp II where the women had been sheltering in slit trenches for 5 hours. Only about four huts escaped out of the seventeen in the camp; the rest were unusable.[30]

'Eight days later the German planes returned to Abbeville and dropped three bombs. Eight [girls] were killed outright and one died later from wounds; six others were wounded.'

Historians Arthur Marwick and Roy Terry have each referred to German bombing raids on Etaples and Abbeville, and Messenger calculated that 'Eight officials and seventy-five members of the QMAAC were killed or died in war theatres'.[31]

Writing some ten years later to share her experience with other members of the WAAC Old Comrades' Association, one girl has given a first-hand account of a bombing raid on the base at Abbeville. She writes how:

At 11 o'clock we were awakened by noise of anti-aircraft guns, with the more muffled and distant one of bombs. So out we dashed, helter-skelter for those blessed trenches, which certainly saved our lives. ... We sat or crouched for five hours, about 200 of us in trenches 5ft. to 6ft. deep and wide enough to allow us to sit single file. The whole camp was lit up with this hateful moonlight and it was light enough to read in the trenches if anyone wanted to ... And the noise ! We had anti-aircraft guns on two sides and a machine gun on a third.

We were in some danger from our own machine gun which kept up a fierce rap-tap-tap all the time. About midnight there was a fierce, lurid light in the south coast sky, we thought the whole of Abbeville was in flames and even at great risk stood up to see the awful sight. It was a petrol dump on fire.

After that it seemed to be intensified a thousand-fold and seemed to endure for hours. I seemed to lose sense of time and was actually dozing when there was a shout, a fearful explosion and the ground shook.

Some WAAC looking upward actually saw the horrible aerial torpedo like a ball of fire in the sky. We all thought the end had come. The next thing I remember was a Sergeant's voice 'Dig that girl out'; that girl was me. I was right at the end of the caved in portion of the trench, it had felt like an earthquake the way the earth rose and fell.

I was soon dragged out, choked and blinded with soil. What a sight met my gaze! A grey dawn was fighting for supremacy with the heavy smoke rising from the wrecked camp. Only about four huts standing out of 17. Some were absolute matchwood, some only half demolished.[32]

It is worth noting that those and other air raids attacks on the WAAC serving in France were not easily forgotten. In 1938 – two decades later –

when delivering an address to a gathering of the QMAAC Old Comrades' Association in London, Dame Helen Gwynne-Vaughan, former Chief Controller in France, referred to what she felt had been one of the 'greatest compliments' the Corps had ever received, which had been generated 'not surprisingly through the medium of Signals'. She was referring to one of the first air raids on a base in France. The bombing attack had been completely unexpected, but the telephonists who were 'on duty in a glass-roofed place, had remained calmly at their posts', and in relating this incident she reminded her audience that 'The young officer who was dealing with the situation quite expected them to faint or something. They did not'. The young army captain had been so impressed that:

> he put it up to Headquarters that they should be mentioned in Orders. The idea was so new that it went right up to GHQ. And GHQ replied: 'We do not thank soldiers for devotion to duty. We do not propose to treat these women differently.'[33]

Her story points up how – far from not wanting to talk about the risks they had taken in that war – those by then middle-aged women still took enormous pride in the contribution they and other colleagues had made on active service. It is a reminder, too, of how the reputation of the signallers' professionalism throughout the campaign gained and retained the greatest of respect in army circles. The GPO's preliminary eighteen months or so of rigorous training into that organization's protocols prior to their acceptance as fully 'appointed' staff members had already attuned these young women to be consistently alert, precise and watchful when on duty at switchboards and telegraph stations in order to preserve the security and confidentially offered as a public service. It was to be a distinct advantage to them when they joined the WAAC that by the twentieth century, the regime and traditions of the late nineteenth-century British Post Office had become 'an efficient bureaucracy run on what was essentially military lines'.[34] These girls would therefore have had no difficulty in adapting to the army-run exchanges. Their understanding of the hierarchy of rank and how to abide by protocols, rules and regulations was a factor that must have greatly assisted the transition from civilian to army life. Not every girl who enrolled to work in other sections of the WAAC had that advantage.

Chapter 5

What Was the Problem in Signals?

*'The most immediate effect of the outbreak of the war in August 1914
was the rapid depletion of the Post Office workforce.'*

A. Clinton[1]

In March 1918, when the last great German offensive of the First
World War threatened the most forward military positions of the
BEF, large numbers of supporting army personnel had already pulled
back to locations of greater safety in view of the escalating danger. The
Signal unit at St. Omer in France was ordered to send its contingent of
WAAC telegraph and telephone operators further back behind the lines,
too, but the Director of Army Signals for France requested that the order
be cancelled, insisting that

> his 142 women had behaved with exemplary calm under air-raids
> and, if removed, he would not be responsible for [maintaining]
> communications between GHQ at Montreuil and Headquarters
> Second army at Cassel, vital to the conduct of the battle.[2]

The protest was valid. His contingent of servicewomen holding out in
St. Omer was clearly indispensable. The counter-order to keep them
in situ was accepted by GHQ and the girls remained on duty, working
side by side with their male army colleagues to keep the L of C running
smoothly until the crisis had passed.

If a situation like that had been envisaged at the outbreak of the hostilities
in 1914, there is no doubt that to suggest such reliance could be placed on a
small sector of female army auxiliaries at a time of great danger would have
raised huge disbelief, if not outrage and alarm in military minds. It may
be argued that what has continued to be equally surprising is the extent
to which little or no acknowledgement of the key contribution made by

hundreds of GPO women – telegraphists and telephonists who served in Signal units on the Western Front – was ever given any special prominence within the decades of historiography that followed.

Irishwomen played their part in volunteering from this sector in much the same proportion as elsewhere – except for the London area – and although a totally accurate assessment of exactly how many Post Office girls drawn from Ireland served in France as signallers is not attainable, there is nonetheless sufficient evidence to confirm that all their working conditions, wartime experiences and postwar grievances ran the exact same course as their colleagues from other regional areas of that organization until 1922, at which time the Irish Post Office became the new Free State Department of Post and Telegraphs.

It can be shown that one of the great advantages attached to an investigation of the work carried out by WAAC in Signals is that their army service records for the most part can provide clear, if basic, data for researchers. Alternative places to look also exist. One of the most valuable sources are files held within British Telecom's Heritage and Archives.

The army's slow acceptance of telephones in 1914

To understand what was going on by the end of 1916, it will be useful to go back to the early days of the war because the core of the problem may be traced back to attitudes in 1914 over the introduction of more up-to-date telephone networks for the BEF in France. Telegraphy systems were being increasingly utilized but there were still clear misgivings in respect of introducing much greater deployment of telephony. The opinion of the General Staff at that time has been recorded by one expert who believed 'the introduction of telephone exchanges was not viewed favourably'.[3] He describes how when beset by this lack of strong support from the top, but determined to find equipment at any cost at the start of the war, RE engineers had descended on evacuated French villages which were then stripped of abandoned telephones and telegraph accessories 'of every description' to provide their Signal units with the wherewithal for constructing army-run exchanges so that 'by the late spring of 1915, an informal military telephone system could be claimed to be in full swing'.

Wartime developments taking place within army and naval communications systems were very much reliant on the willing cooperation of the British government-owned GPO which ran the national telegraph and telephone services in addition to the Royal Mail. The GPO provided the army's Signal units with almost 18,000 of its engineers and male operators, including many from Ireland.[4] Being already established employees of the state, these men held staff positions which carried certain rights and conditions and, as a result, they had been the subject of a specially negotiated system which ensured the men 'received full civil pay in addition to military pay and allowances'.[5] On demobilization they were to be returned to their former employment sectors in the UK, with all their pension rights and other accrued benefits retained.

In reality, when these former GPO men were sent to the front to work on lines at forward positions under continuous shellfire, the risk of them not surviving was high. There is an account which later appeared in their own *Telegraph and Telephone Journal* for October 1916 which relates how, during a visit to France by some senior personnel from the Post Office to inspect new lines being installed in a 'pretty far front position' where one man had been lost, 'killed by a shell' only two hours earlier, a sergeant of the RE came in to where they were sheltering within five minutes of their arrival to report that another corporal in his work party had just been killed by a rifle bullet. Their reply to his comment 'He was the best man I had' was not recorded.[6]

The all-too-frequent losses of these skilled volunteer Post Office servicemen, either killed or wounded, soon created a severe shortage of competent army telecommunication personnel in all L of C units. There was a knock-on effect behind the lines in the far safer core telegraph offices and telephone exchanges, too. Efforts to find enough replacement staff for the relayed messages between the three echelons of GHQ and other bases, using what were often inadequate facilities, soon became an ongoing serious problem and it was clear to many that poor planning by the military had failed to recognize telephone switchboards operating as an army 'trade'.[7]

Some provision for specific technical training for soldiers to work in this sector had begun by 1915 – but its implementation was slow and there were grumbles and letters of complaint claiming the drafts the Army Training Centre were sending to France consisted of insufficiently prepared operators who displayed 'inefficient' or 'indifferent' experience in contrast to all the excellent earlier GPO deployments.[8] The problem was that by then the nationwide UK workforce was so seriously drained of key personnel that the Post Office officials charged with keeping the home service operating efficiently could only spare virtually inexperienced young men – drawn from small offices – who had not yet learned enough technical nonce to be useful. An impending crisis loomed.

A sensible solution was sought

A good place to start an examination of the background to the attachment of the Post Office women to the WAAC in April 1917, is the initial exploratory enquiry made by the about-to-be-promoted Director of Army Signals, GHQ, Brigadier-General J. Fowler who, on 19 December 1916, purposefully set out to find a reliable solution to solve the difficulty of finding fresh personnel capable of operating the army's increasingly important telecommunication systems behind the lines.[9] The Meath-born soon-to-be Major-General Fowler's successful army career was based on his reputation for using 'tact and charm'[10]. It would be needed now, for he had come up with a revolutionary notion for its time.

In a letter addressed to the Postmaster General in London, Liberal Party Member of Parliament, A. H. Illingworth, he asked if it might be possible to consider 'if trained women telephone exchange and telegraph operators could be made available from the Post Office staff?'[11] He was aware that disturbing concerns might be raised over the concept of female staff working shared duty shifts with male army personnel under what was to be later described as such 'novel circumstances'.[12] To this end, Fowler had taken the precaution of adding a cautionary caveat: 'I think it would be necessary that an officer of the Post Office who knows the conditions under which the women could work should come out here and report on the question. Before making any definite proposals will you kindly inform me if you think it is practicable?'[13]

A positive reaction soon came. On 1 January 1917 the Postmaster General sent a careful response to Fowler's letter which agreed the desirability of an investigative report on equipment and conditions in each of the main army bases where the girls would be working in France. He had been aware for some time that an approaching crisis within the army's Signal units was about to cause huge disruption to the army's L of C and it was clear that something radical would have to be done.

The liaison for these arrangements was assigned to two officers who worked under Fowler: Colonel Andrew Ogilvie, Director of Signals Home Defence and his deputy at Army Signals at the BEF's GHQ in France, Colonel E. V. Turner.[14]

Both officers were immediately drawn into the fresh consultation process for introducing women operators into the BEF. Their responsibilities were now to be turned up several notches of anxiety and it is appropriate that due recognition be given to the genuine strong support both men gave to the female GPO staff who were to be put under their care. The weeks that followed saw intensive discussions to assess what had to be done if young women operators were to be introduced into army L of C exchanges.[15] Topping the list was the question whether an upgrading of some of the less efficient equipment currently in use by the army in France might – or might not – be essential.

On 15 February two Post Office officials, John Lee, Deputy Chief Inspector of Telegraph and Telephone Traffic and Herbert G. Corner, a member of the staff of the General Controller of the London Telephone Service were despatched to France to draw up an Inspectors' Report.[16] Twelve days later their preliminary findings were issued. (See tables 5 and 6 in Appendix I) There were to be adjustments made later to the total number of women operators and supervisors needed.

Their initial proposal suggested that women could indeed be allocated to up to forty-eight existing exchange locations but having agreed that the idea was feasible, it was emphasized that most certainly quite substantial work would be necessary in the base exchanges to ensure that facilities and working conditions for twenty-four-hour female staff rosters were adequate. Telegraph work was particularly demanding. The physical effort of 'stick-punching' for hours in the preparation of punched Morse tapes using the army's favoured 'Wheatstone' system, required the operator to thump the keys very hard with a stick. Three keys would produce a dot, a dash or a space.[17] This method had been in general use on the L of C in conjunction with Duplex equipment (which could send two messages over the same wire simultaneously) for all urgent messages since the outbreak of the war.[18]

Several far superior systems had been developed and put in use by the GPO in London in recent years and although their Inspectors' Report in February had included the recommendation that a handful of the existing male signallers might be retained to help out with the shift work on the older methods in use at the bases, there was also the suggestion that the installation of more efficient equipment – which could be used in conjunction with typewriters instead of the stick-punching techniques – might be tried out. (See Appendix II for details of all the alternative keyboard systems under discussion such as Kleinschmidt or Kotyras)

These discussions were clearly focused on the welfare of the GPO female staff in addition to adding greater all-round efficiency. The view of women having to be engaged in hours of stick-punching was that 'it is not considered that this kind of work is good for them as a continuous employment' and it was asked if it might instead be 'feasible to use typewriter keyboard perforators? ... The output is considerably higher'.[19] It can be added here that the introduction of the more easily operated keyboards was to subsequently create a downside in some eyes during the postwar era because of raised fears of what historian Alan Clinton has called 'a new inferior grade of female typists', which was opposed by the Postal and Telegraph Clerks' Association (P&TCA).[20] It would become a concept ripe with complexity and grievances in the early1920s.

In January 1917 the decisions that had to be made over installing appropriate telegraphic equipment for use by women soon made it clear that there would be drawbacks. (Table 5) The changes being envisaged were complicated by difficulties over the availability of new apparatus in wartime conditions and the London Telegraph Office was wary of allowing its best equipment to be shipped off to France.[21] Discussions bounced back and forth, debating the usage of 'three-key tappers' versus 'keyboards'. The working facilities at the bases were primitive and there was limited electric power available for more up-to-date equipment. For example, to overcome the existing scanty provision of power outlet sockets set into walls or near desks, it was finally suggested that the portable three-tapper Kotyra apparatus could be 'worked with 110 volts from electric light power leads'.[22]

Based on their preliminary findings in the report, which covered seven large base areas which held up to forty-eight exchange and office locations

– with already more being planned – the first estimates calculated that the L of C might need around 582 WAAC 'workers' made up of 340 telegraphists and 242 telephonists. In addition, a small number of more senior supervisors – who, it is important to note, ranked within the GPO as that association's own 'officer class' – was suggested for each base area.[23] (Table 5) The report noted that plans for upgraded army telecommunication facilities would require personnel for additional locations in due course.

The two RE Signal unit officers engaged in these negotiations would have been acutely aware – and duly appreciative – that the GPO had their own difficulties in providing sufficient well-trained personnel to keep their own UK service operating efficiently. At one stage, when writing to Colonel Turner at GHQ France, Colonel Ogilvie conceded that to persuade the Post Office negotiators to agree to 'the release of women who are skilled Morse Telegraphists is almost as difficult as the release of skilled [male] Telegraphists of Military age'.[24]

At the same time, behind the scenes at the War Office, there was a deeper underlying concern over the decision to allow matters to go forward. Who would have ultimate control over the women: the Army or the Post Office? Nothing was yet firmed up. Suggestions for an official 'Corps of Auxiliary Army Women' who could undertake other tasks such as catering and clerical work had received approval. Could the scheme to allow GPO girls to work within RE Signal units fit neatly into the plans for a first-ever British Army 'Corps for Women'? There was one big drawback for the Royal Engineers: Earl Haig had not yet been convinced that it was appropriate. That privilege was a far cry from kitchen work or lending a hand with tedious deskbound paperwork and record-keeping.

In the meantime, work went ahead to upgrade exchanges. Weeks passed. No decision was forthcoming. Would female Post Office telephone and telegraph operators be sent over or not?

Finally, on 10 April, Earl Haig's letter of approval was issued. By the end of May, the first signallers were in France. Their arrival had not put an end to every problem, however. A number of further difficulties looked likely to arise over their roster duties. Who was to supervise the long hours those girls would be expected to work?

Movement begins

Despite a hierarchical system devised by the founders of the WAAC to appoint women controllers and administrators (aka officers) to be in command of the new corps, the hard fact existed that the 'general control' over the WAAC was actually 'vested in the Adjutant General's Department'.[25] In other words, the military had to have the final word.[26] Yet, the reluctance of the Post Office to relinquish total control in matters affecting the conditions and general morale of their staff is totally understandable. It may be recognized that their people were taking good care to tread warily. Not only had they to be seen to give every assistance to the War Office, they also had to try and keep a tight rein on the influence and good will of their own institution's traditionally powerful trade unions. Sensibly productive levels of cooperation had to be maintained because, historically, Post Office workers had by then 'became the pioneers of civil service trade unionism and [its] workers were among the first within the trade union movement to actively support their own Parliamentary candidates'.[27]

The first warning shot over the bows was sent in early April in response to a polite enquiry from the General Secretary of the P&TCA, J. G. Newlove.[28] The union man's query had been received by G. E. P. Murray, the Postmaster General's secretary at the GPO in London.[29] Newlove's letter wanted to know if his association could have sight of that February report assessing the arrangements being made in France for staff members who had volunteered. Murray's reply to the union had been guarded, making it clear that: 'The report was made to and at the request of the Military Authorities in France, and in these circumstances I cannot authorise its disclosure'.[30] It was clear that there were sensitive issues that, if possible, might be best left out of any further enquiries.

Despite the presence of so many unresolved matters, when given the green light in April the joint efforts of the postal authorities and the Army Council had swung into action immediately. While several important issues still remained to be settled, there was a great anxiety to press ahead. Six weeks later, the first twelve Post Office girls travelled across the Channel with a group of office clerks. Their destination port was Dieppe, but they would have been dispersed from here to one of just three locations which the RE sappers had made ready to receive them.

That pioneer group included an Irish-born telegraphist, Army Service No. 457 Bertha Castle, mentioned earlier, who had been employed at the GPO in London. Although she was to later remain living in London, Bertha would maintain family links to Newbridge in County Kildare through her sister, who was married to an ex-serviceman who lived there.[31]

The Post Office's February report had anticipated that three areas would be prioritized: Boulogne, Etaples and Le Havre, which between them contained thirty-three exchange locations requiring 286 staff postings. (Table 6)

The earliest contingents were then followed by mixed drafts of WAACs to be later installed at GHQ St. Omer and Montreuil, the GHQ's 2nd Echelon at Hesdin and at the HQ of the Director General of Transport at Wailly, as well as helping to run the Army Pay Department at Wimereux.[32]

What appeared to be a smooth and well-organized process continued through the summer right up until the end of August, but as the sappers and Post Office advisors went about their business making sure everything was being done correctly for their girls, there were still a number of underlying and unsettling matters rumbling within WAAC circles and behind-the-scenes tensions remained high at the GPO.

Questions over the key role of the Post Office supervisors

As the momentum gathered to boost support for WAAC recruitment throughout the summer of 1917, it should be emphasized that individual postmasters had, of course, been required to give their approval to their staff members who wished to volunteer. The minimum age for all was 20 and it was deemed that, for the most part, the more experienced, slightly older young women were preferable. Many were already being groomed for promotion as supervisors – a job that held a higher-ranking 'Officer' status within the Post Office which was an organization run on militaristic lines. As a key employee, a Post Office supervisor earned not only higher pay, but she carried a heavy responsibility for the smooth running of each shift in an exchange or telegraph office. It was she who dealt with any lack of efficiency, technical problems and discipline within the rosters. In civilian life her younger staff telephonists were already attuned to listen with sharp precision for clicks or faults on the lines which might indicate attempts at any interference or wire-tapping from unknown outside sources; they knew how to remain calm under stress and could stay quick-witted when coping with emergencies. Telegraphists, likewise, worked under these same conditions and were fully trained in the essential skills of speed and exactitude. It should not be forgotten that every former Post Office staff member's position within the WAAC was as a civil servant. This meant they were still 'bound by the restrictions of the Official Secrets Act limiting their right to discuss their work with anyone'.[33] A regime of tight security was essential for the army work on the Western Front. Moreover, it was being made clear that a basic understanding of the French language was one of the stated preferences for a Post Office volunteer – albeit not always possible.[34] Supervisors were also trained in the task of identifying and assessing anything reported to them they considered as seriously untoward: system faults, line failures or any other suspicious activities. In peacetime, it was the responsibility of the supervisor to then decide if such matters could be dealt with on the spot or passed on to one of the exchange's senior engineers for further investigation. Accurate identification of any technical issues would have to be drawn up and submitted.

The tasks of supervisors also included working out the duty rosters, breaks and all day-to-day activities of staff under their charge and, to understand the controversies that were to arise over the higher-graded supervisors for France, it is necessary to go back to the early days of the negotiations over pay and conditions.

By the end of March, recruiting for all categories of WAAC volunteers was underway, but it would seem that a serious omission had crept in following the delivery of the February Inspectors' Report to the War Office. Their planning requirements for France had made a clear reference to the possibility of recruiting a few of their staff supervisors. Four were to oversee the telegraph operators and an equal number for the telephone switchboards. It was an entirely inadequate allocation to have a total of only eight assigned for an estimated 574 operators and one may assume this may have been merely a token number to start off with and that future promotions for supervisory roster duties would be drawn from the well-experience staff members who were being selected for France. In the final summarized calculation, nonetheless, the inspectors' figures had most certainly indicated that these eight women were to be added into their recommended total staff requirements. The first rounds of negotiations commenced.

By the middle of March a few adjustments had been made but when the military wrote back to the GPO with the details, the introduction of a serious flaw was immediately spotted. It led to a letter from the GPO to the War Office on 29 March to ask why 'no reference is made to the employment of female Telegraph and Telephone Supervisors?'[35] In the eyes of the officials at the Post Office, there appeared to have been a major blunder – albeit perhaps accidental – because the absence of supervision was entirely contrary to normal GPO working practice. Warning bells had sounded. The letter was tactful, nonetheless. There was no mention of their senior supervisors' specialized knowledge of telecommunication systems. It merely made it very clear that the Postmaster General felt it really would be 'advisable that some Post Office Supervisors should be sent to France for administration and discipline purposes'.

Both sides knew what they were really talking about, however. The suggestion triggered an immediate rebuff. The negative reply received from the War Office on 7 April was quite explicit. A sharp rap over the knuckles, no less: 'I am directed to inform you that it is considered that no technical supervisors from the General Post Office are required.'[36]

Was it, perhaps, that the very notion of a female person holding any kind of technical superior authority in an army-run Signal unit that was felt to be a step too far? In military minds, the daily duty supervision of a roster of girls might have been regarded as a job one of their own RE Signals officers could handle perfectly adequately without any further assistance.

From the GPO's point of view, however, this was not a great start to the new arrangements, but, deciding to be cautious, it would seem that they bided their time. There were people within the organization who knew that this automatic adverse knee-jerk reaction by the army would prove to be too much of a challenge to the more forthright of their female staff members. They were correct. The army's decision had to be completely reversed some months later. WAAC supervisors were given a great amount of technical responsibility in due course when it became obvious that the girls who had been recruited fully expected to have one of their own senior colleagues to oversee each duty shift – and indeed were anticipating that those of them who considered themselves firmly on an upward career ladder would be still working towards their own promotion to this status even if wearing an army uniform. It was an issue that was not to disappear. There would be trouble ahead.

It might be considered that the basis of this dispute was something that had never been foreseen and it was fortunate that by the time that particular row escalated to danger levels, the Post Office authorities was assessing their level of cooperation with the War Office with greater caution. Meanwhile, the War Office, for its part, may have come to realize that compromise occasionally paid off. There would be a need for subtle diplomacy on both sides to ensure the military acquiesced – albeit with deep reservations – on this point.

By mid-June, a memo from the GPO was circulated to all the larger UK exchanges which specifically advised their selectors to take great care over the supervisory staff they approached for the task of taking charge of the operators in France: 'You will know the type of woman who will be wanted – having a thorough knowledge of the work. Having a good influence on staff, and being prompt and trustworthy in decision.'[37] Notably, the writer of this advice also took pains to add, rather tellingly: 'It might be convenient if you gave me the names. We do not want to invite applications.' What seems clear is that the Postmaster General was determined to hold on to as much powerful control as he could in the face of a scheme that was causing more headaches than he had originally bargained for. The agreed release of some of their most highly qualified women to join the ranks of the WAAC was beginning to put a great deal of strain on all their already understaffed exchanges across in the UK.

Consequently, before letting them off to France, the Postmaster General had made certain every girl who enrolled as a WAAC volunteer was guaranteed her job back at the end of the war. But would this be enough to ensure the best and brightest of their girls would not be lost? There were to be more difficulties lying ahead.

A spate of long-dawn-out wrangles

Finding a suitable agreement over the appropriate pay and conditions for the proposed Signals women had commenced in early January 1917. The idea was still only being regarded as a possibility. At that time, the

Plate 1: A typical mixed draft of WAACs ready to embark for France. (*Author's Collection*)

Plate 2: The Signals telephonists at work on the Western Front from 1917 onwards included a number of Irishwomen. Note their special brassards/armbands worn by all male and female members of a Royal Engineers' Signal unit in France. (*National Army Museum catalogue ref. 1995-01-29-76*)

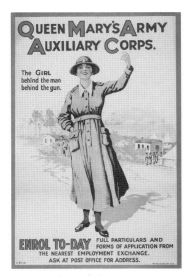

Plate 3: One of the many different recruitment posters. (*Imperial War Museum catalogue ref. Art.IWM PST 13167*)

Plate 4: WAAC clerical workers on duty in an ordnance office. (*National Army Museum catalogue ref. NAM 1995-01-24-20*)

Plate 5: A camp's catering and cleaning workers line up for that day's orders, supervised by a forewoman. (*National Army Museum catalogue ref. 1995-01-28-88*)

Plate 6: Inspection parade by Chief Controller of the QMAAC, held in Dublin, 1918. (*National Army Museum catalogue ref. 1995-01-30-88*)

Plate 7: Faded images from the past. Matilda (Tillie) Nevin (second from left) and lifelong friend Marjorie Simmons with army pals in France. (*Courtesy Hart Family Collection*)

Plate 8: The camp at Moore Park, Fermoy, County Cork, in 1917. (*Author's Collection*)

Plate 9: WAAC/QMAAC forewomen are lined up by an administrator. (*Author's Collection*)

Plate 10: The staff of the Rouen Signal office mustered for an inspection 1 September 1917 included several from Ireland with more to follow. (*National Army Museum catalogue ref. 1994-07-242-126*)

Plate 11: Attempts to make things homely included the creation of many similar WAAC camp gardens in army bases and depots. (*National Army Museum catalogue ref. 1994-07-238 -5*)

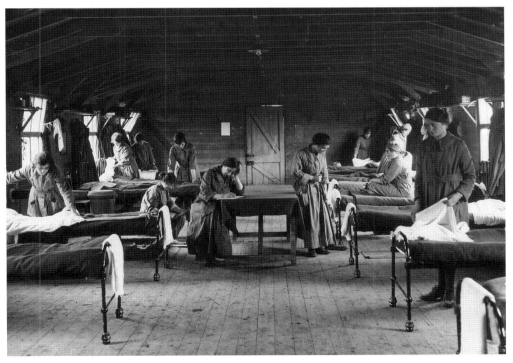

Plate 12: The dormitory-style sleeping quarters in the huts were basic. (*National Army Museum catalogue ref. 1995-01-28-91*)

Plate 13: WAAC administrators from landed families in rural Ireland could always find a horse to ride on off–duty days. (*National Army Museum catalogue ref. 1995-01-30-122*)

Plate 14: No socializing rules broken: Signaller Mollie Crook (on the right) seen here with two pals from the Rouen Signal unit, 1918 (*Author's Collection*)

Plate 15: A quayside in Rouen, home to the 3rd Echelon of GHQ. (*Author's Collection*)

Plate 16: Air raid drill: WAACs take cover in trenches, Rouen. (*National Army Museum catalogue ref. 1995-01-28-89*)

Plate 17: Working with the Royal Engineers to cover twenty-four hours of roster duties, L of C telephone operators in France. (*National Army Museum catalogue ref. 1995-01-29-75*)

Plate 18: L of C telegraphists at work at a BEF Boulogne base exchange. (*National Army Museum catalogue ref. 1995-01-29-83*)

Plate 19: Winifred Dennett (middle row far right) and fellow Signal unit colleagues from England, Ireland and Scotland. (*Courtesy Flett Family Collection*)

Plate 20: A formal photograph of forewomen who served in Rouen. (*National Army Museum catalogue ref: 1995-01-30-121*)

Plate 21: Armistice Day, 1924. Standing third from the left beside the highest-ranking 'Officials' representing each separate WAAC sector, a medal-decorated forewoman signaller wears her simple 'worker's' uniform. (QMAAC Old Comrades' Association Gazette, *December 1924*)

Plate 22: Off-duty companionship in a camp hut. (*National Army Museum catalogue ref. 1995-01-28-90*)

Plate 23: Forewomen at the Rouen base celebrate the Armistice in their mess hall, November 1918. (*National Army Museum catalogue ref. 2005-08-44-2*)

Plate 24: Evidence suggests this group are the Rouen Signal unit's principle soloists and understudies for the production of *HMS Pinafore* who had gathered for an informal photo in December 1918. (*Courtesy Dale Family Collection*)

Plate 25: When home on leave in 1918, Mollie Crook strikes a pose that pokes fun at the concept of a 'military woman' who emerged between her mother's generation and her sister's hobble-skirted future. (*Author's Collection*)

Plate 26: WAAC clerks at work in the 61st Advanced Motor Transport Section, Abbeville. (*National Army Museum catalogue ref. 1994-07-235-4*)

were Tomorrow, Thursday, I shall see The Secy of The Post Office Ireland, and insist on being put in funds To The extent of the amount due To me by The Army, in order That I can pay The debts I owe on account of living, medical Treatment etc, and Then The Postmaster General can settle The whole question with The Army.

I have Taken full notes of the muddling, and incompetence displayed in dealing with my case and if necessary will use them Through The Head of the Irish Government.

Plate 27: Telegraphist Mullally writes that she can seek help from 'the Head of the Irish Government' over disputed remunerations due. (*National Archives. Army Service record 2054 Mullally*)

Plate 28: Plenty of bread but other rations had been severely cut back by 1918. (*National Army Museum catalogue ref. 1994-07-235-13*)

Plate 29: Catering and other kitchen duties accounted for over half the tasks taken on by enrolled WAAC members as an essential contribution to the war effort. (*National Army Museum catalogue ref. 1994-07-235-11*)

Plate 30: Application paperwork for a free passage to Canada for servicewomen was made available to QMAAC members from their headquarters. (*Author's Collection*)

Plate 31: A pre-1920s contemporary view of Canadian wheat being harvested, (Children's Encyclopedia *published by The Educational Book Company Ltd., Tallis House, Whitefriars, London, 1920 edition*)

Plate 32: A pre-1920s contemporary view of a newly planted Australian fruit farm. (*Children's Encyclopedia published by The Educational Book Company Ltd., Tallis House, Whitefriars, London, 1920 edition*)

Plate 34: A typical settler's house in Australia's Mildura's Red Cliffs dried-fruit area, 1926. (*State Library, Victoria, Australia catalogue ref. H2011.134/13*)

Plate 33: The two military war medals issued for service 'Overseas' in France matched those issued to the soldiers who served in 1914–1918. (*Author's Collection*)

Plate 35: Wedding portrait of Martha Hanna and George Fisher in Australia, 1927. (*Courtesy Hanna Family Collection*)

Plate 36: Winifred Dennett. (*Courtesy Flett Family Collection*)

Plate 37: Tillie Nevin: an early portrait depicts her as a one of the typically demure and well-brought-up young women working in an Irish post office. (*Courtesy Hart Family Collection*)

Plate 38: Mollie Crook, 1924. (*Author's Collection*)

Plate 39: Armistice Day, College Green, Dublin, 11 November 1924. (*National Library of Ireland* catalogue ref. *HOG131*)

Plate 40: The Celtic cross in memory of the 16th (Irish) Division. (*National Library of Ireland* (*extracted close-up*) *catalogue ref. HOG131*)

Secretary at the GPO when writing to the War Office had made it very clear to the Army Council: 'As regards pay, the Postmaster General's view is that the Telegraphists and Telephonists employed should continue to receive their Post Office pay together with some additional allowance to meet the special circumstances of their employment.'[38] However, that particular assumption was soon fated to be challenged, which is an aspect of these women's army service that has rarely, if ever, attracted any later attention from historians.

Although discussions over pay had been thought by both sides to have been finally settled in March prior to the formal approval for the recruitment of category 'E' postal workers by Field Marshal Sir Douglas Haig in early April, it later became clear that a number of grave misunderstandings had occurred.[39] Anxiety was exacerbated when the terms and conditions attached to the original enrolment form for WAAC – known as Army Council Instruction No. 537 for 1917 – were targeted for a number of changes due to be issued in July as Army Council Instruction No. 1069 for 1917. The revisions it contained soon brought about a flurry of fresh correspondence between the Army Council and the GPO officials who wrote to announce that they had received 'complaints from France'.[40] The original No. 537 Army Council instruction form had required a commitment from these Post Office women to serve in the WAAC for just twelve months. This was now changed to a more open-ended period described as 'for the duration' of the war. The former rates of pay they had signed up for – which included extra payment for overtime and for Sunday duties – were gone. They would now be expected to work a forty-eight-hour week at a fixed rate and there was some dispute over whether this included time off for meals or not. Lastly, the promised £5 bonus following a year of continuous service was to be entirely abandoned. The War Office had been obdurate on that point. As one of their negotiators put it: 'The £5 was a waste of money from the start. We see no reason for any equivalent to be given now.'[41]

These proposed changes led to a spate of wrangling and recriminations between the Army Council and the specially appointed Post Office officials. Finding mutual ground for agreement was plainly not being much helped by some of the attitudes that the recent change of government in London in December had introduced. The new parliamentary coalition in

Westminster was marking 'a definitive stage towards direct State control of all aspects of the war effort'.[42] As the discussions went back and forth in an attempt to find some satisfactory agreement over the GPO's female telegraphists' and telephonists' army pay and conditions, there were occasions when misunderstandings caused patience to get badly frayed.

Writing to the War Office on 26 July 1917 in a response to these announced changes, the clearly almost exasperated GPO spokesman started off by observing that:

> I must confess that your letter of the 20th [July 1917] leaves me even more disturbed about Post Office women for France. We had not realised that the Army Council Instruction cuts away any claim to overtime or Sunday pay. This makes the new conditions far less favourable than we supposed, as it was thought the Post Office staff would be required to perform quite a lot of Sunday duty.[43]

He further complained that: 'It may be that the Post Office staff are more difficult to deal with than outsiders, but the War Office cannot expect the Postmaster General to play fast and loose with them', adding the reminder that in contrast to all their GPO men who had volunteered for RE Signals work 'the women are going out on far less favourable terms. From a trade union point of view 'they are black-legs [strike-breakers or 'scabs'] and this makes it especially desirable not to worsen the conditions'.[44]

Pertinent to the problem at that time was a series of hitherto unforeseen pay rises within their UK staff pay scales. To settle the differences between GPO staff members at home and those 'on loan' to the military in France, some form of parity had to be addressed and it should be kept in mind that, in all these negotiations, the GPO officials were very conscious of the difficulties that their organization's employees' union, the P&TCA, could cause if grievances over unfair conditions and pay were to seriously escalate.

From one point of view it was to the advantage of the negotiations that, having been formed in 1914, the P&TCA had become seriously weakened during the war years owing to the ill-health of Secretary Newlove, who continued to be paid a salary but was effectively inactive and retired until he was replaced in 1919.[45] On the other hand, no one could assume that all WAAC Post Office women were members of this union, especially those from the Irish exchanges, although the membership was still rising steadily.[46]

There would have been an awareness, too, that the scene for postal workers in Ireland was rather more convoluted and difficult in recent times. A number of breakaway unions with Irish nationalist sympathies – such as the powerful Association of Irish Post Office Telegraph Clerks, which, back in 1912, had remained 'traditionally strong with a membership which totalled 75 per cent of this grade' – were coming to the fore. (It was to be one of several bodies that united with others into the Irish Postal Workers' Union in 1922.)[47] This body's executive was extremely vocal. It had weathered several setbacks and, for example, as Clinton recalls: 'they had protested about the dismissal of some of its members for being involved in the Easter Nationalist rising of 1916 and in later years took part in a number of strikes in support of Ireland's national independence' when the political scene in Ireland became more seriously fraught.

Espousing loyalty to the Irish nationalist cause did not, of course, preclude anyone from offering support to end the fighting in France. As is now being more widely realized, there were plenty of Irish nationalists who were keen to help put an end to the conflict in France, as evidenced by the large numbers of enlisted Irish soldiers with nationalist sympathies who had believed that the plans for Irish Home Rule could go ahead unhindered if the fighting was ended. It can be validly argued, therefore, that among the diversity of Irishwomen joining the WAAC there were many within every category of their recruitment patterns who were just as likely to have held the same view.

How exactly the difficulties surrounding signallers' pay rates and working hours were finally overcome by the negotiators remains difficult to unravel given the voluminous correspondence generated by claims and counter-claims on each side. Having been a government-run organization, telephonists' and telegraphists' wage structures came under the control of the Treasury (which inevitably meant underlying political connotations) and a compromise was finally reached by way of some convoluted strategies to allow for incremental adjustments.

These guaranteed that each GPO girl who returned to work within the organization after demobilization would gain a number of benefits not only from some appropriate remuneration, but from the promise that her career's qualifying promotions would be held as intact as they would have been had she remained doing her job in a home-based exchange. For the most part, the arrangement worked, although the postwar changes in working practice brought about by the introduction of new technology were to bring an escalation of difficulties in due course.

Ripples of agitation continue

Soon after the first drafts of signallers had settled into the military bases, signs of rather more radical attitudes were beginning to emerge. Employee union membership was to gain increasing strength and although there were conscientious senior people within the GPO who expressed genuine concern for the sacrifices being made by their girls in France and the need for fair play, the final wartime years were undoubtedly heading into even more difficult times. Research by Helen Glew into women's employment issues on the horizon within the GPO holds that: 'By 1918, the P&TCA had a membership of 28,000, of whom 12,000 were women'.[48] Militant socialism was on the rise. By 1919 there were stronger demands for more equal pay rates for women within the GPO. Also, as Glew observed, no one was forgetting 'the stormy applause at a 1917 (P&TCA) Conference for a resolution supporting the Russian (February) Revolution'.[49]

For those in France in the late summer of that, their first year, 1917, army life had soon settled into a steady routine. The L of C Signal units were keeping the machinery of war running smoothly by relying on hundreds of Post Office women working twenty-four-hour shifts seven days a week – and the girls' attitudes remained stoic. It was wartime. There was a job that had to be done, a duty not to be shirked. New foundations of solidarity had been formed, nonetheless.

Chapter 6

The Status of Signaller Forewomen

The rules are often callous, and its dictates always plain,
But, you know, there is a war on, and we've got to see it through.

I. Grindlay, 1918[1]

By August 1917, just as the GPO women's pay problems appeared to be reaching some acceptable level of settlement, there was yet another ripple of unease starting to surface. The new issue concerned the ranking status of their own higher-rated officers who worked as female telephone and telephone supervisors, many more of whom would be needed in France. The decision to reach agreement over the necessity for the supervisors – on whom the WAAC conferred the title of 'Forewoman' – was a battle which the GPO people thought they had already won during the early planning period back in April.

At that time, the Army Council's initial negativity in regard to the desirability of employing these skilled senior women in the army bases had been swiftly challenged by the GPO when it was proposed that 'no technical supervisors from the General Post Office are required'.[2] Strong rebukes had been issued and, as has been shown, the assumption was hastily dropped when the GPO insisted that it was the customary practice for all their telephonists and telegraphists to work shifts under their own officers' strict supervision. The practical value of the system had been grasped, albeit if reluctantly, but it would seem that the army had not fully understood the true value gradual graded upward promotions brought to the career prospects of GPO staff. Bright girls with ambition who had gained a promotion to one of these better paid and far more prestigious supervisory roles still held high hopes of gaining even more elevated positions within the GPO's own ranking hierarchy. Enlightenment was soon to come when a formidable middle-aged Liverpool telegraphist, who was well placed on her own career ladder within the organization, sent a letter to her former postmaster on 31 July to raise a serious problem.[3]

After the war, Alice Clarke was to be awarded an OBE for her war service in France and went on to hold appointments as a member of the Executive and of the General Council of the Post Office Controlling Officers' Association.[4] In July 1917 she was an ambitious GPO supervisor, by then just short of 50 years of age, about to travel out as a forewoman to take up duties at one of the larger base exchanges in France accompanied by a draft of colleagues that included four Irishwomen who have already been described in Chapter 3. (Table 4)

Her letter clarifies the essence of a worrying situation that was being more frequently discussed and questioned by her younger companions and herself. They had been all handpicked by their postmasters to take on heavy responsibilities with the army and were willing to do their best – but questions yet remained.

The concerns she raised were to cause not a few ripples to travel though those experimental waters they had embarked upon. It is well worth repeating in full:[5]

D Square, Stanhope Lines,
Aldershot, 31 July 1917

R.A. Dalzell, Esq.,

Sir,

Mr. John Lee, Postmaster of Belfast has suggested I communicate with you in reference to the position of Telegraph and Telephone Supervisors taking up duty in France.

We are anxious to know if you can give us any information as to our corresponding army rank when we get out there.

When we arrived at Aldershot we were received by an Administrator who put us in a house of whom the head was said to be a Supervisor also (she is amongst the Tempy [sic] and Postal Sorting Women) an N.C.O. This proves how little our position as Established Supervising Officers – which position we have gained only after years of tried Service with outstanding abilities and qualifications – are recognised by the Army Administrators.

After our explaining that with the presence of so many young Telegraphists and Telephonists being with us, who we had and would again Supervise, the prestige of our own Service was not being maintained, they made us NCOs which in their opinion made us the same level as the Tempy [sic] staff.

As these NCOs here are very young and for the greater part have been given this rank for having tidy houses and looking after same and are liable at any time should their attitude not meet with approval to be reduced in rank, we feel our position is unsatisfactory.

In the matter of drill for instance, which is foreign to us, we might not be considered so good as one of our junior staff and might be reduced and they put over us. It seems strange to us to scrub, clean and do fatigue work generally amongst our staffs, but quite recognise it is Army life and are most anxious to make the French business a success and a credit to our own respective Departments.

Questions have arisen about one or two matters which I will not trouble you now about, but when making any enquiry we are always asked "Have you any written document about it", of course we had nothing but a formal letter of introduction, and we are wondering if we could be supplied with a detailed account of the Rank, pay etc, on which our services have been loaned to be military before we enrol.

Being the pioneers of the Female Supervising Force, we think it is essential for those who follow us to have our position clearly defined. Whilst understanding that the women officers (Administrators) who are concerned with clothing, housing, food etc., are given a very superior rank and that our training not being on these lines we could in no way correspond with them, still we feel we are experts in our own Departments and have given up much to help make this section of the WAAC turn out a real success as "Our Service" Administrators.

We trust that the Post Office has claimed for us at least rank equivalent to that of Subordinate Commissioned Officers – as only in some such position will it be possible for us to maintain discipline, efficiency and the Status of our Civil rank in the Service.
Awaiting your reply,

Yours faithfully,
Alice C. Clarke (Assist. Supr. Liverpool)

Having applied to enrol mid–May, her offer to serve had been well endorsed by her Liverpool postmaster, who had unhesitatingly endorsed her for her experience and competence, describing her as 'very strong and capable and well recommended' when asked for his opinion as to her suitability.[6] Years later, when retiring from her long career it was noted by her ex-Post Office colleagues that 'she had been and has always been an enthusiastic champion of the claims of her sex in the service'.[7] To have a voice of a telegraphist raised over her personal issues of concern may be seen as a not-uncommon occurrence in Post Office circles and Alan Clinton , who has delved deep into Post Office labour relations, has taken pains to point out that, historically: 'The telegraphists were always to some degree "outsiders" within the Post Office structure'. Staunchly supportive of their once-strong English-based P&TCA for the past decade or so, this section 'became the most persistent of Parliamentary lobbyists, a fact that infuriated opponents of their "interference"'.[8]

The reaction to Clarke's letter

Clarke's letter to her postmaster was taken very seriously. He had forwarded it to the officials in London who were involved in the negotiations over the girls' pay and conditions and the issue was investigated on all sides but, as has been already indicated, it was to be the Army Council who was to take the responsibility of making a final decision. They did not rush. It was to be months before an answer was forthcoming.

At one stage, one of the GPO negotiators approached the WAAC Chief Controller in London, Mona Chalmers Watson, to gather her opinion over the issue of commissions for the Signal forewomen – possibly half-expecting the lady to agree with the Army Council that ordinary GPO working women were inappropriate candidates for inclusion within the ranks of her mainly upper-class 'Officials'. However, the response she gave was quite to the contrary. She was a Scottish physician, a lady who herself had striven to make her mark as a career woman. When the negotiator returned to his office he wrote a memo recording the meeting for his GPO colleagues which makes her views very clear:

She is convinced that an error has been made in classifying the Departments' Supervisors selected from the Establishment Staff as Forewomen.... She stated that, in her opinion, considering their technical qualifications and duties, they should be classified as Assistant Administrators and so rank as junior commissioned officers. The pay would be £120 with an allowance of £20 for uniform and a deduction of 15s 6d per week for board and lodging.[9]

As one of the women leaders who conceived the idea of the Corps, the view she espoused on that occasion certainly projects an underlying desire to grant full recognition of ability and equal talent among those who volunteered to serve. Any suggestion that army chiefs wanted to implement some form of class discrimination to exclude Post Office staff deemed worthy of receiving commissions was being firmly rejected. It was an opinion that was to be entirely ignored, of course. Was it time that an alternative strategy might be launched?

A 'cunning ploy' or a 'mistake'? Confusion is caused

Close examination of the Post Offices files for this period reveal that a diversionary ploy may have been already hatched by someone to slide a couple of senior Post Office women into the ranks of the aforesaid 'Administrators' – either as an experiment or – far more probable – in sheer desperation because not enough suitable volunteers for assignments in France as supervisors were coming forward. Rumours of the dispute had been circulating.

Since 3 July and 3 August, respectively, GPO officials had identified two staff supervisors from London as particularly ideal candidates. Their application forms reveal both had been already officially commended by the Post Office for remaining cool and taking on 'highly important work' in exchanges in the UK when on duty during the air raids in 1915, 1916 and early 1917.[10] So, while on the one hand, they were exactly the type of senior women who were extremely suitable for conditions in France, on the other hand, it was clear that the role of a GPO supervisor was very different to that of the existing administrators who were all essentially younger women engaged in housekeeping-style supervision and logistics. By contrast, every GPO supervisor was a well experienced woman whose duties – either in civilian life or while serving with the army alike – required them to have the ability to keep disciplinary control of each roster in addition to dealing with technical problems or outside interference which might breach security.

In the arrangements made when setting up the Corps it was envisaged that to gain promotion to the rank of an assistant administrator, a member of the Corps who was serving as a 'worker' had to undergo a specially designed short training course to cover all the tasks needed for tackling a number of responsibilities similar to that of a school or small hospital. Costs had to be kept under control. Rules could not be broken. Reports would have to be submitted to those who were superior in rank and it was obvious that the existing training course for administrators which included how kitchen waste was to be handled, how rosters and timekeeping should conform to army regulations, and how to cope with an endless stream of form-filling was clearly unsuited to the supervisory duties and expertise of the GPO women's day-to-day work. Would a special course have to be designed for them? Would it be necessary to insist it interfaced neatly with the existing training courses for administrators?

The problem still hinged on the difficulty of setting an appropriate level of pay for this grade of employee while serving with the army. Nothing had yet been firmly agreed and objections raised by the GPO negotiators who held that the rate that was being offered 'was not sufficiently attractive' would seem to have remained up in the air.[11] Nonetheless, it is curious to discover a note from the WAAC Controller on 7 August which refers to the status of two members described as 'one Telegraph and one Telephone' – no names were supplied – who were to carry out 'Home Service' duties at the WAAC London Connaught Club Hostel.[12] Their arrival had raised complaints from the hostel because they had not been advised that these young women 'were of superior rank'. So who was by then 'calling the shots' in this matter: the Army War Council, the WAAC or the GPO?

The two girls may have been a pair who were later despatched to France but what was deemed later to have been 'a mistake' was not widely spoken about at the time and, within another couple of weeks, the opposition of the War Office to granting commissions appears to have been crumbling. But it was a false alarm. On 21 August, it was thought possible 'to accede to the appointment of suitable women occupying positions as Assistant Administrators (or Technical Assistant Controllers) instead of being

Forewomen [but] this is conditional on their fulfilling all the qualifications which we require for appointment as an "officer"'.[13] This suggested that the GPO girls seeking a commission would need to adhere to the existing training qualifications which were pitched towards hostel-running and the management of units. The writer then deliberately takes care to draw the line on any subsequent promotions being offered within the Corps hierarchy: 'I am afraid this is as far as we can go.'

So had a deal then taken place or not? The story does not end here. The summer rolled on into late autumn and there are no further official comments until – on 27 October – almost three months later – when Charles Peel at the Post Office wrote to A.G.11 – Adjutant-General Department 11 (or XI) – in London to enquire about the position of a staff member who had enrolled.[14] Their reply on the 31st of that month informed him: 'Miss Reid has now been told she may take up duties as an Assistant Administrator provided she is prepared to accept the £110 rate with a chance of an increase to £5.' On 2 November, Mr Peel then received another enquiry which came from a Post Office colleague in the Telephone Service at 144a Queen Victoria Street, E.C.4 asking about another supervisor selected as suitable, a Miss Izant. He wanted to know 'if the proposed arrangements for Reid could also apply to her?'[15]

So what had his understanding of those arrangements have been? Were these girls to be employed as telecommunication supervisors in France or not? Had a balance to everyone's satisfaction been struck between Post Office expectations of adequate pay rates and status for their supervisors and the decisions being made by WAAC controllers and GHQ in France as to what they felt was appropriate? Unfortunately, it seems those negotiations must have somehow faltered. Swirls of unsettling, undercurrent argument and counter-argument rose to the surface. It was almost the end of the year and high time a solution was found, once and for all.

In the last week of November, the Chief Controller of the WAAC received a letter that was accompanied by a copy of the army's standing orders to remind her:

The forewoman's place is among the telegraphists and telephonists at their work; the Signal-master NCO's must definitely remain in charge of, and remain responsible for, the whole of the staff working in the Signal Office and it is therefore not considered practicable that the forewomen should hold rank equal to that of commissioned officers.[16]

In other words, such a situation would be a complete topsy-turvy of army protocols. Meanwhile, there were still questions flying back and forth between the Army Council, the Post Office and Army GHQ in France over pay rates and status. One note asked: 'Have any of them actually been granted commissions or promised them?'[17] The answer would come in due course but not until a firm and final end to all the controversy had been announced by some formal, stiff words issued from the very top by the end of the year.

The contents of a letter from Fowler, the head of Signals writing to the Secretary at the War Office on behalf of Field Marshal Earl Haig, Commander-in-Chief British Armies in France, on 1 December 1917, was unequivocal: 'It is now recommended that the proposal to grade certain Forewomen Telegraphists and Telephonists as Assistant Administrators should be abandoned. Having regard to all the circumstances of the case it is now considered that their duties will be best carried out if they remain as Forewomen.'[18]

It was hoped there would be no more discussion. No more rumours. No further speculations. On that same day, 1 December 1917, a similar message was sent from the War Office to Mr Charles Peel, at the GPO in London which repeats the request 'to abandon the scheme of grading the telephonists and telegraphists forewomen as officers. The matter appears to have been given some careful consideration and we propose to agree'.[19]

For a few, it would seem the decision brought about some perplexity. About ten days later, a correspondent commenting in a reply to a question that had been posed, reveals that:

According to L.T.S. [the London Telephone Service] one at least of the women, Miss Reid, actually holds a commission. I believe she is still in this country. I don't think any promises have been made to the others but they have been led to hope for commissions.[20]

Not surprisingly this received an instant reaction which was less than happy. The scrawled reply from the recipient is revealing: 'News very awkward. Surely Turner ought to have consulted us?'[21] It will be recalled that Colonel E. V. Turner was the Deputy Director of Signals at GHQ in France. Others were less worried. A ray of light was about to be cast on the whole debacle.

In a clearly approving tone to show that the circumstances surrounding the supervisory work of Miss Reid presented no serious ideological problem, the correspondent reported back immediately that the lady in question was already hard at work in France:

> Miss Reid, the one commissioned woman, is in charge of telephones at Abbeville. As there are no men on Telephone work (NCOs) – her OC confirms her presence presents no direct difficulty.

The writer goes on to say there had also been problems in the telegraph room at the same base. It had become necessary to bring in some of the older women to take charge in there, too.[22]

To add to these circumstances, it is certainly very clear from available data that the additional girl earlier taken on for a commission, 30-year-old Mary Isabel Mease Izant – who had been a telephone supervisor at the Gerrard Road Post Office Exchange – was to also subsequently serve as an administrator in the WAAC in France from 12 January 1918 until almost the end of 1919.[23] However, although originally recruited as a telephone supervisor, might she have been quietly assigned to other duties in France? She could legitimately claim to also have some experience of the type of work required of administrators, having parents who ran what was described as a catering business from their home and she could have passed the standard 'test' for admission as an officer probably without any difficulty.[24] In her case, it is possible that some appropriate 'string-pulling' may have been put underway by Colonel Ogilvie with the help of a sympathizer in the GPO, if only to comply with the army's standing orders that administrators had to prove they could pass the existing qualifications. Will the truth ever emerge? Further research may be needed to bring forth a definite conclusion.

Alice Clarke – more repercussions

As for how all of these events impacted on the telegraph supervisor, Alice Clarke, who despite her complaints remained conscientious in fulfilling her duties in the base at Wimereux as a forewoman, another month was to pass before she was to receive a final formal reply to her July complaint. The letter was sent on the first or second day of January 1918. The message it contained was short and stark:

> I am directed by the Postmaster General that in view of administrative duties it has been found impracticable to offer commissioned rank to Post Office Supervisors serving in the WAAC. I am to express the Postmaster General's regret that it is not possible to fulfil the expectation of a commissioned rank held out to you.[25]

So that was that.

Alice Clarke – who would not have been aware of the struggles going on in the background – would have long since resigned herself to waiting patiently for a response from those in authority. Nonetheless, she was not to be easily disheartened or deflected from a course of action she felt was worth fighting for and, on receiving the news, she must have felt that another push was needed. On 3 January, she wrote to voice her disappointment to her former postmaster at the Liverpool Exchange, W. F. Webber, who was someone she trusted and respected. Her comment 'We feel most strongly that the decision about us is an insult to the whole Telegraph Service' provided an eloquent signpost in that thoughtfully put-together letter:

Posted at: Army PO 1
3 January 1918

Dear Mr. Webber,
I expect your Christmas run is now over and that you are very glad. It seems to have been a very busy one judging by all the overseas parcels.

Our Xmas brought us a great disappointment, for Mr. Dalzell has written that it has been decided not to give the Telegraph Supervisors Commissions.

We have faced our many difficulties with hope and constant assurance that the matter would be settled to our satisfaction, and for the decision to now be arrested leaves us almost desperate, more especially as we heard Commissions had been given to Telephone supervisors – a lower grade of woman in our own Service than ourselves. We feel most strongly that the decision about us is an insult to the whole Telegraph Service.

I understand the excuse, so far as we are concerned, is that the Signal Masters are being retained, and that a woman graded as an officer would create difficulty. This is absurd as our duties in no way interfere with his, and a WAAC officer has no jurisdiction over the Male Army whatsoever.

I personally am engaged at one of the largest Signal Offices on the Lines of Communication, and have entire charge of the female personnel of the office – both Telegraph and Telephone.

The traditions of the Army are being adhered to where women had not to be considered, but now in this new emergency new methods are necessary.

On every hand young girls are applying to Commissions in the WAAC, and I should like to know if we are at liberty to so apply, or if we are tied down to act only through the Post Office.

I think that the Post Office, which has the monopoly of the Telegraphists who are required, should insist that their women have the opportunity of rising to Commissioned rank, and that the women recruited as Supervisors should be accorded the recognition of the status they already occupied when they joined up. At Present the Supervisor on Active Service has to live with her staff under Military discipline, as the equal of those she is expected to supervise.

The decision arrived at makes the whole position hopeless for all Signal women. I am wondering if you could put forth the suggestion to Colonel Ogilvy to represent to the WAAC that if there are insurmountable difficulties in the Signals, we shall be given the Commission on the Hostel side, and have a dual duty, for a great deal of our time is spent in making duty charts, and giving information to the Administrators so that they may arrange the necessary meals etc. They cannot possibly understand the peculiarities of Telegraph work and the strain involved. We do, and the staff have been very surprised that they had not Matrons from the Home Offices to look after their welfare in the Hostels.

I feel very loath to trouble you with all this, but the few Supervisors out here are asking my advice and some suggesting we should ask to be withdrawn, that I feel I must use every effort to try and get things right if possible.

I shall be very grateful if you can do anything in this matter as it is not only for myself but for the sake of every Telegraphist who has given up everything – even a large share of her salary – to come out to make this a success, and who will return at the end of the war without having had a chance, or opportunity, to show the world at large any capabilities which merited promotion.

With best wishes to Mrs. Webber and yourself for 1918,

Yours sincerely,
A. C. Clarke[26]

As might be expected, Mr Webber did the decent thing and passed on her letter to a higher authority, viz the Director of Army Signals, Home Defence, Colonel A. M. Ogilvie, writing to him on 7 January that

it seems somehow wrong that so important a branch of the WAAC should have no share in the commissioned ranks, especially if it be the case that telephone Supervisors officers have been recognised.[27]

When it landed on the Colonel's desk the next day, Ogilvie appears to be badly taken aback by this later development. He drops a scribbled note to the Post Office official with whom he liaises:

Dear Raven,
You should see this. I did not know that any of our women had sacrificed pay to go out. I am afraid there will be a lot of disappointment in Telegraph circles. Of course, it was only an accident that a Telephone Supervisor got the commission.[28]

Accidents do happen, of course, but might the granting of those two commissions have been an attempt to stage a fait accompli? It is well worth noting that Ogilvie's note to Raven went on to say: 'If the War Office had not written we might consider if something cannot be done. I don't see how Commissions can be given for Hostel work without withdrawing the women from their ordinary duties.'

Further note may be taken that Ogilvie's word had carried serious clout.[29] Within a week, Mary Izant had been sent to France, to take up duties for the duration as an AA until the formal termination of her 'Engagement' as an 'Assistant Administrator' in October 1919.[30]

It might be worth considering if the refusal to grant WAAC commissions to GPO supervisors had rankled quite deeply, seeds of resentment may have been sown and – more crucially – might there have been damage to the former sense of trust many of them had held in regard to future opportunities their chosen career could offer? Collateral damage was to resurface in due course when the demobilization process got going, and the impression that lingers suggests that their experiences was to boost membership of their supportive post office union, the P&TCA, which, while not seen to be actively interfering, was hovering in the background throughout those wartime years.

The foundations of distrust were disturbing

Very little imagination is needed to understand how accommodating special arrangements for the Post Office staff may have played havoc with the army's paperwork. It must have led to huge confusion on all sides. There's even, at times, a distinct whiff of tetchiness accompanying some of the memos being passed back and forth between the backroom offices. One thinly veiled rebuke sent to Colonel Turner sharply pulls him up over a request he made about wanting copies of the application forms for the volunteer telephonists and telegraphists. He was told rather sharply: 'I gather you are under the impression that the form is a Post Office form. You will see that on the contrary that it is a War Office form and the responsibility to supply copies must rest with A.G.11.'[31]

With plenty of sniping like this going on, there should have been no doubt left in anyone's mind on either side of the English Channel as to who called the shots.

Otherwise, the only other possible suggestion to be made as to the reason behind the curious denial of officer status to the Post Office supervisors is that it would seem that by the end of the year tension was becoming increasingly fraught between what Signals in France felt was necessary and what the opinion of the Director of Home Signals felt was appropriate. Was it therefore left to the Army Council in London to make a decision as to what would be best? There were still plenty of people around who probably felt that having army women involved in the whole delicate business of security within telecommunications was not worth the trouble it caused.

In due course, when the time came for dispersals of the WAAC signallers in 1919, there is – not entirely unexpectedly – evidence of a considerable number of written disputes over final calculations, delays in back pay and incorrect deductions. Investigation of these details and from whom they could appeal to for help will be covered when we turn to examine each girl's case history. The war had changed the strength of their background employee support systems by then, which points to question the extent to which the War Office's A.G.11 managed to hold onto having the last word on everything relating to the administration of the GPO staff within their new Women's Auxiliary Army Corps.[32] It makes for a difficult issue to assess when viewed in hindsight, as there was to be no lessening up of the difficulties.

How many Irishwomen served in BEF Signal units?

Despite the military's essential need for their expertise, the number of women who served in Signal units can be measured in hundreds rather than in thousands, which may account to some extent for having been so neglected by historians.

Table 3 in Appendix I lays out a list of 'Signallers' who have been identified as having an Irish address at the time of their enrolment. The list is, of necessity, incomplete and additional research may improve matters in due course. One problem is that there are probably quite a number of others who have Irish parents who had moved to England before their birth date who are now almost impossible to trace, and there are other similar cases of girls who had moved to England for work either with or without their families, as well as many who gained promotion to supervisor aka forewoman who cannot always be identified owing to the loss of most of those senior women's archived files in the Second World War.

One excellent example of the latter whose records have not survived is that of Limerick-born Kathleen Hegarty who served as a telegraphist in Boulogne 1918–1919. Her Cork-born father and Tipperary-born mother had migrated to Lancashire some years earlier and, by 1912, Kathleen had been trained and appointed to the Post Office in Manchester. After the war, having gained promotion to assistant supervisor while serving in France, by 1921 she had returned to work for the Post Office and had been appointed to the telegraph exchange in Dublin at the time the Irish Post Office was starting to switch over from London to form a separate organization. Two years later, 1923, she was sent, or chose to move, back to England for an appointment in the Central Telegraph Office in London.[33] She remained there until her retirement in 1953, but can now provide a good example of the strong links to WAAC friends that were retained by many of the Irish-born ex-army colleagues in the postwar period. In 1963, following a car accident, her obituary describes her as 'a staunch supporter, she gave invaluable [voluntary] help in the Association office each week, where her quiet efficiency and kindly good nature were always much appreciated'.[34] Army life had brought out a sense of purpose to many young women like her, and there were to be many more in the troubled postwar era.

Postwar recognition of status from their peers

While it may be argued that the disputes over the correct status denied to the Signal unit forewomen might have been due either to the military's reluctance to employ any women under terms they could not entirely control, or by the concern of GPO men to keep their employee union demands at bay, the same issues can be tinged with a recognition that 'gender' or 'class' prejudices might have also come into play.

At the same time, what can be clear is that these young women who served in the L of C under the direction of Colonel Turner, the RE head of Signals for France, were undoubtedly always regarded within their own women's corps with enormous respect from the top down. In the postwar era, fellow ex-members of the WAAC/QMAAC displayed assiduous tribute to them by making a point of affording a retrospective equality of status as commissioned officers in all their formal ceremonial occasions such as marking the Remembrance Day ceremonies of the First World War.

Wearing their simple rank and file 'Forewoman' coat-frock, complete with the distinctive RE brassard and service medals, a uniformed representative of the GPO women in Signal units would be invited to stand shoulder to shoulder beside WAAC officer colleagues who each headed up their own individual sectors: the WRNS, the WRAF, the Forestry Division, the Transport Section, and so on. It was a display of recognized status, a silent acknowledgement that spoke volumes of the enormous respect still afforded them by all their former army colleagues.

Chapter 7

Lighter Moments and Winds of Change

'Change is not constant and not always in one direction.'

Marwick[1]

A s 1918 rolled on, the women who arrived to take up duties in army depots and camps across the breadth of Ireland became accustomed to the same routines and restrictions that applied to other WAACs serving elsewhere. Unless specifically enrolled as 'non-mobile' (who could be given permission to remain living at home) there was a distinct aim to deploy girls in camps and barracks that were well distant from their local area. Recruits from Monaghan were sent down to Cork; those from Kerry came up to the Curragh in Newbridge; others from Dublin or Limerick might go to a camp in Ulster and Belfast girls could be posted to Tipperary. By far the greater number were made up of cooks, waitresses, kitchen staff and 'general domestics', but Irish army installations also had a contingent of clerks, especially in the larger barracks. Recruits from these categories continued to be regularly sent across the Irish Sea – until quite late in 1919. They were attached to barracks and camps in England in addition to serving in all the BEF bases there. Chapter 2 has discussed percentages and regional origins of the girls based mainly on army records. (Table 2) One English base which received a great number of Irishwomen – mostly working in the 'B' catering and domestic category – was the large army camp at Bostall Heath. Quite a large body of clerical staff was needed for various section of the WAAC HQ in London, too, and their day-to-day routines were much the same as for similar 'workers' posted to the Curragh Camp, or to the military barracks in Fermoy, Belfast, Dublin and elsewhere. They had all conformed to Corps 'regulations' in the same way as the girls sent off to Bristol in Gloucestershire or to one of other command locations in England or France. Accommodation in suitable billets supplied at WAAC camps within army installations was similar. Sometimes, it comprised of a number of wooden huts ('hutments'), which were relatively easy to construct and about the same size as the sandbagged Nissen huts being used by the BEF behind the front. Separate mess halls and wash-houses for the use of rank-and-file girls were provided, while administrators and controllers were billeted in accommodation which varied in comfort. Strenuous efforts were made to keep the living quarters of all female personnel as far distant as possible from any areas used by army men.

Their leisure time ran on pre-organized lines, too. Despite the imposition of morning and evening roll calls, regular inspections and the other restraints of army life, determined efforts were made by unit administrators to make life a bit more tolerable for their girls by arranging sports and other off-duty activities. Bouts of homesickness were often countered by giving permission for a girl to keep a small pet dog or cat – but the concession was only to a limited degree – which occasionally led to some young WAACs to display a rebellious streak which signposts something of the spirit of determined assertiveness that was to colour a great deal of these women's lives in the postwar years.

Four-legged pals
There was one occasion when the popularity of keeping four-legged pals in one of the camp hutments had clearly got out of hand and, even years later, one unnamed former WAAC could still recall the trauma created on one occasion when her camp had 'boasted no fewer than twenty-eight dogs and cats besides other pets'. Orders had been received from GHQ that 'the keeping of pets in camp was detrimental to the health of the troops and the practice had to cease'.[2] Her account went on to explain: 'Even though "Orders were Orders", with animals being rounded up every now and then, somehow they were never actually destroyed, in spite of the threats from GHQ downwards.' The animals would be collected and locked up into one of the huts to await the arrival of an army man 'who was to remove them for execution [and] a report went to the camp's Orderly Room to confirm that the order had been carried out'. As the account puts it, however, on hearing the news on one particular occasion, there had been 'a hurried consultation and a whisper' among themselves which 'resulted in a window being left slightly open, just enough to let

the hand of one broken-hearted WAAC slip through to undo the catch'. A word was then circulated to inform owners that they were allowed to go and take a final farewell of their pets and, as the report happily recollects: 'the rest was easy'. When an army sergeant arrived to find there were 'no victims he soon forgot his murderous intentions' when handed a cup of tea, followed by a 'nice chat with the girls' before he went 'on his way on other business'. The crisis had passed – but in recollecting the incident the writer was prompted to add, perhaps tongue-in-cheek, that 'it only goes to prove that even women could beat the British Army'.

Written in 1929 – by which time many ex-servicewomen favoured pacifism and had raised critical voices over many aspects of military life and what the glory of waging war really meant to its rank and file servicemen and servicewomen – it is nonetheless interesting to note that the piece's concluding words had not met with any editorial disapproval at the time.

The incident may not have been an isolated one. Informal photographs of WAAC friends to mark special occasions had frequently included one or more of the canine or feline companions who had helped new friendships to be formed and common interests shared. For example, a 1918 picture of a mixed group of friends from the Signal unit in Rouen includes one telephonist, Clara Thornton, who had managed to acquire a little terrier puppy for herself when posted to Rouen.[3] (See plate no. 24)

Clara had grown up in a Yorkshire home that had always cherished these much-loved Jack Russell terriers in much the same way that many Irish families also favoured that friendly breed of little dogs. Meanwhile, sitting not far away in the informal photo, one of her army companions, Lilian Mycock, an inveterate cat-lover from a farming family in the Staffordshire town of Leek is making sure to keep tight hold of a fluffier ball of fur that is sitting contentedly on her lap.[4] Decades later, Lilian's relatives would remember how her house 'always had a cat around the place'.[5] By 1918, true to form, Lilian had soon found one to share camp life with her in France.

When dispersed from the WAAC in 1919 Lilian had quietly returned to her local rural GPO exchange to receive deserved promotion and extra pay as a supervisor and thereafter was content to remain here for the rest of her career. She never married but kept her links with the Corps by becoming a life member of the North Staffordshire branch of the Old Comrades' Association. Unlike so many of the Irish-born fellow workers with whom she had shared long roster hours in the Rouen Signal unit, the rare technical importance of her war service days during the final, decisive battles on the Western Front was never forgotten by her local community. When she passed away at the great age of 90, some sixty years later in 1980, her obituary in the local newspaper, *The Leek Post and Times*, made a point of reminding its readers of Lilian's work in telecommunications with the army during the 1914–18 war.

By contrast, Jack Russell owner, Clara Thornton, was one of the girls who did not return to her GPO work when demobilized. Having already been engaged to be married when she enrolled in the Corps, her future was already mapped out well before 1919. Her fiancé was serving with the Royal Flying Corps as an air mechanic and was afterwards also posted to France as a driver in the motor transport section. When released from army service, he went back to his work as an estate agent and, as soon as Clara was dispersed from the WAAC in 1919, their marriage plans went ahead in Huddersfield. Typical of the many 'army couples' who would return to civilian life to embrace a quiet and uneventful family life for themselves and their children, they were afterwards proud of the contribution made during the First World War. Like many others who returned to homes in Ireland, Scotland or elsewhere, they had neither a burning desire nor any need to embark for exotic foreign parts and were happy to leave postwar adventures to other former service colleagues.

As in the story of the pets, several devious ways to counter some of the more irksome of the petty rules and restrictions soon became almost a game for girls who yearned for a little less army regimentation. One unpopular order had instructed that the wearing of any form of jewellery was strictly forbidden, although a young woman who was engaged to be married was allowed to display a signet or modest betrothal ring. Plain wristwatches would seem to have been tolerated and it was not very long before the mandatory wearing of army-issue metal identity bracelets bearing their name, army number and religion for those serving in France began to provoke signs of ingenuity. Soon, imaginative ways to transform that heavy bracelet into a more attractive item for the wearer to display had been found: to overcome the enforcement of the no-jewellery regulation, young women were having the bracelet sneakily replaced by an identical 'gold-plated' one, often bestowed on a girl by an ardent admirer. It was quite blatant. No rule had been broken. One of Rouen's most popular WAAC administrators was even presented with a gold version of her identity bracelet by her signallers as a token of their admiration and thanks when she was moved to another posting, and there are others of less exalted rank whose families still retain an example of this 'jewellery' as tangible evidence to this day.[6]

The arrival of American army women in 1918 raised a challenge
Despite all the stringent rules and regulations laid down by army life, that new sense of self-confidence gained by women who had served with the Corps can be compared to the attitudes of girls from the United States and Canada who arrived in the summer of 1918 some months following the first drafts of US troops who formed the American Expeditionary Forces (AEF).

It was deemed necessary that these newcomers should fit into the existing administrative protocols for army women working on the Western Front, and to help them settle into bases they were joined by a large number of former WAAC/QMAAC members who had been transferred into the AEF as a newly formed sector to 'show them the ropes'. The new arrangement had its own separate controller directly answerable to the Chief Controller in London.[7]

It is not known how many Irishwomen may have been among those who were transferred from the work they were doing for the BEF to the sector created under the new arrangements but there is one excellent example of a young woman who had served in both France and in London as a 'qualified shorthand typist' who was moved into the AEF.

Katharine Fitzpatrick, born in Waterford and educated there by the Ursuline nuns, had been working in England for some twelve years prior to her enrolment in the WAAC in early May 1917. As will be shown, the contribution being made by her and others at that difficult time was to be particularly valued.[8]

That decision to muster all these girls under their own separate controller, appointed by the Chief Controller in London, might have been thought to be excellent in principle – but the arrangement had produced a number of headaches. The new corps was put under the command of the WAAC former Assistant Controller of Inspection, Hilda Horniblow, who had become well accustomed to organizing other new sectors of the Corps. (She had been the official sent to inspect the setting up of Irish WAAC units which had their own HQ in Dublin in 1917.) However, this new assignment became a rather more challenging task, afterwards described by former colleagues as 'a difficult post which she filled with great success'.[9] Her efforts to maintain discipline and a satisfactory standard of control over the young women from the United States was an issue that was to become quite tense. There were grumbles on all sides, apparently provoked not only by the clash of cultures, but on account of the inexperience of administrators sent from UK home service units who had no prior experience of the strict working conditions that existed behind the lines on the Western Front. Bending rules to suit the more relaxed and sometimes contentious attitudes that arose may have led to the initial difficulties. Compromises had to be made.

At the onset, the WAAC Chief Controller in London, Helen Gwynne-Vaughan, later admitted she 'had not liked having to send one hundred of her best clerks to the Americans'.[10] They were followed by a great many more, including quite a large number from the records centre at the Rouen base; it was later claimed by Gwynne-Vaughan that the Corps had sent altogether about a thousand serving WAACs to help the American girls who had been posted to Bourges and Tours, as well as for some administration work in Paris.[11] The work to be done by the AEF women members would have been mixture of tasks that included 223 women telephonists, who deserve mention because Canadian historian Jill Frahm has argued that the success of the US First Army communications through the last battles of the war was largely due to the abilities of the telephone operators and points out that they 'provided vital support to American military operations'.[12]

Another recent work by historian Elizabeth Cobbs has also investigated how they were recruited and trained at home in the United States prior to being despatched to France.[13] She makes it clear that these American girls were set to work under a very different set of conditions of service, pay levels and status to that of their British WAAC counterparts in Signal units. They had none of those squabbles over their perceived role as trained telephonists. According to Cobbs, they bore ranked titles as 'Operator', 'Supervisor' and 'Chief Operator' and wore individually tailored uniforms which had to be paid for out of their own pockets (a sum which might total half a year's army salary and, if loans were obtained to pay for them, might result in their being in debt to the American Telephone and Telegraph Company for the duration of their service days).[14] In an observation to explain their identifiable higher status, Cobbs comments that: 'by contrast, the other American "yeomanettes" [i.e. rank and file clerical or domestic workers] received standard issue suits at no cost'.

The Irish WAAC forewoman clerk Katharine Fitzpatrick mentioned earlier was one of the experienced young WAACs allocated to help supervise the AEF newcomers who were given office work. Soon singled out for promotion to the commissioned rank of an assistant administrator, the additional role she had taken on had included being 'in charge of certain works for the American Labor Bureau', a responsibility which was deemed by her boss, Lieutenant-Colonel Frank E. Estes (US Army), to have been 'of most excellent character and highly satisfactory'. His endorsement of her rise in ranking status 'in your [QMAAC] service' was, moreover, accompanied by a clear reluctance to forego her help when the time for her dispersal had arrived, and he had suggested: 'Should it be possible that Miss Fitzpatrick be assigned to the American EF as an officer, we would be glad to have her services.'[15] But Katharine had been ordered to return to London. She received her discharge on 22 September 1919 and there is no indication in her army file that that she took up that offer from the AEF. It would be intriguing to discover what became of her life afterwards.

So what had been the problem that arose over the behaviour of the American girls she had assisted with so efficiently? The military–style WAAC operational systems in France required a rigidity of obedience and deference to senior ranking colleagues that was dictated by the intense pressure of working within a war zone. As one early commentator has pointed out, those working there had grown accustomed to

the close control of the Administration [and they] did not appreciate the laxer methods of their new [American] employers, nor were they tolerant of the [WAAC] women and officials newly arrived from England. There were grumbles and complaints and a general patronising disparagement by the old hands of the efforts of the new. It did not make for happiness or efficiency.[16]

One must concede, however, that the observations of Elizabeth Cobbs have demonstrated why the American girls were not only shocked to find what they must have thought as 'old fashioned', strict social class divisions being upheld by WAAC controllers, but how they found much more to criticize in what they called the 'treatment' of their British colleagues 'under rigid army rules' and were quite upset to discover that 'WAAC were not allowed to associate with officers'.[17] It may be further observed that their disconcertion and difficulties over these constraints can be better understood if consideration is given to the chasm that existed in those days between American and European social mores within the workplace for young women. For example, studies have shown that the attitudes of girls in regard to serving customers from behind a counter in an American department store or similar business was rather more 'driven by a "work ethic of independence" and, consequently, the US employees were happy to "sell but they would not serve."'[18]

Such attitudes would have found little sympathy within the hierarchy of top WAAC personnel either on the Western Front or in London in 1918, but times were changing.

Awaiting good news: in France

It was the first week of November 1918. In France, the atmosphere had been very strange for days. The telephonists at GHQ base in Rouen were being kept just as busy as usual but there was a buzz of unspoken anticipation, quite different from the hectic days earlier that year when the pressure of the army's huge spring offensive saw workloads building up and nerves strung tight. Now, all the exchanges in that large, sprawling base were alert to each nuance of news 'coming down the lines'. Rumours were flying and, as the tension heightened, none dared voice their thoughts despite the knowledge that the duty telephonists must all have known what this exciting news was going to be, but not one of them let even a whisper escape.

One evening, just as the late afternoon's shift was to go off duty to be replaced by the next roster, the tension in the air became so electric with restrained suspense that the girls who were finished for the day collectively decided to remain behind with the colleagues who were taking over for the night.[19] No one wanted to miss the big announcement they knew was surely coming shortly. Midnight came and went – but they were quite determined to be there when the news broke. Finally, shortly after 2 o'clock in the morning there was a nod from the switchboard.[20] The waiting girls rushed outside but instead of heading back to their nearby billet, they together made their way to the hill overlooking the town.[21] It was a very cold night – possibly a hint of frost in the air – pitch black all around and a sky that was bright with stars. Silence enveloped them; patience and excitement were stretched to their limits; could they half-dare to hope for a public signal to put an end to the horrors?

Finally – just as dawn started to break, the group up on the hill heard the sound of a single church bell drifting up into the silence. Then more bells followed – celebratory, pealing bells – the signal! It was true! The waiting was over. They hugged each other and wept. What was being called 'The War to end War' had come to an end.

Somewhere down in the town, the BEF Chief Ordnance Officer in Rouen, Lieutenant-Colonel G. C. Blackburn, was writing in his confidential war diary: 'Armistice signed at 5 a.m. this morning.'[22]

It had been a night those girls were never to forget. For many it was to become the most important turning point in their whole lives. They had then slowly drifted back to their billet to have a quick nap before breakfast. They were due to report back on duty by lunchtime. They could not have known that the journey from that morning to each of their individual dispersal dates in 1919 was going to stretch for long weary weeks and months ahead. The arrival of peace was going to be a very trying experience, not without some disillusionment.

The 11th hour of the 11th day of the 11th month: 1918

On hearing the news on the morning the Armistice was announced in Dublin, a local VAD, who had spent the whole war with one of the Irish teams who prepared 'sphagnum moss' – peat moss – hospital dressings for wounded soldiers at the front, raced out with all the others from her workplace to join the celebrations. She later wrote a diary account of the reaction in the city that morning:[23]

> Flags were already waving out of many windows. It was a glorious clear bright sunny day and Grafton Street looked quite lovely, decked all the way down both sides. Boys were yelling 'Stop Press', and everyone buying and then running off to buy a flag. Woolworths was besieged.

She went on to recall how:

> Grafton Street was thronged with excited people. Trinity College students commandeered laundry carts and jumped on them 20 at a time, terrifying the drivers and even more so the horses. The military of every degree simply beamed.

She and her friends 'bought a tin trumpet and took turns to blow', and she afterwards relates how a large four-wheeled horse cab going down the street was hailed by an important-looking army officer who looked like 'a General'. He had stopped the cab to 'stuff three or four WAAC inside, followed by himself' and the cab had proceeded onwards with 'several Tommies sitting on the roof'. It must have been an extraordinary sight.

Outside of Dublin, there are similar accounts of celebrations, particularly in Ireland's garrison towns such as Maryborough (now Portlaoise) or Birr where military parades were held and flags flown. Yet elsewhere, a number of quite different scenes were displaying a far less jubilant, but equally valid reaction. The work of John Dorney, an independent historian, provides usefully balanced and insightful analyses of those times. He draws attention as to how the upheaval of Irish society during the Great War interfaced with the transition to republican-versus-home rule ambitions and civil war in a reflective way which takes cognizance of all aspects of those struggles that are important to consider.[24] He describes how, by nightfall on Armistice Day 1918, some of the jubilant scenes in Dublin had tapped into existing areas of bitter dispute and protest. Not unexpectedly, divisions within Irish society had been stirred up by the deeply embedded and genuinely held aspirations of opposing views that had continued to endure throughout the war years. He cites how some of the street celebrations with waving Union Jacks were to become in the eyes of another commentator 'less an expression of thankfulness for peace than a jingo demonstration against Sinn Féin in Dublin'. A mob had gathered. The crowd went on to attack Sinn Féin headquarters at No. 6 Harcourt Street:

> A dance crowd, singing British war songs, collected, in front of Sinn Féin headquarters and attacked the building. The police made faint-hearted efforts to disperse the mob, which grew larger by the hour. In the evening, reinforced by many hundreds they attempted to set fire to the building. A section of the third Battalion of the Volunteers was called out to defend the building and a very lively fight ensued.

Dorney takes care to add the important point that the senior Irish Republican Brotherhood and Volunteer leader in Dublin, Michael Collins, when reporting on 'the serious rioting between republican activists and British troops, wrote how "as a result of various encounters, there were 125 cases of wounded soldiers treated at Dublin Hospitals that night ... before morning, three soldiers and one officer had ceased to need any attention and another died the following day"'.[25] Similar ominous disturbances had erupted elsewhere.

For the Irish members of the WAAC who were serving in France a long way from their families, word filtering back from anyone who had been home on leave at that time, or who had brothers or future husbands serving with the Allied forces, such stories of disturbances would have left them nursing a great deal of heartache. The Corps had deliberately drawn women together from a wide divergence of backgrounds which would have included passionate supporters of home rule and unionists, as well as many who were entirely apolitical and just wanted their loved ones safely home with their families which represented every stratum of their communities.

Meanwhile, there were no wild celebrations laid on for those Rouen girls who had waited up through the night to hear the first bell ringing in the sign of peace. They had reported back on duty as usual for their shift the following day, so it is unlikely they saw any of the celebrations that took place in the town later on, unlike one talented colleague working on a different roster schedule. Having aspirations of a career as a journalist, she recorded her own take on the scene to capture an atmosphere that embodies the truly non-sectarian and international composition of the Allied Expeditionary Forces that morning. Published in her local East Fife newspaper, she describes a parade that carried a particular Scottish flavour, writing that: 'An Aussie, a Tommie and a French soldier were standing on the bonnet of their car, singing lustily'. She recounts how they were shouting at a Gordon soldier in the crowd to join them, when:

> suddenly above the shouting and noise, the skirl of the bagpipes was heard and the Jocks mobilised without a moment's delay and fell in behind the piper. They swarmed around and after him, keeping step to "Hielan' Laddie". In behind French soldiers in their picturesque blue uniform, wounded Belgians, Aussies in hospital suits, step to step, Americans, Portuguese and Chinese swelled the procession and crowding behind them came swarthy South African Scottish, in Atholl tartan, stalwart Canadian Highlanders and Indians.'[26]

For army personnel in Rouen it was a day no one could forget. The question now was what outcomes lay in the future? In BEF bases, the girls' army routines continued as before. How fast did things move to bring them home after the Armistice? The answer is: very slowly. Evidence suggests there may have been a tiny relaxation of some of the rules such as allowing personnel to use cameras for their own informal photographs to record some of their off-duty service days, but otherwise, and certainly, as indicated by the imposition of the twenty-four-hour daily rosters for the signallers, everything continued exactly as before. The atmosphere may have been a mite more relaxed, but there were still huge levels of administration work to be undertaken. For clerks and caterers the work went on and, with no respite in workloads for months to come, it would continue thus until well into the following year.

In the meantime Christmas was around the corner and serious attention had to be given to the preparation of light entertainments. It was generally agreed there was much to celebrate. They had done a good job and it was time the signallers gathered up the courage to take a small tilt at stultified and outdated class distinctions within army-run institutions.

A tilt at class distinctions comes in Christmas wrapping

Throughout their time in France behind the lines, the organization of concerts and theatrical performances of all kinds by the WAAC was a common occurrence, although many reminiscences and photographs of those days reveal how such events were at first restricted to 'women only'. When the rules eventually relaxed enough to allow 'mixed' musical performances and productions, the talents of the former Post Office employees provided far more scope in introducing these off-duty activities because these servicemen and servicewomen already worked so closely together in Signal units. In their prewar days the GPO had already gained quite a reputation for encouraging staff to engage in cultural and sporting interests outside of work and their own staff musical societies were very much part of that effort. A continuation of that tradition while serving in the army may be looked back on as having been inevitable. Fifty years later, a former hostel forewoman who had served with these girls in Boulogne wrote how she still recalled their musical societies and how 'the Signals women ... went to various hospitals and sang for the patients'.[27]

Entertaining productions of Gilbert and Sullivan operettas that were put on during the first Christmas of peacetime had nonetheless often carried not-too-subtle subversive messages of rebellion, when viewed in the clarity of retrospect. That Christmas 1918, for example, the Rouen Signal unit's choice of the popular operetta *HMS Pinafore*, or *The Lass that Loved a Sailor*, was an interesting one for them to have selected, having received the full approval of one of their unit administrators, Edinburgh-born former member of the D'Oyly Carte Opera Company, Miss Christian Lorrimer.[28] Its libretto carries a typically Gilbert and Sullivan theme which derides the snobbery of class divisions by wrapping it up in an intentionally silly and fun-filled story.

WAAC members' frequent discomfort with the rigid social divisions that army rules imposed upon their lives was patently echoed by one of the refrains: 'Things are seldom as they seem, skim milk masquerades as cream', when the story relates how a 'common sailor' turns out to be of much higher birth and social standing than the daughter of the snobbish Admiral of the Fleet he wants to marry.

Was the choice quite a deliberately rebellious one? It looks likely that their unit administrator may have taken it upon herself to disregard the rules preventing 'workers' from associating socially with their own commissioned 'Officials' and RE officers, so that a cast of singers could be assembled for a high-standard production. The unit was fortunate to have an experienced professional singer, Tom Purvis, serving with them who could act as director as well as contributing as a tenor.

Sapper Purvis was an RE signalman and one of several talented wireless operators who were later transferred by the GPO to BBC Radio when it was founded after the war. Among the many strands of a career which paralleled his other part-time work which became dedicated to choral music for the rest of his life, he would become not only a Vicar Choral in St. Paul's Cathedral but was soon also to become a star with the BBC Wireless Singers.[29]

One question which remains unanswerable, must be whether the part of 'Little Buttercup' in *Pinafore* might have been sung or, at least coached, by the unit's administrator, Miss Lorrimer. The role was one she would soon be returning to when resuming her stage career after the war as 'Christine Lorimer', having switched to a company called the Gilbert and Sullivan Opera Company for a tour of South Africa which lasted from mid–1920 to 1923. Clearly proud of her army days, the publicity for that show had included a photograph of her wearing her army uniform which appeared in a Johannesburg newspaper.[30]

Hints that rules may have been bent for practical purposes might be suggested by a rare surviving photograph of what may have been the leading soloists, their understudies and others helping the Signal unit in Rouen to produce their performance of extracts from *Pinafore* in December 1918. For the male soloists – all identified as RE members of the unit – bearing a mixture of ranks, the wearing of casual off-duty army uniforms, possibly some not their own, but borrowed ones to wear when gathered for a rehearsal, is worth pondering upon.[31]

There is a sense that among groups like this that they were very conscious of the enormous changes that might await them when they returned home to 'normal' life, having left behind the rigidity of army ranks and rules. The girls were aware that the experience might change their perception of the past as well their expectations of the future. A new style of women had emerged and sometimes laughter was the best way to come to terms with how people were reacting to the greater emergence of authority that the war had given them.

When Mollie Crook had her first week of leave to visit her family, she dressed up in a brother's army uniform to pose as a WAAC returning from the front whom the war had transformed into an open-shirted, hands-in-trouser-pockets, pipe-smoking 'military woman'. Her two sisters joined in the jokey fashion statement, one pretending to be their mother's generation wearing an air of down-trodden servility in a long skirt that swept the floor, while the other donned one of the restrictively tight 'hobble skirts' that had become a fashion statement for 'modernism'. Their tableau raised a lot of laughs and the brother who was the owner of the borrowed uniform took a photograph to show his pals. The little snapshot became a treasured memento of one of the lighter moments her war service had created.

Looming problems in the Cork garrisons
Before pressing on with the broader story of what lay ahead for young Irishwomen and other members of the WAAC/QMAAC in the postwar era, events surrounding their attachments as clerks in the British army garrisons at Cork Harbour may have some relevance to later events and changing attitudes.

The situation here has already been touched on briefly in Chapter 2. By early 1918, the lack of trained soldiers capable of operating telephone systems in barracks and camps everywhere had become such an enormous problem that in April that year the harbour garrisons in Cork had been obliged to seek help under a set of new rules about to be enforced by the updated Army Council Instruction No. 652 of 1918 for the women's corps (officially issued just over a month or so later in June 1918). The new rules re-endorsed the practice of using 'A' section 'General Clerks' for telephone duties in local military exchanges in the UK. Records have survived for at least sixteen of the WAAC 'clerks' who were enrolled by the army in Cork in April 1918 for that specific work. The WAAC recruitment unit would have been contacted and the employment of suitable candidates was duly processed through one of Cork's labour exchanges. Signed up to serve for an undisclosed period under the new rules which stated it would be 'for the duration', their service days continued unbroken until the end of October 1919.

For the WAAC/QMAAC recruitment unit in Dublin, all the months of 1918 up to and even after the declaration of the Armistice in November remained as busy as they had ever been. The welcomed end to the fighting in France and Flanders had not triggered a swift winding-down of the number of young women being sought to enrol and fresh intakes were still badly needed. The repatriation of troops and equipment from France back to their home bases was planned to commence but it would be months before it gained any traction and, in the interim, the level of assistance being given by army women engaged in camps and depots could not be wound down. Organizing the widespread demobilization was creating additional work for WAAC clerks in all the regimental HQs and the huge volume of telegraph traffic that continued to be generated by all this activity saw the Signal units in France becoming even more hard-pressed. It was anticipated that it would not be until the autumn that major dispersals of all WAAC/QMAAC staff from home commands and French bases could be completed. A handful of maintenance members was to be kept on at a base in France or assigned to other duties elsewhere in Europe – which included their attendance at the Paris Peace Conference. After that, all WAAC/QMAAC administration was thereafter centralized at the HQ in London.

Winds of change

In the meantime, in Dublin, from the very onset of the New Year in 1919, the political scene was about to be utterly transformed. On 21 January, the First Dáil met in the Round Room of the Mansion House and the declaration of independence was passed unanimously. A polarization of ideologies had emerged that was to pose a serious challenge for the women who had been attached to the army.

Almost twelve months after Armistice Day, on 18 October 1919, a captain of the 33rd (Queenstown) Fortress Company, Royal Engineers (RE) in Cork had written to the QMAAC Controller at her HQ in Jury's Hotel, Dublin, to clarify his position as regards how to go about replacing his WAAC staff in the military telephone exchanges in his area when the agreed period of their appointments came to an end.[32] The girls he had taken on in April 1918 were soon to be gone and he had two questions to be solved. The first was to ask if these 'immobile' telephone clerks were 'entitled to one weeks or one months notice of discharge', explaining that if they were entitled to only one week's notice he could discharge them 'with effect from October 31, 1919'. His second query reveals that he needed to immediately retain eleven of them as 'Civilian Subordinates' from 1 November because he still had no military staff to replace them for telephone work onwards, adding that he was going to be so short-staffed that: 'it is impossible to grant these eleven members the seven days leave prior to discharge to which they are entitled. It would, however, be possible to relieve them individually and grant leave later'. If he took this course did she think there would be 'any objection?'

The Irish Controller, Miss Lace Pritchard, recognized his dilemma immediately. She confirmed that he could indeed retain their services as civilians at the same rates of pay laid down by Army Council Instruction No. 653 of 1918, plus a total war bonus of 14s per week. From her point of point of view she may have felt that those former female staff members would probably think themselves extremely lucky to be kept on the pay roll because to get work again as civilians in the locality might prove difficult. Jobs were scarce and, while on the one hand she would have known that there was a growing climate of resentment surrounding anyone who had worked for the army, the garrisons would have to assume those girls in Cork would remain as loyal to their work as WAACs were assumed to have been. On the other hand, if the military was going to be forced to take on new civilian clerks or office workers, to what extent were they comfortable with the obvious dangers that might have accompanied that course of action? There was already evidence that telephone and postal security was extremely vulnerable. As investigations by historian John Borgonovo show, the military was not unaware that: 'The Sixth Division Headquarters had warned: "servants, orderlies, etc., overhear scraps of conversation and gossip … this information leaks out"'. Indeed, by then, many military garrisons in Ireland were being successfully infiltrated by the Irish Republican Army (IRA).[33] Intelligence and telephone exchanges and postal services operated by civilians in Cork and elsewhere had been targeted and even well-vetted employees such as ex-WAAC clerks were to become a matter of concern as rumours circulated that the local Cork convents of Presentation Sisters were suspected of having been 'in league with the Sinn Féiners'.[34] The records for the WAAC clerk telephonists the Cork garrisons had employed reveal that, indeed, several of these young women had been educated by that local community of nuns, so how deep had these girls' loyalties run following their discharge from the Corps? There is no evidence yet to say one way or another in regard to that specific batch of employees.

As increasing civil unrest encouraged more sophisticated intrusions of public telephone and telegraph communication networks, all forms of communication became increasingly fragile in Ireland. As Borgonovo has noted, it was the opinion of the GPO officials in London that 'the [Irish] postal and telegraph systems were manifestly corrupt, and it was felt their staff undoubtedly included officials in the pay and service of the British government [who] are not true to their employer'.[35]

One question may be asked is that even if there was a suspicion that their phone lines might be open to abuses such as wire-tapping and information being passed on from listeners within the Post Office organization, did the Cork garrisons' still-loyal former WAAC general clerks have sufficient technical telephony expertise to recognize outside interference on their lines? They had not had the benefit of the professional training and experience of those ex-GPO signallers who worked in France and knew how to detect attempted encroachments of wire-carried messages.

There were, of course, plenty of others at work in the Cork garrisons whose political sympathies were making inroads into security. For example, to cite Borgonova's work once more, there were the successful activities of Josephine McCoy O'Donoghue, a young woman, codename 'G', who held a supervisory post over the typists' pool at the Victoria Barracks in Cork City and who 'eventually would take charge of the Divisional Sergeant Major's office in his absence'.[36] Josephine's father 'was a retired head constable in the Royal Irish Constabulary and her [late] husband had died fighting with the British Army in Flanders in 1917. Beneath the loyal exterior, however, McCoy was an Irish separatist'.

The mother of two small boys, she and her youngest child were already back living in Cork when her English husband was killed at the front. The elder child had remained with his grandparents in Wales but they were reluctant to allow him to be repatriated and she had sought the help of Father Dominic, a radical Republican priest. Her work at the barracks gave her access to secret army documents and Father Dominic arranged for her to be enrolled as an IRA spy so that she could pass on information and, in return for her help, the IRA, arranged for the child to be 'abducted' and returned to her. She was never suspected.[37]

There were to be others, too, whose stories have since been investigated in Borgonovo's study. The goings-on in Mallow Post Office, for example, whose employees included Siobhan Creedon Lankford, an intelligence officer in the IRA who was dismissed when her activities were discovered, while her colleague, Annie Barrett, 'a supervising telephonist who began working for the IRA in 1918', was never suspected and, according to surviving local lore, 'carried on working here until the Post Office was taken over after independence'.[38] Annie had 'monitored Crown Forces' telephone conversations, recorded phone messages and intercepted ciphered police communiqués for decoding by IRA Intelligence'.[39] Likewise, investigation of intelligence work in the Cork area reveals how the contents of telephone conversations, recorded phone messages and 'intercepted ciphered police communiqués for decoding by IRA Intelligence' were increasingly successfully passed on to their brigades.[40]

For the ex-WAACs/QMAACs about to arrive back home from serving in Signal units in France at a time when the issue of covert intelligence actions was arising more frequently, their return to Irish post offices in 1919 and 1920 was likely to carry far more serious challenges than they had anticipated. The atmosphere had changed in more ways than one and when dispersals commenced in 1919 a great number of Ireland's Post Office staff were probably reluctant to return to their former jobs. In the meantime, having been glad to get back home to what they hoped was to be a more normal existence, there was very often a long period of disconcerting worries over army back-pay errors, an issue being shared with many of their former army pals from homes in England and Scotland.

Chapter 8

An Unsettling Atmosphere Gathers

'Women who can lead women are ... fearless, frank and outspoken'
Good Housekeeping, Issue No. 1, 1922[1]

Revisionist historians have increasingly revealed much more information on the spate of strikes and protests that occurred in France in the months leading up to the declaration of the Armistice in November 1918 and thereafter. The reports of these problems were kept for the most part from wider public knowledge at the time and rarely, if ever, mentioned decades later. Nevertheless, those gravely disturbing events being witnessed behind the scenes in some of the French bases would have been well within the cognizance of the serving WAACs in those areas. Now being viewed as justifiable complaints, the grumbles of rank and file soldiers serving in France had grown into serious demonstrations and even mutiny so that 'protest and dissent became commonplace ... and in January 1919 these grievances exploded into agitation for improved conditions and speedier demobilisation'.[2]

As can be shown, those protests had been supported in some instances by women serving in WAAC/QMAAC units. From that time onwards, evidence begins to turn up in their files and other accounts which indeed demonstrates how challenges to the rules began to surface. With the arrival of spring in 1919, the wait for word that they could leave for home became intolerable. When some members posted to the Boulogne area had been informed to expect their discharge from the Corps to begin by June 1919, the good news must have triggered an even greater streak of insubordination. Movements when off duty were still very restricted by permissions and the issue of passes to visit anywhere outside of their camps was mandatory. Risks began to be taken. A couple of enterprising Boulogne girls once managed to get to Paris for an outing despite being in full knowledge that 'Passes for the capital had been stopped a fortnight previously'.[3] To overcome the restriction, they had cunningly headed first for Rouen – probably by train – and then 'went on from there'. However, the escapade had not escaped discovery by their unit administrator. Rigorous punishment followed: 'The two girls were court martialled.'

Another rebellious girl from that base had been caught in the town: 'out motoring with an officer'. It might have seemed a trivial matter – but it had broken protocol. She was 'fined and given two days' Removal or Restriction of Privileges [R of P]', while someone else who committed a much more disturbing offence, having been 'found stealing from her fellows', was also fined 2s 6d and then 'removed to another camp'.

Rather more serious undercurrents of insubordination were gathering, too. For example, by May 1919, a few unhappy members of the QMAAC at the Boulogne base telegraph office were keen to pursue answers to a number of questions over the exact terms and timing of their dispersal orders. Several Irishwomen had served in this office. Had they been among the rebels? It is hard not to speculate. The row had been going on for some time and they had grown annoyed when they did not receive as full an answer as they had wished. Some of them took it upon themselves to send 'an ultimatum to Colonel Turner asking for a final answer re. bonus and demobilization and, if he failed to do that, they were willing to refuse all work on Tuesday morning'.[4]

Not all their fellows were quite as militant, of course. Feelings were mixed. The news of the ultimatum came as a shock to the girls operating the exchange in Pourville, a location just outside Boulogne, and the response from staff members had been to declare themselves, on principle, to be 'opposed to stoppages' and consequently, their firm message back to their rebellious colleagues in the Boulogne base was to say that they would *not* cease work in support of the issue, but instead 'press the matter in every way we know – but nothing in the way of a strike'. To have displayed discord among themselves was not a good sign and the WAAC member who had taken note of the incident was right to have been disconcerted over the possibility of any upset that might disrupt her plan 'to return to Canada' just as soon as possible following her 'awaited discharge from the Corps'.

In the same way that a number of her Irish colleagues were looking to the future, the writer had keenly desired change and although her original home place was deep in rural England not far from Wales, she had already laid plans for a new life on a small farm in Ontario for herself and her sister. Their decision to leave England was very much in the spirit of the times. A similar yearning for adventure under new skies was a trend that was to emerge very frequently for that generation and Canada was to be a popular choice.

In May 1919, yet another disruption in the military's rank and file over conditions had gone ahead in France. It had been supported by some WAAC units, but considering all the disputes with the girls' back pay and disappointments over war bonus payments that were about to erupt in a few months' time, it may be suggested that the refusal of some of the women to be pushed into a course of action that they did not agree with indicates they were not slow to voice opinions when views differed, while maintaining a level of tolerance. It was an attitude that was to be of value to hold onto in later life, whenever outraged protests ran high.

Discharge often brought dismay and disappointments
With thousands of girls being let go at a rate of 300 to 400 a week, it was inevitable that small glitches would occur as the pressures grew behind the scenes to tidy up service records and pay-book account balances. Waiting for solutions became a patience-breaking process and a great amount of postwar disquiet was being evidenced by the assertiveness of former WAACs on both sides of the Irish Sea, especially when some of the explanations for late or non-remittance of monies due offered by the Corps paymasters put blame on the complainants' misunderstanding of bureaucratic procedures. As levels of dismay increased, letters which once had been polite and understandably deferential changed their tone. When sometimes weeks and even months went by without receiving a satisfactory response, the mood changed. The flow of correspondence into the WAAC HQ in London was soon beset by repeated reminders arriving by every post. Infuriated by delays and unexplained mistakes, the complaints grew even less respectful. They carried acerbic tones and even threats emerged.

One of the immediately noticeable features of those times was manifested in the numerous arguments that escalated within all categories of former rank and file WAAC workers. Complaints were widespread.

Irish-born members of the Corps were as vocal as their English and Scottish fellows. The problems which arose were concerned with delays in receiving permission to leave the service, errors in the calculation of pay settlements, unnecessary deductions and almost always a long waiting time before any satisfaction could be gained. As time went on, the list of disconcerted enquiries being generated acquired the appearance of an endless rant. There was the instance of an 'Immobile' 'General Clerk', Florence McBeth, a local girl enrolled into the WAAC via the Limerick Labour Exchange who was working as a shorthand typist in the Templemore 'Bombing School'. Florence was sent home in early February 1919 but had not been officially 'struck off' the roll due to a mix-up between the QMAAC in Dublin and HQ London over her discharge.[5] Her pay had ceased on leaving, but no civilian dole was forthcoming being considered still listed as 'serving'. Having no other source of income, she wrote looking for help, claiming to be financially 'in very bad circumstances', while pointing out that 'suitable employment cannot be obtained'.[6] Six months were to elapse before the error was corrected. By then, a proliferation of enquiries from other former WAACs with disputes over errors in back pay, mistaken deductions or the slow receipt of gratuities had been gathering momentum.

It is noticeable that the earliest enquiries over errors were mostly restrained and deferential in tone. For instance, Donegal-born telegraphist, Teresa Mary Black, who had been assigned to duties in a Signal office in Le Havre in early August 1917 and had served just over two years there before being granted a discharge 'on compassionate grounds' to allow her return home to her father who was in very poor health, had patiently held back for weeks before gently enquiring again about the delay in receiving money due, explaining: 'I would like to be able to help my father financially.'[7] The hold-up of her back pay was then almost two months in arrears. Similar difficulties became a recurrent theme throughout 1919 and into early 1920. Young women were finding that transferring back to civilian life had been often less then easy, and it can be shown that most of the serious problems were over an immediate shortage of money – not just in homes in Ireland, where a downturn in the economy was evident, but just as frequently the case for families in Scotland, England and Wales.

What becomes noticeable within the exchanges of correspondence is that although the formality of the earliest letters voicing dissatisfaction most often bore the habitual humility of those times when writing to personages perceived as of higher status, e.g., rounding off with a 'Yours obediently' or 'Yours respectfully', there is soon plenty of evidence to display the use of the more egalitarian 'Yours truly' or 'Yours faithfully', or even no polite valediction at all, especially when satisfactory answers to questions had not been received. Displays of overt subservience were losing ground fast and once they had moved beyond the strictures of their army service days, a quiet movement was gathering – no doubt rallied by the rising vocal exhortations of activists on all sides for 'women's rights', of which there will be more to say.

The picture is clear. A rebellious atmosphere was developing. There was a girl from Longford, sent to Etaples as a waitress in June 1918, who had served there for just over a year before being dispersed in mid-September 1919. Her indignation was very genuine when writing for a second time months later over the non-payment of back pay, although her plea 'Surely, by now I should have some news?' was a mild rebuke by comparison to many of the other complaints being received.[8]

She was not an isolated case. Ex-GPO girls from every region were finding it difficult to adjust to the rising cost of living in those postwar days. A former signaller from the Le Havre base, a Dublin girl from Blessington Street whose brother had been killed in France, who had come home to care for her widowed mother, was a typical one who was not afraid to stand up for her 'rights'. She wrote to HQ in London warning: 'The delay is unpardonable! Please see to it immediately, or must I get my solicitor to take up the matter?'[9] As the daughter of a deceased engineer she had the education and confidence to speak up. Similar strident tones were sent from other former army colleagues, although it is striking that while from every location and background, the complaints came mainly from clerical or telecommunication workers and not as a rule from former domestic workers.

On the other hand, there were rare occasions when apologies were forthcoming. In one case, the clearly embarrassed Chief Controller for France informs those in charge of a London pay unit: 'the official concerned … should be held responsible for this deficiency,' having noted that the member 'had been put to the expense of informing you of the error by telegrams'.[10] It is interesting to note how that ex-WAAC complainant had lived in the North City Dublin middle-class suburb of Glasnevin. Her father was a senior overseer in the GPO Sorting Office, a post that may have had carried some local clout with either that organization's officials or their employees' union.

Other instances of successful claims and fulsome recompense being insisted upon by the QMAAC chief controllers included one for a Manchester girl, Florence Jackson, who wrote reminding for the second time: 'I was informed at the Medical Board on 30 October 1919 that I was recommended for discharge and 6 weeks sick leave [but] my sick leave has been terminated after 4 weeks only. Kindly rectify the oversight.'[11] It can be noted that, in her case, her questioning of the accuracy of their calculations was deemed correct. The system was reliant on a long-standing army rule that all discharges recommended by a Medical Board carried a twenty-eight-day delay before a dispersal certificate was issued – and in recalculating the sick leave, the paymasters had to admit that an adjustment of pay was indeed due to her. Nevertheless, despite admittance of an error, by 14 January 1920, with a long delay in responding and still no sign of any compensation money after weeks of waiting, her patience had worn very thin. Clearly very angry, Florence writes for the third time, echoing the dilemma being faced by so many former army colleagues:

> As previously stated, I have a widowed mother to maintain and I wish to impress upon you the urgency of this request being complied with as it is absolutely necessary that I should have what I am justly entitled to at once if the home is to be kept intact. I would point out that I have had no pay since November and I think it is grossly unfair that payment should be withheld in this fashion.

The response from QMAAC HQ for the case was more enlightening. By then, the winding-down of many of their own HQ administrative tasks had concluded. No longer armed with any power, they were obliged to write back in January 1920 to tell her they now had no authority to issue any further pay, as, from that time on, the War Office would be taking responsibility for all queries over money. However, they had managed to get for her a confirmation that the twenty-eight-day delay rule before a discharge applied in her case so that she 'will actually receive pay or compensation up to 7 January 1920'. The Manchester girl's dogged perseverance had finally paid off – but not before a determined struggle and a long and anxious wait. Others with less patience were not so fortunate and it is clear that the procedures for claiming funds that were still due when leaving the service on 'Compassionate Grounds' were often complicated.

There has to be some sympathy, nonetheless, for those tackling the overwhelming workload that such widespread demobilization was imposing on military paymasters at that time. One of the main contentions of inadequate back pay had come about because of a change to the current National Health Insurance (NHI) rules in 1919, which introduced increased insurance benefits for a wider range of workers – both Irish and English – but which was also accompanied by the need for a weekly contribution to be collected from many more workers. The rule applied to several categories of the WAAC such as former office workers and catering staff who had been under the NHI Act of 1911. By May 1919 the sum of 7s 6d a week was being deducted from these army pay-packets. The changes to the rule did not apply for recruits who had held prewar jobs as government civil servants and there are numerous cases of grievous arguments over the final pay settlements of the latter which, of course, included all the telecommunication women who had been brought in under their own specially separate, negotiated arrangements for pay and conditions which have been already described.

A new twist to the controversy was soon to come. A Glasgow-born WAAC who had received no response to her explanation that 'I am a government servant and getting no payment from any other source' had been quite ready to do battle. She had sent a 'demand that money be refunded as it ought never to have been deducted' and, soon ready to snap from frustration, her next letter announced: 'if not attended to and a satisfying answer given, I shall have to appeal to someone in Higher Authority.'[12] What she meant, of course, was that there were several parliamentarians who had become actively engaged and willing to speak up for them and questions were being raised in Westminster. She would not be the only one to take a similar course of action. The Dublin girl from

Blessington Street who had threatened to get legal advice had not gone to her solicitor but had instead written to the paymasters to announce she had appealed for political help: 'Failing satisfaction, Sir Maurice Dockrell MP is taking my case in hand.'[13] Sir Maurice at that time was an Irish Unionist MP and there were other politicians keen to be involved, such as the recently elected Labour MP Frederick O. Roberts, who was to go on to have a long and distinguished career in British Labour politics.

One of the more noteworthy Irish voices to be raised in this context was a volunteer from the Dublin GPO's telegraph office, Florence Mullally, a girl from a North Circular Road Catholic family. Her father, originally from Bog of Allen in Kildare, had been a Post Office overseer. Sent out to France in August 1917, she had travelled with three other Irish girls from the Aldershot Camp in the same draft as the activist supervisor, Alice Clarke, who led that protest over the lack of higher-ranking commissions for the Post Office officers, discussed in Chapter 6.[14] Florence was attached to one of the BEF exchanges in the Le Havre area until March 1919. Her health had suffered badly while in France and she had been sent back to Dublin and granted three months' sick leave. By 29 June a discharge was granted but she was still seeking what she felt was the correct amount of sick-leave pay she was entitled to under the agreements drawn up between the Army Council and the Post Office in 1917. Her letters to QMAAC paymasters at first voiced annoyance and dismay: 'you will find a mistake in your calculations no doubt on investigation,' but as the weeks passed with no satisfactory redress received following her return home to her job in the GPO, she had finally issued an ultimatum several months later:

> To make the matter quite clear, I demand payment by return of post for my services to the army up to the 29th June plus 28 days on discharge and in addition the money due to me overseas and credits there ... I have taken full notes of the muddling and incompetence displayed in dealing with my case and if necessary will use them through the Head of the Irish Government.

Six months earlier, the First Dáil Éireann had been convened in the Round Room of the Mansion House on 21 January 1919. The threat worked. She was told that an adjustment would be made and an extra allowance of eighteen days' pay was to be sent to her. However, that issue was not her only gripe. It was her firm conviction that her employers should be held responsible for sorting things out with the army and, right enough, her case had been noted. It was later considered sufficiently important to have been preserved in the Post Office's own UK archives, especially as she was claiming to have been a victim of what she called 'a clear breach of faith' over the terms of her contract to serve with the Women's Army Auxiliaries.[15]

In all these cases, what appears to have been mainly one particularly difficult sticking point was the non-payment of the £5 war bonus which had featured in the 1917 wrangles over pay and conditions. Although the 1917 negotiations between the War Office and the GPO authorities had eventually cancelled that promise of the war bonus, that decision must not have been afterwards efficiently conveyed, nor fully understood by many of the early recruits such as Mullally. It is interesting, though, that in this instance, the correspondence relating to her disputes with the army paymasters was kept on GPO files possibly for political expediency. These were diplomatically delicate times for an emerging new relationship between the British and Irish postal authorities.

Also significant had been her decision to avoid seeking help from a Unionist MP in Westminster, but had a mind, instead, to call upon 'the Head of the new Irish Government'. It implied that she was carrying sympathy, if not closer connection, to seriously powerful politically active circles following the Republican Sinn Féin's election victory in December 1918, which may have been a factor which raised concern in many minds. Those in the know were aware of the tinderbox that was on the point of being lit. The threat of claiming to get powerful help for her case from the new government must have created some uneasiness within an increasingly dangerous Irish situation.

Nonetheless, a formal internal report on Miss Mullally's problems was, indeed, drawn up on her behalf by the office of the Postmaster General in London in February 1920. No further immediate action was likely to be considered, probably because by that time some delicate negotiations had commenced over the possibility of the British and Irish postal services parting company under the proposed political introduction of a separate Irish Free State. With such uncertainty in the air, decision-making was difficult.

Throughout the rest of February and into April 1920, internal GPO notes and correspondence from Miss Mullally continued to be exchanged without any sign of reaching any satisfactory solution, although some sympathetic 'off the cuff' background noises of support from at least one of her her superiors had felt her claims had been 'justly so'. Finally by the end of April, it became clear that as no further help was possible and, as one of the correspondents comments with obvious relief, 'She will now let the matter drop as far as the Department is concerned.'[16]

Within the next three years work to bisect the British and Irish postal and telegraphs and telephone services from each other was to continue. Southern Ireland was to function separately under the Free State Parliament's newly created Department of Posts and Telegraphs; the existing Irish Postmaster General, James J. Walsh – a member of the centre right Cumann na nGaedheal – continued to hold his post and was appointed as the new minister for this department.

Meanwhile, one of the earliest telegraphists to be sent to France, Maude Onions, who had served there since June 1917, had contacted her Liverpool postmaster in 1919 when home on leave from 'L' Signals GHQ. Her letter dated 16 July had come straight to the point, warning him in the strongest possible terms that Post Office personnel were being 'retained in France under conditions less favourable than those of the staff which remained in England' and she points out that 'apart from the lack of material comforts, their pay was below that of the staff in the Home Service and also compared unfavourably with the women sent to Paris'.[17] Her letter sounding the alert was kept on file – but there was not much joy in the reply they sent to her on 6 August, even though: 'The question of an increase in the pay is under active consideration, and pending a decision the Postmaster General is unable to take any action'.[18] To which it was added: 'The question of the eligibility of members of the QMAAC to receive war service gratuity and the bonus granted to men retained for matching demobilisation is entirely for the War Office, and the Postmaster General regrets he does not see his way to take any steps in this matter.' There was nothing more to be said.

A letter to General Sir Douglas Haig, Commander-in-Chief BEF

In that same summer, a ferocious warning rocket was being launched by a girl from Lancashire, Southport-born Ellen Thompson.[19] She was still a serving WAAC at the Rouen base when she raised her own gripe over the lack of a war bonus being paid. The 27-year-old signaller had aimed high – and it might be asked could her missive have been deliberately also coordinated with Maud Onions's hand-written complaints to her postmaster? Posted in July 1919, Ellen's letter was addressed simply to General Sir Douglas Haig, the BEF Commander-in-Chief at the War Office.

Its contents caused such a flurry that copies went flying from one office to another across Whitehall. The points she was raising were the same complaints being put by both Florence Mullally and Maud Onions: the poor rates of pay, despite their willingness over Sundays and night duties being filled for no extra money; their otherwise poor working and living conditions; and the refusal to grant either a war bonus or gratuity to the signallers on dispersal. She writes that:

> All that we receive on demobilisation is one month's leave with pay. No clothing allowance or gratuity. Considering that clerks, telegraphists and telephonists who are employed at the Peace Conference for only a very short period receive a dress allowance of £25, besides living in comfort and without any risks, surely the women who have spent two years and more are entitled to share some consideration?

The letter was delivered to A.G.11. A copy was shown to the QMAAC Controller-in-Chief, Dame Florence Leach and it then reached the desk of Lieutenant-General Sir J. J Asser, Director of the L of C: his only response was to send some stiff words to the War Office to convey that:

> The necessary action has been taken to inform this member, 2039 Asst. Forewoman E. Thompson, of the correct channels of correspondence.

Ellen was discharged in November. She made one more effort by writing directly to QMAAC Chief Controller Florence Leach outlining personal details of her financial difficulties, likening it to 'bankruptcy':

> I recommenced my civilian work with a debt of £17.19s. 9d. This alone is sufficient to dishearten even the strongest-minded of

womenfolk [and] I beg you to place this case as an example to the Authorities …

The letter was replied to courteously from the C.C.'s office. It conveyed to her that 'the matter has been submitted to the War Office, and it is regretted that no increase can be made in the rate of demobilisation benefit now issuable to members'. For Ellen, the time had come to rest her case. Further protest was useless.

It is intriguing, nonetheless, to note from this exchange of correspondence that, by January 1920, both writers had drifted into colloquial, if still unofficial QMAAC terminology: 'demobilisation' when referring to the termination of women's wartime service days with the Corps. Attitudes were changing.

Postwar life was to treat Ellen Thompson rather better. She overcame that shaky postwar start by seeking a better future far from home. Within a week or two of the final letter of complaint, she married an ambitious ex-serviceman who saw a future in the motor industry and she and her husband set sail for the United States twelve months later. He found work in Manhattan as an insurance assessor and New York became their home. By 1940 they were naturalized US citizens.[20]

As will be shown, there would be many of her fellow servicewomen who, like her, were to seek new lives abroad – including those from Ireland – who were now armed with the additional confidence that army life had provided. They were full of spirit and determination to 'make it', come what may.

There is an interesting aside to be added to Ellen Thompson's grievances. Her younger brother had also served in the Great War as a Signals engineer attached to the Fleet Air Arm which was at that time heavily engaged in the development of experimental aviation wireless communication techniques. When Ellen's sibling, George, came to be demobbed, he had continued to work at the cutting edge of Post Office technology and, twenty-five years later, at the outbreak of the Second World War when he was, by then, one of their senior engineers, his hi-tech communication skills were called upon to provide specialist advice at Bletchley Park, the Allied facility centre for codebreaking and monitoring of all telecommunication traffic. It was probably not a completely unique coincidence. Young people with technical nous of all kinds who were called upon to serve in the Great War went on to become the 'movers and shakers' of the mid-twentieth century and remained very much attuned to radically changing times.

Women's role within a peacetime workplace is questioned

The new decade, later dubbed as the 'The Roaring Twenties', was to give yet another shake-up to the changing kaleidoscope of society. Can it be confidently assumed that everyone was to cheerfully embrace the age that introduced bobbed hair, shorter skirts and greater freedom for women? There were some who were doubtful if was wise to be too quick to anticipate changes which promised to introduce improved lives for all.

According to a contemporary Edinburgh academic, Nora Milnes, when speaking some three years into the decade, the postwar atmosphere was regressing once more into an unfair arena for women. It was her view that 'the men are not always fair to the women'. Writing in generalized terms for a Post Office staff journal in 1923 on the topic of opportunities in the workplace, she was careful to make it clear to her readers that she was not referring specifically to that organization's employment terms and conditions, but rather more to other sectors of industry and commercial life that were pulling back on well-paid career opportunities for women after the war and asking:

> I wonder if we have not accepted too meekly the attempt at gradual return to prewar conditions as far as women are concerned. ... We find little consideration – little appreciation of the fact that woman must also live.[21]

As has been demonstrated by the financial difficulties being faced by so many of the girls being demobbed, it is clear that all was not well in the battle for rights and equality. Young women looking forward to being married had little option but to accept a life of busy home-based domesticity. That it also brought loneliness and sometimes utter desperation was rarely addressed by the majority of people who regarded young men as total failures if they could not 'support' a wife who stayed at home. As for the girls who remained single, they had to get along as well as they could on lower wages and less opportunity for advancement. It was an uneven playing field and it would remain so.

Chapter 9

The Roaring Twenties

'Cynicism became fashionable and disenchantment was smart.'

Hattersley[1]

In the months that followed the declaration of the Armistice in November 1918 there was little immediate change to the 'Overseas' and 'At Home' work being carried out by the WAAC. The fighting was over, but there were plenty of busy days ahead. Yet as the ensuing winding-down of all former wartime priorities commenced, it was now accompanied by a weariness on all sides. The stringent shortage of basic foodstuffs across Britain had not been lifted and, by then, even the army personnel in France – men and women alike – had begun to complain about deteriorating standards of their daily rations.

Fresh recruits from Ireland continued to be deployed in all locations because the army's gradual repatriation of troops was complicated and their reliance on WAAC background support was still required. It would not be until Christmas 1919, or soon after, that WAAC demobilizations had been significantly, but not completely, finished. By then many of their members had served well over two years.

As has already been indicated, when enrolments from Ireland commenced in March 1917 many of the girls who were keen had not waited for the Dublin WAAC HQ to get all the depots and hostels in Dublin and Belfast up and running but, instead, had made their own way to England to enrol. The young woman who became the Recruiting Controller for Ireland was one of those early applicants (see Chapter 2) and another of the many shorthand-typists who had immediately come forward was a girl from the Dublin suburb of Cabra, who had filled in an application in April 1917.[2] She had been working as a shorthand-typist for a solicitor and was one of the first WAACs to be despatched to the forward GHQ base in St. Omer. Later assigned to the lieutenant-colonel, head of the Heavy Repair Shop in Rouen, as soon as the Armistice was announced, she had sought a move back to the Irish HQ unit in Dublin so that she could help cope with a family crisis. Her brother-in-law had died, leaving her sister with three small children and no income. She asked if she might be allowed to serve in Dublin as an 'Immobile' member of the Corps, which would allow her to provide her sister with financial and practical help and it provides a good example of how army sections other than the Signal units were usually helpful, but sometimes ran into difficulties in allowing their WAAC staff to be repatriated. In her case, her army boss had no objection to allowing her home, but it was on the proviso that the Corps replace her with 'a thoroughly efficient substitute', adding: 'I shall be sorry to lose Worker Lowe, as she has carried out her duties in a competent and satisfactory manner, and is my only shorthand typist.' The request was received sympathetically by the Assistant Chief Controller, but the pressure on finding available staff in France by that time was so great that there was no replacement to be found. The move had to be refused and her service days did not end until mid-October 1919, almost a year following her request for a transfer. The following weeks and months kept the depot busier than ever with the movement of military equipment back across the Channel and there was nothing for it but for Florence to stoically endure those extra eight months of service with the BEF before final dispersal.

Other examples of early enrolments who may have been extremely thankful for a discharge from duties as early as March 1919 include two sisters, the daughters of a clergyman in Clonegal, on the border of Wexford and Carlow, who applied in July 1917 but were later formally enrolled in Hastings. Despatched from there to France, they served together at the Le Havre base as cooks from November 1917 to March 1919. For these refined young ladies, having to toil in the sometimes rough conditions of army kitchens in France must have been quite an experience, especially as the pay at £26 a year being offered was only equivalent to what they had been receiving for household positions in gentrified families. One had worked for seven years for a lady as 'a governess for my children' and the other was engaged in housekeeping work for 'a retired judge'.[3]

There was also a young woman, born in Cork, who was eager to resume a career in journalism. She was already pursuing this ambition when she enrolled in London where she was studying for a BA degree while holding down a part-time job at a newspaper office.[4] At that time she had been staying with an aunt in Chiswick but, having been spurred by fresh appeals for more recruits, had decided to come forward in May 1918. Taken on as a WAAC shorthand typist, she was sent immediately to France. About twelve months later, when home on leave in May 1919, the editor of the *Daily Mail* newspaper offered to take her on trial as a reporter if she could 'obtain a demobilisation within a month'. The job would have allowed her to finish her BA studies on a part-time basis. She appealed for a discharge, pleading that she would only have a few days to respond to the offer. She was fortunate on two counts: the WAAC controllers held a definite ethos of support for women wishing to make their way in professions, and the major who was her OC at the base in Boulogne was sympathetic and full of praise for her abilities. Suggesting he had a girl on his staff who could step in to take her place, the major swiftly backed up the request. The discharge was granted. She was one of the lucky ones.

Office workers, clerks, typists and record-keepers in addition to the girls working in Signal units were still very much in demand by the army right up to the end of 1919. Colossal stacks of military records were building up over the demobilization of troops in every sector and such was the pressure that there were many requests for a discharge that were not being granted until the end of the year. Added to this was the growing volume of telecommunication traffic which ensured that the pressure to keep on top of operational needs remained burdensome, even when the end of the war was in sight. For instance, when a lieutenant in RE Signals, Rouen, was being pushed to allow one of his Scottish girls to leave, he was adamant in regard to the need to keep her in situ for several more months, reporting higher up: 'she cannot be released at present without a relief. My technical minimum for telephonists is 23, and on account of Leave and sickness, my present actual working staff including Forewomen is only 21.'[5]

In another case, even though the young woman's 'grounds for discharge' were deemed 'genuine' following her mother's death, which was backed up with her local postmaster at home, who was also short-staffed and anxious to have her back to her job in Essex, the final outcome of her repeated appeals for release was stark. The answer from GHQ declared her application was 'not recommend[ed] … in view of the difficulty of her replacement', followed by an updated review when she again pleaded her need to be at home, which once more ruled: 'it is considered the circumstances are not of such an exceptional nature as to justify the application being granted.'[6] She was wanted in France and that was that. It would be another year before she was released from duty and allowed to go home.

In the meantime, telegraph and telephone traffic had not lessened and although several signallers had been granted discharges with what were deemed more valid pleas – mostly requests to get married – the rest were being desperately held on to by the army. Staff shortages continued and as late as mid-September 1918 new intakes of signallers were still arriving from Dublin. Most of those girls were posted to the Calais and Boulogne army telephone and telegraph offices. The final large-scale return of the 'E' sector back to their former exchanges and post offices did not take place until October/November 1919.[7]

The push to accelerate dispersals was very evident in Dublin, despite the slowness of the process at HQ in London. Already, by 21 July 1919, a parade 'of demobilised soldiers' which included all ranks of the army, Royal Navy, nursing sisters and Women's Auxiliary troops participated in a march-past which terminated at College Green. They were sent a special message congratulating them on 'the special appearance they presented'.[8] But the work was far from over.

In France, following the closure of their last base at Wimereux on 31 October 1919, it was planned to have a small contingent of WAAC gardeners remain in situ to tend war graves until deemed no longer needed. In addition, there was some support work for the army's continued presence in Europe for some time ahead. This included a 'party of Administrators engaged in Intelligence work', which had been moved to 'the Army of Occupation in Cologne in 1919' and 'a group of five or six Officials from the home service attached to the Military Mission in Berlin, where they were also being used for encoding, decoding and other highly confidential work'.[9] At least another twelve months' commitment was given by these groups.

In London, copious administrative correspondence lay ahead and before the end of the year, all regional commands, including the one in Dublin had been closed and their controllers dispensed with one by one. The former Controller for Ireland, Miss Lace Pritchard, left Dublin to return home in 1920 and by Christmas that year it was reported she 'was teaching Domestic Science under the London County Council'.[10]

Finally, when all was done, the war service days of the WAAC/QMAAC were to reach their official end. Their very last unit, based in Saint Pol, which had been engaged in tending war graves and the final administration work in northern France, was welcomed back to London by a crowd of former comrades, press representatives and cameras on 26 September 1921.[11] The official disbandment of the Corps took place at the War Office the following day.

From that time on the sharing of memories and support would take place solely under the auspices of a body called 'The QMAAC Old Comrades' Association' which had already been in existence since the previous summer. It was hoped the Association would become a thriving permanent organization – open to all ranks – offering companionship and useful contacts to assist in the transition to peacetime. Their first published 'Newsletter', issued in July 1920, invited members to form local branches of the Association. The idea gained popularity very quickly and within the next few years twenty-two 'flourishing branches' were formed.

Likewise, a number of overseas branches were created. The spread of those links are evidence of the amount of subsequent emigration of members that was to take place. By 1921 the first overseas branch was opened in Sydney, Australia. It was followed in 1922 by two in Canada, one in Winnipeg and one in Vancouver, as well as one in New Zealand, founded in Wellington that same year. Yet another Canadian branch started life in Montreal in June 1923 and, in Australia, a second branch was opened in Melbourne in September 1923. In South Africa, 1925 saw a branch convened in Johannesburg, Transvaal.[12] Thereafter, the networking of these young women's support systems went from strength to strength. The majority of the Corps' members may have returned to family life at home, but there were a great number who embarked on a myriad of new careers at home and abroad.

Adapting to life back at home

It has been held that the freedoms achieved by women during the war were subsequently stifled by 'a postwar backlash against women's new roles [that] extended far beyond the question of women's paid work'.[13] In Ireland, the scene was rather different and this situation was to remain for decades to come. There were not the same opportunities for girls to find employment outside of farm or home in that largely non-industrial society, as studies to provide analysis of women's lives in the twentieth century have shown.

To keep a dwelling-place warm, coal or turf fires had to be set, fuel had to be carried and ashes cleared. Built-up urban areas may have had town gasworks for ovens and lighting, but the use of other appliances was rare. To cook, bake, wash and clean without the help of any modern equipment and facilities were tasks that required a pair of hands to be engaged in an unrelenting routine, seven days a week. For working-class families, middle-class homes and wealthier households alike, the sweeping brush, manual carpet sweeper, bucket, mop, scrubbing brush, washtub and wringer were all most average households could rely upon. Electric-driven equipment such as vacuum cleaners only slowly made their appearance in wealthy urban households. With no kitchen devices such as electric toasters and refrigerators, meals had to be freshly prepared and eaten without undue delay. In rural and urban areas alike, there might still be a need to draw water for household use; clothes had to be washed, dried, ironed and aired. Home dressmaking, sewing, mending and darning was not so much *de rigueur* but a practical necessity at every level of society. Running a household was a full-time, hands-on job and for the greater majority of the girls who came back from the war to their homes in Ireland this was the reality of living, whether single or married and most households were a traditionally reliant on partnerships of one breadwinner and one homemaker. Employment for most men was available. For middle-class women – especially married women – it was less easy. Efforts to overcome the strictures on the earning capacity of women tied into household chores had always existed, however. For stay-at-home wives, to conduct a small business venture from her front sitting-room was not an uncommon situation, and occupations such as dressmaking or millinery for private customers, piano or singing lessons and instruction classes in other skills such as needlework, embroidery, knitting, crochet and similar home-based occupations were run by married and single women alike. These earnings usefully supported family finances and the practice was to continue for decades.

A not too dissimilar scenario can be found in all the other regions, and the campaigns being mounted for fairer wage equality were obviously valid. A single daughter very often had to become the breadwinner for a household which had lost menfolk in the war, and had aged parents or younger siblings to care for, and in those instances, the effort to undertake household management in addition to holding down a job became an even more problematic. For married and unmarried women alike, if they were lucky enough to have a garden, the growing of all-year-round vegetables and fruit for the table or the keeping of hens and pigs was not at all rare. For working-class as much as for middle-class urban and rural families, the partnership of a marriage was for the most part reliant on essential work outside and inside the home so that living standards and benefits for all could be provided. Samples of those patterns for life will be addressed in Chapter 11.

A return to normal working hours for the former 'Signallers'

By Christmas 1919 former members of the Signal units, female telegraphists and telephonists, had all had the opportunity of being welcomed back from war service by their local postmasters. There were guaranteed openings for gaining further promotion, their secure pensions had remained in situ and if they were leaving the organization to get married, they qualified for a marriage gratuity. They had also a firm assurance that their their seniority positions and pay rates within the GPO ranking systems were to be in line with the level a girl 'would have reached if she had remained at home' and it had been made clear how the calculations for their remuneration were to be managed: 'The period of their absence [in the WAAC was to] account for pension and marriage gratuity and for incremental purposes.'[14]

But times were hard. In Ireland by 1920, Republican intelligence work was widespread throughout the Post Office organization. By the end of that year, IRA Brigade instructions recommended that 'a reliable person be placed in each Post Office to be constantly on the look-out for letters' going through the system which might be useful for information-gathering. They ordered that 'telephone and telegram messages sent by enemy police, soldiers or agents should be copied and recorded'.[15]

For ex-WAACs who were lucky enough to return to former jobs at home in Britain the scene had changed, too. A rampant growth of inflation had taken place during wartime years. Prices were still increasing and people were struggling. For the former 'Signallers':

> The familiar characteristics of the Post Office had begun to disappear. … The Department for the first time in its history announced a deficit of expenditure over income. … Prices had approximately doubled and though it was thought at the time as temporary and abnormal, it was never reversed.[16]

Moreover, since the end of the war there had been a severe decline in inland telegraph traffic and this section continued to lose money, mainly because of much greater competition from the Telephone Service.[17]

Comments to be found in a Post Office staff journal in 1917 reflect much of the thinking within that organization at that time, with one anonymous writer holding forth the hope that:

> The old doctrine that women's occupation must be sheltered, with different scales of pay, different methods of discipline is crumbling away faster than any of the prewar shibboleths maintained by the authorities, of course, because it was thought to produce economies in the public service, but I believe that to be a great delusion.[18]

These were strong words. The writer goes to refer to how the war opened up opportunities to 'hundreds of clever, ambitious women' who were 'breathing the free air which comes with equal opportunities for both sexes'.

For those who were returning from the war, it must have seemed that normal working hours and set routines were quietly reverting to the way they had always been. The telegraphists were especially fortunate in that they had gained plenty of experience in working with some of the newer methods of communication the army had installed in BEF bases. However, it should be noted that they were not going back to a buoyant sector of public service. The immediate postwar years were not a good time for the postal services either in either Ireland or England. The economic situation everywhere was in a bad way – and in Ireland, especially, the political circumstances were to bring an overall disruptive effect. The atmosphere was soon charged with anxiety. Not only were they once more surrounded by wartime tensions, but the equipment and working conditions in Irish exchanges were way behind the times and there was little likelihood anything would change for a long time.

For those who returned to London and the larger English exchanges, their problems were rather different. Telegraphy systems in post offices which had formerly used 'the old Morse and Baudot systems' were beginning to be replaced by teleprinters from 1921 onwards, and not everyone was happy about this. (See Appendix II) Postal historian Clinton had identified one of the difficulties arising for its female staff as being due to so many of the 'older telegraphists refusing to come to terms with new technology and had deliberately changed to non-operational duties instead of mastering the new techniques of the teleprinter'.[19] In referring to these women as 'older', it is likely he was indicating those Post Office women who did not volunteer to go to France. By contrast, the girls returning from their army service days were well honed in facing the challenges of new technology and had no fear of what might be introduced into postal telegraph offices in the coming years. The levels of responsibility that had been thrust upon some had boosted their ambitions, and there were some who made noteworthy achievements within the organization.

For example, a former WAAC/QMAAC telegraphist, Bessie Reid, who had served in Etaples and Boulogne, was to become the first-ever woman manager of a telegraph office in Britain when she was promoted to this position in Oxford in 1924.[20] When she returned from the front to her former position in Oxford, armed with the high standards she had become accustomed to in France, Bessie is reputed to have found the local GPO 'equipment very primitive, so she frequently carried out running repairs'. She then took it upon herself to seek a higher management job – and successfully achieved it – although apparently not without a fierce struggle and she was later to be unequivocal in her view that it had generated 'much male opposition' at that time.

Bessie typifies the attitudes that so many former WAACs would adopt following their wartime experiences. After her retirement, she continued to acquire new skills that needed dexterity coupled with sensitivity and, at the age of 66, she learned to play the organ so well that she eventually became respected enough to become chairman of the local Diocesan Organists' Association.

There were other successes, too. Another equally skilled former signaller who made a significant advance in her career at the GPO was Gertrude Hall – whose return from serving in France resulted in an eventual appointment to 'the highest possible position for women in the telegraph service as Chief Supervisor at the Central Telegraph Office in London'.[21] By the time Gertrude retired in 1932, she had celebrated forty-two years with the Post Office.

No evidence has yet been found to show if equally good career progress was ever made by any of the Irish signallers who returned to the Irish Post Office. Those who went back to work were soon to be employees of the new Irish Free State's Department of Posts and Telegraphs. Constraints on expenditure lay ahead. There was to be no investment in new equipment for some time to come and the newly acquired skills of telegraphists were of little immediate use. Instead, the ability to adapt and similar character traits were to be put to good use in other ways, either at home or abroad.

By the time the Director of the School of Social Study in Edinburgh University, a woman, was commenting in a GPO staff journal in 1923 on what she felt was a serious reversal for women in the postwar workplace, the Irish Post Office administration and staff had become a civil service sector of the Free State government. Her view is nonetheless relevant in that she made sure to reiterate the fundamental point of the arguments being made at that time on both sides of the Irish Sea. It was her view that:

During the war women were able to live according to a totally different standard, owing to their greatly increased earning capacity. This increase, coupled with the remarkable change in the field of employment, naturally changed their whole outlook. Before the war they had very little 'freedom'. During the war they realised the opportunity of carrying out their own lives, living as 'self dependent' individuals.[22]

She is obviously quite pessimistic that equal pay would be immediately achievable but pins her hopes that her readers would not lose sight of the gains women made during wartime, so that they may in the future 'maintain with greater honour and greater justice, the position that we try to insist upon in our demands for practical equality'. It was an aspiration which continued to be debated into the next century.

An uncertain future for WAAC administrators?

For other professions and occupations a commissioned rank as an 'Official' within the Corps did not automatically bring about any easier transition back to civilian life. Former administrators often saw the privileges temporarily afforded by their army roles being almost entirely reversed.

A great number of these young, well-educated women, who had held high positions within the hierarchal structure of the Corps, left their army service with nothing of any substance ahead of them. Their wartime responsibilities had been onerous. What now faced them was often a void and these girls would have to fend for themselves from that time on. This was certainly true for all the former WAACs who returned home to Ireland. There was a great deal of adjusting to be done and they were to be surrounded by conflict again in the struggle, first for Irish independence and then the bitter civil war that caused deep rifts within society, often splitting apart whole families and groups of former close friends.

Those who had served in army Signals who held hopes of a smooth return to their former GPO careers in Ireland would have found the atmosphere particularly hard to handle. Some did stay on, regardless of the difficulties, but there were others whose lives moved on in a different direction in very much the same way as many of their fellow WAAC comrades from elsewhere. Were these women prepared to take all that uncertainty lying down? It would seem not. The Corps' *Old Comrades' Association Gazette* (*OCA Gazette*) was just six months old when it published a review of the variety of work being tackled by members who had recently set off to carve out new lives for themselves. Having been inundated with letters to report successes and/or failures, requests for support and other messages offering suggestions and help, the Old Comrades committee was determined to do what it could. They aimed to sound positive, commenting: 'The achievements of ex-QMAAC in every field of enterprise make extraordinarily interesting reading.'[23] The article had supplied a description of the number of employment opportunities that had been taken up by ex-members of the Corps which included missionary work in China, growing tomatoes in the Channel Islands, poultry farming, appointments as secretaries for a number of distinguished people or returning to their former lives as actresses or singers. It may have been considered that such employment 'situations' were far less prestigious than the status those young women had formerly enjoyed as commissioned WAAC officers in uniform, but they certainly reflected some of the enterprising activities that lay ahead.

For the Irish members of the Corps who served at the same level of rank and responsibility, a report which appeared in an earlier 1920s issue of the *OCA Gazette* reveals that, as yet, nothing quite as exciting as their wartime experiences had impacted on their postwar lives. One former unit administrator in charge of the women who were serving in the Curragh Camp at Newbridge, a Miss Beatty, had begun 'training as a solicitor', which it was claimed would 'make her one of the pioneers in that profession for women'.[24] Another administrator, Miss Haskins, who had served at the Irish Command HQ, had just finished a course of 'secretarial training' and a girl called Miss Fish (who had worked in the Rouen base) had returned to Dublin for the same reason. Meanwhile, the former unit administrator of the Dublin Depot, a Miss Lloyd, together with a Miss Eva Finny, a doctor's daughter from Merrion Square, whose service days had been spent in the London District, had both obtained secretarial posts in a Dublin hospital. The political and economic situation in Ireland in that summer of 1920 was, nonetheless, becoming more uncertain and volatile by the day. All they could do was wait and watch. Their days as servicewomen had nurtured tolerance and non-judgemental attitudes because of the need to work with such a mixture of beliefs, cultures and social backgrounds for a common cause. There would probably have been no desire to become embroiled in bitter controversy and, certainly, for those who had been exposed to the horror of armed conflict in France and Flanders, there must have been a determined effort to put their worst memories of blood and bullets far behind them.

By February the following year, 1921, Eva Finny had answered several enquiries from old friends she once served with, by dropping a note into the Old Comrades monthly newsletter to let everyone know she had moved from the city centre to live in Sandymount in addition to having acquired some new employment: 'I am in a Government job, in the Treasury, and work in Dublin Castle, behind barbed wire and bayonets. I can't be more definite here, but it's not really quite as thrilling as it sounds.'[25]

Eva was one of half a dozen or more identifiable Irishwomen who had originally enrolled for work as a hostel forewomen but who soon proved themselves suitable candidates to be granted a full commission. Some would remain to work in Ireland and others in the UK or France. They would form the backbone of the subsequent spread of Old Comrades local branches everywhere across the world – a network that became both an international and a long-lived 'help-line' of support for each other.

Within two years, by which time the civil service has been taken over by the new Free State, Eva Finny had left her 'government job' to become a staff member of a large secretarial training college. She reports to old friends that 'the work is very interesting, but [she is] is naturally a good deal depressed by the state of the country'.[26] In the following issue of the *Gazette*, she explains that her job now entails 'teaching the young to the accompaniment of bursting bombs and whistling bullets', to which she added enigmatically with what may be visualized as a shrug of either impatience or philosophical resignation over violent struggles to gain power: 'it is all in the game.'[27]

Eva was to remain a very loyal friend of her old army pals for the rest of her life. She was to soon become the secretary of their own Old Comrades Irish branch. Another former unit administrator, Honor Connelly, who oversaw the work of WAAC clerks and cooks in the Fermoy unit and who had praised the Moore Park Camp for its setting and tidiness, presents an example of one of the many who created new lives for themselves abroad in Canada and elsewhere following their dispersal from the corps. Originally from Wicklow, Honor had lived briefly at the rectory in Rathangan before leaving to be married in the city of Montreal in 1927. She returned to Dublin to visit cousins in 1928 and, when widowed not long afterwards, she had married for a second time in 1932. Although she kept in regular touch with her army friends like many others, Canada became her permanent home thereafter. She was just one of many former army women from both England and Ireland to have migrated in that direction in the 1920s.

The membership of the Corps, being a well-mixed diversity of all-comers had its own contingent of several later extremely colourful Irish characters within its ranks, some of whom later became famous, such as the famous woman aviator, Sophie Peirce-Evans from Knockaderry, County Limerick, better known in later life as 'Lady Mary', a sportswoman and amateur woman pilot who had served as an army driver in France and then emulated another former WAAC from Ireland, Mary Bailey neé Westenra from Roscommon (Hon. Lady Bailey), another adventurous woman flyer who had been a WAAC aviation mechanic and who would later serve as a Second World War officer in the WAAF.[28]

Chapter 10

Call of the Wild:
The Assisted Passage Scheme

Together, then, when Peace comes, we will find
A home and, having found it, rove no more.

Grindlay, 1918[1]

Irish servicemen and servicewomen alike were to find it difficult to obtain work as civilians on their return home unless they had a job already lined up. Those from farming households or who had a family business to which they could return were the most fortunate but for the majority of the WAAC who were still in their early twenties, there was a clear problem ahead. The ones who had no work awaiting them were the last to be demobilized. That was the rule.

The surviving records of WAAC women shows that applications for a British government-run assisted passage scheme was soon being put to use by servicewomen from every region – including Ireland – and often in conjunction with the applications of ex-servicemen they had met during the war and planned to marry.[2] When the scheme for granting an assisted or free passage was set up in April 1919 it was originally intended that it would end on 31 December 1921, but the delays over the dispersals had caused such frustration for everyone that the closing date was subsequently extended for twelve months. Further concessions lasted up to the end of the following year, 1923: 'e.g., the dependents of men who proceeded overseas in advance of their families. Reasonable latitude was also allowed to late applicants who, owing to pressure on the shipping accommodation, were unable to sail before the end of that year.'[3]

The initial response was good but there had not been as great a rush as had been anticipated. By December 1920 it was claimed that 'only 687 ex-servicewomen had availed of the scheme: 334 had gone to Canada, 210 to Australia and New Zealand, 85 to Africa, 15 to India and the remainder to New Guinea, Ceylon, West Indies, Hong Kong, Egypt, Malay States and Straits'.[4]

The proportion of applicants who emanated from Ireland is not known, although there are plenty of examples to be found in surviving army records. Priority was given to all migrants who were willing to work 'on the land' or in 'domestic employment'. The applications had to be accompanied by references – and girls who were 'educated' or had good secretarial skills were far less welcome than young women willing to undertake less skilled work. Despite that drawback, as will be shown, there were plenty of Irish girls who were willing to go out in any capacity in order to qualify for the 'Assisted Passage' who then later left these jobs and reverted to deskbound office or other employments.

Likewise, the dispersed officials were just as keen to lay down new roots. Former unit administrators were often chosen to accompany groups of women travelling abroad.[5] Even the technically skilled former 'Signallers' whom the Post Office was anxious to see back at work were joining the exodus to foreign parts. In Chapter 11, the lives of two young women – one from Ireland and one from England – who had similar WAAC wartime service years in France and who made the choice to emigrate will be examined in some depth to compare/contrast with another pair of ex-WAACs, also Irish and English, who chose to stay at home.

Marriage to an ex-servicemen – quite a few of whom were from overseas regiments – became a significant factor which boosted migration. For Irish girls there was often a link to family members who had already moved to North America and evidence pointing to the popularity of Canada not only prior to the outbreak of the Great War but from 1920 onwards is particular strong. In 1917, the *Church of Ireland Gazette*, for example, was still carrying regular advertisements offering business and farming opportunities in Quebec.[6]

Quite a number of those enquiring did not understand that the scheme only applied to locations within the British Empire or the Dominions. When told the grant for travel was not being offered for the United States, the girls promptly switched to an alternative destination and reapplied. Most had ambitions to 'better themselves', having been pushed by their army experience to consider what opportunities might have existed in the wider world.

For example, a desire to leave Ireland was being pursued with enormous determination by one young woman from Inchicore in Dublin, Annie Delaney.[7] Following a brief spell in the Bostall Heath Camp in 1918, she had been transferred back to Dublin to be upgraded from her category as a 'B' waitress to work as an 'A' clerk for the Irish Command until dispersed in October 1919. Her postwar plans were to go to Vancouver with her friend Florence Doogan from Monaghan, who had also applied for the scheme. The latter girl, Florence, who had described herself as a 'land worker' was successful and duly arrived in Newfoundland on the SS *Metagama*, on 20 April 1920. However, Annie had not been accepted by the scheme's organizers – probably because her occupation was unequivocally a 'clerk'. Determined not to have her plans thwarted by the rules, she travelled to Quebec at her own expense three months later.

Not everyone was lucky enough to get away to start a new life so swiftly. Ethel Flynn from Ballina, County Mayo, who had worked in the kitchens of a Royal Field Artillery depot in Woolwich up to November 1919, was one of many who was accepted as a suitable candidate for an assisted passage by May 1920.[8] A great deal of patient waiting lay ahead, nonetheless. It was to be almost twelve months before she received a sailing date. The delay was likely to have been brought about because the selection committee had queried the Canadian job she had been offered as it had come from a firm with retail premises in Winnipeg, Manitoba. She may have possibly presented herself as willing to take up a situation as cleaner, cook or matron for shop girls who often 'lived in' on the premises of such retail establishments in those days, which may have been valid enough to comply with the scheme. Had she realized that the postwar years in that city were going to be a lot bleaker than had been anticipated? Possibly not. By the mid-1920s Winnipeg had sunk into a period of serious economic unrest and depression that was to last for some time to come. It was probably just as well that Ethel was unaware of that situation when she had been left facing that long and frustrating twelve months' wait for a passage. In the end, she and an older sister – most likely to have been a former servicewoman, too – travelled together from Liverpool to New Brunswick from where they took a train bound for Winnipeg.[9] There were opportunities to grab for everyone who went out to Canada – but it was tough and adapting to a new way of life came with rather more challenges than expected.

One Irish WAAC, Mary Moynihan, who found the experience initially far less satisfying, was honest enough to admit to deep-felt disappointment and anger to find that some of the glowing pictures painted for settlers by Canadian agents in London proved less than accurate. She later shared her thoughts with friends in London and in doing so indicates she had probably served as a forewoman clerk in Brighton and may have been one of the WAACs sent to Europe for administrative work at the time of the Paris Peace Conference in 1919.[10]

She and two ex-WAAC colleagues arrived in Saskatchewan in western Canada in August 1920, but her comments some years later reveal regrets for having opted for the offer of a free passage, admitting that she was now 'so envious' of other old army friends who were still in London and able to meet up with each other. On looking back to those days, she strikes a rueful note in her comment: 'like thousands of others I found it difficult to adapt to civil life after the glamour of the army and having seen the greater part of Europe, I thought I'd like to explore this end of the globe.'

Clearly more used to city urban living, her first taste of western Canada in 1920 had been a much greater shock that she could ever have envisaged. To qualify for the passage all three girls had offered to tackle 'domestic' positions, and she had ended up on an isolated grain-growing farm sixty miles out from the capital in the middle of the prairie.

Her greatest problem had been coping with the summer heat, describing it as 'simply unbearable, not a vestige of shelter'. Her employers were a young couple in serious financial straits. The wife was suffering from ill-health, there were two small children and the family was utterly reliant on the outcome of the forthcoming harvest for their very survival. Mary was given space for a bed in a corner of the upstairs area, partitioned off with cardboard-like board with only 'a curtain to serve as a doorway' in their still-to-be-completed wooden house. Recalling how 'our life in the army was luxurious, compared to this mode of living', she likened the hard straw mattress on her bed to one of the stiff army 'biscuits' the WAAC slept on without any grumbles when in camp. When out on the prairie, she always found each night-time hard to bear. It was impossible to keep cool: 'Were it not for the mosquitoes and the fear of grass snakes

I would have wrapped myself in a rug and slept outside in the open like the Canadian Indians do.'

She was determined to stick it out, nonetheless, and confessed that she had only stayed because 'her soft Irish heart' was reluctant to abandon the couple to their plight until the harvest was saved. Looking back at her seven-week stay which became 'one long nightmare', she afterwards felt some pride in having 'mastered the art of bread and butter-making' in addition to learning how to cook for a large gang of hungry harvesters, even though she admits those skills were 'never needed to be used again' following her move back to Regina, the capital of Saskatchewan, to find employment more suited to her qualification as an office worker.

It should be considered that Mary's less-than-rosy account may have been merely an aberration and, certainly stories like this one came to be vigorously countered by other more fortunate ex-WAAC migrants to Canada, whose experiences had been entirely different. One respondent who firmly held that 'Such conditions did not obtain in Alberta' when she had gone out to Canada went on to explain that, by contrast, her new life as a farmer's wife was compensated by the fun she was having from horse-riding and other healthy rural pleasures.[11] When on a trip home in 1927 she and her husband were congratulated on 'how fit and well we looked [and] I was supposed to look younger as a result, even if it is hard work' but she graciously conceded that Mary was correct over the 'terrible loneliness and home-sickness at times', suggesting there was 'something very worthwhile in building a comfortable home in a new country'. Her message was unequivocal: 'Don't come out only for the dollars. ... As men found their manhood in the war, so have I found my womanhood on the Canadian prairie.'

The frustration of delays

Attention has been already drawn to the long delay that was endured by one applicant to go overseas from Ballina. It was a difficulty met by many other would-be emigrants. One case in point was the attempt made by three sisters from a Catholic family of ten children who lived in the town of Monasterevin in Kildare where their father was self-employed as a 'fruit and vegetable merchant'. The youngest of his three elder daughters, Mary, had attended the local Mercy convent and, on leaving school, she had been employed as a cook for a resident in the town. She had joined the WAAC in September 1918 and had been sent to Chadderton Camp near Manchester, where she had worked as a waitress. Two other sisters had followed her leadership and had also enrolled. When discharged in November 1919, she wrote to the QMAAC in London to seek three application forms so that they all might benefit from the scheme.[12] The eldest of the siblings was to be let go from the Dublin Depot by Miss Lace Pritchard in November 1919, and the third sister due her exit from an army training camp at Oswestry in Shropshire around the same time. By Christmas 1919 they were all back on home ground without any employment prospects and a clear economic necessity to find themselves work. Canada looked to be a much better prospect than the current scene at home. What they would not have been aware of, however, was that they might have to wait an inordinate length of time before being issued with a sailing date. Clear evidence of any of them eventually getting away to Canada still remains elusive.

While there should have been plenty of local contacts who could have been approached for a job, it may be posited that for girls like these there may have been a less-than-warm welcome for them when they returned to Ireland as former 'army women'. Attitudes were changing. It is a point that Fionnuala Walsh's study has investigated more fully and her observations on one case provide an excellent example which she believes 'illustrates the prejudice encountered by some such women on their return home'. Her account reveals that a young woman called Annie Kelly was sexually assaulted when on leave from the WAAC in Dublin in 1919. Her assailant justified his actions with the belief that 'she had a bad character as he believed no decent Irish girl would be in the army'. When the case came to court, the defendant's solicitor allegedly attempted to cast doubt on Kelly's testimony by pointing out that she was 'only a WAAC' and consequently that her 'word could not be relied upon'. Kelly sought help from the QMAAC as to how to obtain protection from those 'people whose wrath I have incurred by serving my King and Country'.[13]

This is clearly an account that can convey the existence of the political connotations that coloured society's perception of why men and women made the decision to serve in the war and it is understandable that similar incidents of hostility would not have been widely publicized, but kept very quiet for fear of acerbating increasing tensions.

Group travel to Australia for single girls
In 1920 an arrangement was made for a group of sixty ex-WAACs to travel out together to Sydney, New South Wales, to take up some of the well-paid opportunities that Australia offered.[14] They were led by former District Administrator M. Munro Mathews, who had undertaken to accompany them and help them settle into the adventure they had embarked on. The highest proportion of the Corps' 'workers' employed in army depots and barracks everywhere had been cooks and kitchen staff and most of the migrants in that group were carrying hopes of being able to move on from that scene. It was believed that civilian jobs 'as nurses or governesses' were much preferable. They had been strongly advised that for life in Australia they should concentrate instead on perfecting their cooking skills. The wages being offered in New South Wales in 1920 could be as much as 35s a week. It was a good wage when compared to what could be then earned in Ireland or England, and it was suggested that female migrants would be able to save up, learn from the experience, and then either 'return home with a modest competence' or else acquire land and houses for themselves in Australia – which would have been an almost unheard-of opportunity for women before the war.

Specific examples had been cited in this report in order to further raise enthusiasm. It was explained how two girls working as cooks who went out earlier had been able to 'in one case, buy a fruit farm with a cottage and a horse and sulky [a popular lightweight cart]. In the other case [they bought] two houses, which are let at good rentals'.

News of similar satisfying progress being made included a reference to how another girl's heartbreak and determination to build a new life had turned out well. It was asked: 'Does anyone remember Forewoman Flynn, who served in France? She came from near Kildare, lost two brothers and fiancé in France and sold up her little farm in Ireland.'

Flynn's move to an Australian country setting was presented as having been a successful decision. It was implied she had an enthusiastic love of horses and how she was now able to ride out in Australia 'and is very happy in her country place'. The commentary adds, nonetheless, that

Flynn had migrated because she 'could not stand the prevailing disloyalty' at home and the observation carries the uncomfortable suggestion that there would have been many other heartbroken cases like Flynn's, who had unwittingly been made feel unwelcome on their return to their local neighbourhoods following their war service as a WAAC.

It cannot be denied that there was a downside to the farming life in countries like Australia and Canada, of course, but it might be argued that ex-WAAC girls from families in rural Ireland were probably better able to cope than many of their city- or town-bound former wartime colleagues from England. Warnings were issued that anyone accepting work on one of the isolated Australian stations would need to be prepared 'to understand existing conditions. They have sometimes to carry logs for the fires, carry water from distances, wash sheep shearers' overalls, and cook for big numbers at unearthly hours'. For anyone used to farm work anywhere, the news that it was usually demanding would have come as no great surprise.

As that group demonstrates, there was no shortage of cooks and domestic workers among those willing to build on career opportunities their army life had improved. For example, a Catholic girl whose home had been a tiny artisan dwelling in a working-class area just off the South Circular Road in Dublin had been immediately appointed as a hostel forewomen when she enrolled as a WAAC in Plymouth in October 1917. She was then 29 and had been previously employed in household work. She went on to serve in Devonport Plymouth and Warwick until July 1919. Seizing the chance of a new life, she had applied for a passage under the free scheme in October that year. There had been no delay to processing her application. By early March 1920, she, too, was on her way to Australia and what must surely have been a better life with an opportunity to improve her standard of living.[15]

Old Comrades' network

For every ex-WAAC who moved around the world in the years to come, there was the assurance of knowing there were people 'at the other end' with whom girls could make contact on arrival. The Association has been largely ignored by researchers who have put little credence on the value of this body's focus on the social and benevolent support they generated and clearer recognition is due. The monthly newsletters sent out to members maintained a lifeline to past companionships in addition to being a conduit for information. As one ex-WAAC cook who had served in France and who was working in Montreal by 1920 puts it: 'How can I ever thank you for those magazines. I devoured every word of them over and over again.'[16] So delighted by all 'the news', she writes in to urge others to 'come over here. You can have £100 a year, working as a cook-general – that is the average – but I get more than that and I have all my indoor clothes found me.'

For the overseas Old Comrades the networking formed a tangible link which could always be called upon in times of need. The message was clear:

Should you happen to live miles away from civilisation overseas, let us know at Headquarters and we will send you a list of Old Comrades living in your part of the country. We may even be able to supply an ex-WAAC neighbour quite near.[17]

In the years that followed, overseas membership of the QMAAC Old Comrades' Association continued to grow. The UK branches' shared news of activities nurtured by the Corps' deliberately egalitarian ethos would keep alive and reinforce all the valued affinities these like-minded girls had uncovered during their army service days.

Ex-signallers had the advantage over many former WAAC members because, apart from being members of the Association, they could also keep in touch with old work colleagues by way of the Post Office's staff journals, which occasionally carried news and items of interest for those who had served in the war.

What is clear is that the efforts of the Old Comrades' Association had been actively constructive in allowing their Irish, Scottish and English women to keep firmly in touch with each other. Newsworthy items included regular news of 'visitors' from the far side of the Atlantic throughout the interwar decades and encouragement for emigration continued despite the signs of a serious slow-down ahead. Optimism was hard to crush and by 1930, the secretary of the Society for Oversea Settlement of British Women (SOSBW), by then ten years in existence, was still publishing pieces of advice for those who might still be looking for opportunities in Canada.[18] Apart from work as shorthand-typists – who had to be 'really proficient and who can do book-keeping' – there were sometimes unusual openings, for example, there was also a 'very considerable demand for social workers'.

British colonial life continued to be attractive

In the interwar years of the 1920s and 1930s, life in Britain's colonies had continued for those who already had a prewar connection, but there was not an immediate flood of migration by contrast to the popularity of movements to one of the British Dominions such as Australia and Canada. These were difficult economic times, not only in Ireland but also across England, Scotland and Wales. When the Great Depression began to cast deeper economic gloom across the northern hemisphere the effect had been widespread. Life abroad had always presented an attractive option for hundreds of young people but, by then, even families living abroad had been hit hard.

Until more research is conducted into the postwar lives of the Irish ex-WAACs, only shadowy impressions can be glimpsed to compare the lives of those who stayed at home to those who sought an alternative future. What is clear is that, at first, Irish patterns of migration soon returned to prewar levels and the traditional constant movement between homes in Ireland and employments in England continued as it had done for centuries. Apart from the unquestioned approval Irish families gave to the recruitment of women into religious life in one of the proliferating orders or congregations of nuns and sisters which reached its peak in 1970, a female workforce that had never received encouragement to work outside the home continued to float back and forth across the the Irish Sea. It was driven, as always, by the needs, enterprise and generations of close family links between the two islands.[19]

The Central Committee for Women's Training and Employment

In 1920, governmental bodies had attempted to ease hundreds of recently demobbed ex-service personnel into career paths and lifestyles that the war years had denied all these young people. Former members of the WAAC who qualified for assistance had been able to apply to the Central

Committee for Women's Training and Employment for the South of Ireland. Fionnuala Walsh has put a clear outline of the scheme and her work is once more useful to cite:

> This was a government scheme introduced in January 1920. It enabled training of women for new employment who had suffered financial hardship or loss of employment opportunity due to the war. Applicants for the scheme were required to be unskilled, unemployed on time of application, but normally in employment.[20]

She cites some case studies for both successful and unsuccessful applicants and provides examples of the committee's refusal for more expensive training courses such as a 'medical education at Trinity College, Dublin', while options for a career as a shorthand typist, in midwifery or as a gardener had received approval. The scheme came to an end in 1922.

For ex-WAACs living on both sides of the Irish Sea the final years of the 1920s and early 1930s had most certainly accelerated a decline in employment opportunities. Soon even opportunities abroad became clouded with pessimism and a number of societies dedicated to the overseas settlement of women began to slowly wind down their efforts. By 1931, it was being announced that the: 'pressure of unparalleled economic depression [had] compelled the virtual cessation of British State-aided migration and settlement', and it was thought doubtful that there was to be 'a revival on any appreciable scale in the near future'.[21]

The awarding of war medals

All women who served in France in whatever capacity were awarded the same military campaign medals that were given to their male companions: the British War Medal and the Victory Medal. Their names, army service number and Corps were individually engraved on the rim and it is sad to think that many have been left languishing unrecognized at the back of a drawer or stashed up in the attic. The succeeding generations who have come across those First World War medals often mistakenly thought them to have belonged to an unidentifiable male relative, not realizing that they had belonged to a grandmother or grand-aunt or other female relative.

To be entitled to those medals, a girl would have had to serve 'overseas' in one of the BEF bases, but the ruling had a sting in its tail which could sometimes cause later disappointment. Gladys Blain was enrolled as a forewoman clerk and had been kitted out in her uniform in her native Belfast by the end of April 1918.[22] By early May, she was posted to the army training camp in Randalstown, County Antrim, and served here for a year until transferred to Dublin in June 1919. By July she had been sent across the Channel to the army base in Calais where she remained until four days before Christmas, by which time most of the WAAC had left northern France. Several years later, when she enquired if she was entitled to receive the war medals that several of her former wartime companions had applied for, she received a short, standard note of reply from a lieutenant working in War Office. It conveyed the news that although she had worked for the army in France for six months, she was 'not eligible' because she had not served before Armistice Day, 11 November 1918. The large number of Irishwomen who were recruited during 1918 included many who were sent 'overseas' for up to a year following 11 November. They, too, never received medals despite being fully enrolled and under army discipline until their dispersal in 1919 and 1920.

Chapter 11

Life 'Down Under' or Adventures at Home?

'Ours is the earth, and health and wealth – and youth – the gifts of the gods'.

J. Rich[1]

The 1920s ushered in radical life changes for the many Irish-born former members of the WAAC who migrated to Australia. Their experiences often ran in parallel with their English army colleagues who made the same decision at that time. For example, the outcome of a move 'Down Under' for Martha Hanna, a young woman from a farming family in Poyntzpass, five miles north of Newry in County Armagh, was to take a similar course to that of English-born Winifred Dennett, from the town of Sandown on the Isle of Wight, who had likewise moved to Australia when dispersed from the WAAC/QMAAC.[2]

Both girls had brothers who saw action in the war and one can understand their keenness to offer any help they could to ensure a swift ending to the slaughter. When she enrolled Martha Hanna's younger brother, Willie, had already been wounded by shrapnel at the battle of the Somme in 1916.[3] Her Hampshire-born English colleague, GPO telephonist Winifred, had suffered the greater loss of one of her brothers, killed in the battle of Loos in 1915.[4] When she had volunteered for France, another of her brothers, a former professional photographer, was in France working with a field ambulance as a non-combatant volunteer with the Royal Army Medical Corps. He, too, was to lose his life barely a month before the end of the war.

At the time of their enrolment in the WAAC in the summer of 1917, both girls were already 'established' Post Office staff members. Martha had been taken on as a 'learner' in 1908 and, eighteen months later, she had become a fully qualified GPO telegraphist with a permanent position within the organization. Sent by her employers at the Post Office to Dublin, she had remained working there, although keeping close links to her home in Ulster. In 1917, at the age of 26 she was still working in the city and staying at a house in the pleasant southern city suburb of Ranelagh with her younger Post Office colleague, another farmer's daughter, Matilda Jackson from Clones in County Monaghan.

A girl from Armagh: Martha Hanna (1891–1969)

Martha Hanna arrived in France on 22 July 1917 in a draft which included her workmate Matilda Jackson. There were two other young Irishwomen in this batch, one from Limerick, the other from Cork. All of them subsequently served in a Signal unit at the BEF base in the channel port of Le Havre until September or October 1919.

Following their demobilization, by November she and Matilda Jackson were back in Ireland. They had found accommodation at the same address in Kingstown (later Dun Laoghaire) not far from the port. Hanna was soon sending an appeal to the Corps HQ in London for a final payment of the £8 to £9 due that was still delayed. She was worried that she had 'no money for winter clothing'.[5] The transition back home must have been difficult. It had coincided with her being struck down by a bad attack of that era's virulent flu, and it would seem that, when fully recovered, she had no desire to return to Post Office work but instead, decided to train as a nurse in London. On her return to Ireland a few years later, she made the decision to stay on in Dublin as a maternity nurse working for a city mission that cared for the poor.

Romance may have only seriously blossomed for her when a boy she had been at school with came back into her life in the mid-1920s with the suggestion that they might start a completely new life together in Australia. George Fisher, the son of a neighbouring farming family not far from Newry, was one of the thousands of Irishmen who had seen action with the British army in the war. By 1925 he was considering an ongoing Australian government scheme for the settlement of ex-soldiers in Victoria, and was making plans to accept the offer of a block of land on affordable terms. The scheme was accompanied by advances of money to allow the new owners to make the necessary improvements to allow fruit trees to be planted on what was virtually virgin land. The areas chosen were usually in a very poor condition –but farming life was not unknown to him and while he would have understood that virgin land in Australia might prove to be more demanding than the green, well-tended fields of Ulster, he was ready to have a go. This was pioneering at its best.

With her newly acquired nursing expertise and wartime experiences Martha was ready to take on a new set of challenges. Decisions were made and George left for south-east Australia ahead of his fiancée in 1926. Martha followed shortly afterwards and the couple was married in Melbourne the following year.

Showing great determination, they eventually made good because George had soon recognized the scale of the challenge that lay ahead. His assigned plot of land lay on the outskirts of Mildura in Victoria, 336 miles north-west of Melbourne. It was an area that had gained a reputation as a major centre for the production of citrus and grapes, but there had been problems with the supply of water, and farmers were placing enormous reliance on irrigation from the Murray River. The methods being used to do this were not altogether satisfactory because as the flow from the river basin grew in response to demand, the shallow deposits of salts being left behind on the surface of the land by these waters had also been increased, thereby reducing soil fertility. George was soon seriously reassessing the situation that faced him.

The plot was not promising. He had built a house for himself and Martha but had sensibly added a small general store that sold everything including groceries. Lack of water was a serious drawback. Cultivation would be difficult and a wise decision was soon made to forego the land. The shop was dismantled; they moved it and its contents into the fast-expanding town nearby, and he and Martha set up home in the upper storey of the building. Plans were made to start a family but it was not until September 1930 that their only child, Betty, was born.

Business did well. They worked hard and nine years later Martha and George could afford to take a trip home to Ireland with their 9-year-old daughter on a visit to meet her two grandmothers. Little did they suspect that an unforeseen setback lay ahead. When the Second World War broke out in September of that year they found themselves trapped in Belfast with no hope of returning to Mildura until the war was over. However, George once more displayed a streak of enterprise. He took a job as an inspector of weights and measures in the Belfast area. When German bombing of the city became too dangerous, Martha and Betty went to live with an elderly aunt in County Armagh, who needed some care and, in a year or two when Betty was old enough to start her secondary education, she was sent off to school in Dublin, where Martha still had old friends.

They remained in Ireland until after the war had ended, and it was not until 1946 that they were finally able to return home to Australia. Within a few years of their return, George bought another store and they moved to Porepunkah, a tobacco-growing area about a hundred miles from Melbourne. Here, their daughter grew up and – following in the footsteps of her mother – went on to train as a nurse and midwife before she married. Not long after that, Martha and George retired to Melbourne.

In 1969, the couple made another visit to Ireland and while they were here, Martha – who was 78 by then – suffered a fatal stroke and was laid to rest beside her parents, near her birthplace in Poyntzpass, County Armagh.

A girl from Hampshire: Winifred Dennett (1890–1987)

Unlike Martha, the anticipation of a life ahead on the other side of the world for English girl Winifred Dennett had looked to be a far more certain prospect in 1919. Attached to the 3rd Echelon of Army HQ in Rouen for over two years as one of those telecommunication 'Forewomen' who had been denied a WAAC commission, she was already engaged to be married to an Australian ex-serviceman she had met in 1915. When the Armistice was announced, Winifred had sought demobilization just as soon as possible.

Her fiancé, Hedley William (Bill) Moore, of Eaglehawk, Victoria, had seen action in the Gallipoli Campaign (1915–1916) and, although not directly wounded, his health had suffered badly. By September 1916 he had been sent home from Europe and delisted from any further service. The couple were not to meet again for almost another three years.

Before he left Europe, Bill Moore and Winifred made careful plans for their future. As an ex-serviceman he had applied to become a registered fruit grower under a similar Australian government settlement scheme that Martha Hanna's husband, George, was to later take up. Prior to the war, Bill had worked as a baker and pastry cook. Winifred's only employment experience was as a Post Office telephonist in a well-populated urban area. It was going to be a challenge – but having made the choice, she was determined to join him out there just as soon as the war was over.

It was not easy for WAAC signallers to swiftly extract themselves from their overseas service when the conflict had ended. Their contribution to the smooth running of army communication systems had been essential but the pressure continued. Millions of men and mountains of military hardware, together with all the accompanying administrative work, had to be efficiently returned to the UK in a controlled manner. It was quite fortunate, therefore, that because of her imminent marriage and confirmed travel plans, the request Winifred put in for an early demobilization was to receive an extremely fast response compared to the delays suffered by others who were anxious to get away. She was sent back to London on 30 April 1919 and her formal letter of discharge was received in the third week of May. By 6 July she was able to set sail for Victoria.

When her boat docked at the port of Melbourne she was met on the quayside by her fiancé with a horse and buggy and they set off on a slow 230-mile-long journey to where he was living in the district of Piangil, in the state of Victoria. The closest town, Nyah, lay eight miles away. Within a few months' time – by then 1920 – the pioneering pair was married at the Anglican Cathedral in Bendigo, the nearest city. Life was going to be very different, often fraught with difficulties, but subsequently successful.

For the greater part of the past three years Winifred had coped with the challenge of working long hours in France, the inherent danger of enemy bombing attacks and the rigidity of military rule which brought little or no privacy. It was a life tightly filled by constant movement, noise and stressed-out people. One of the first things she would have had to come to terms with was the empty vastness and silence of this new land, which, despite the upheaval of her most recent wartime experiences, was to present a huge contrast to her earlier upbringing as a daughter of a self-employed carpenter in Sandown and one of five siblings, two girls and three boys. Her hometown in the Isle of Wight had been always filled with the throngs of fashionable visitors, bustling shops and ferry boats coming and going. Life on the far side of the world within the isolation of a tiny but vibrant pioneering community would require a significant adjustment.

For Bill, too, the Australian government's returned soldiers' settlement scheme had brought enormous challenges for someone unused to a farming life. While waiting for Winifred to join him, his first task had been to clear his allocated block of virgin land to make it ready for the planting of fruit trees. The work to prepare the ground for cultivation required cutting or ripping out bushes and shrub-land growth, usually by horses or oxen working in pairs, dragging a heavy chain between and behind them. The rough bush and tree growth then had to be burned prior to making the soil ready for planting. There was also basic housing accommodation to be built.

As the weeks and months passed by, it was becoming disappointingly clear that all their work – and that of others in this area – was not going to yield a viable enterprise. All the planning and physical hard work that had followed was not going to be enough. Within a year or two it became obvious that many of the 'blocks' in the preselected locations were turning out to be unsuitable for commercial fruit-growing. Some were turning out to be too small, as was the case with the first settlers who planned to develop Nyah.[6] Elsewhere, as outlined in Martha's and George's experiences, there were problems with water supplies. For many of those ex-servicemen who went out with high hopes, there were often similar truly heartbreaking setbacks. Hard lessons had been learned.

Nonetheless, Bill and Winifred were determined not to be beaten. Winifred soon encouraged Bill to turn to his prewar trade. They moved to a small nearby settlement, Nyah West, opened a bakery and began to supply and deliver bread locally. Business thrived. It had been a wise move. Before long, Bill had a fully operational bakery up and running and, by the early 1930s, by then with a family of four children, the couple had rented out the bakery business and moved to the town of Eaglehawk, about 130 miles away, where they were able to extend their activities which included setting up a poultry farm to supply eggs and chickens. Life was good.

Shortly after the onset of the Second World War they moved again – this time to the prosperous town of Hamilton, where Bill opened another bakery and supplied the army with fresh bread for the duration. When the war was over they returned once more to Eaglehawk, where they made further wise investments in property. Blessed with children and grandchildren, their lives centred around hard work and family life, but it was not without enjoyable community activities such as the local bowling club. In due course, in much the same way that Martha's daughter may have inherited something of her mother's instinctively caring nature in her choice of career, Winifred's daughter, Peg, may have also been influenced by the contribution made by both of her parents during the First World War. When the Second World War broke out in 1939 she enlisted in the Australian Women's Army Service and served in Hamilton, Queensland.

Unlike Martha, however, Winifred's close family ties to her home on the Isle of Wight had been broken by that time. Winifred's husband, Bill, passed away in 1973 but Winifred was to live on for many more years. When she died in 1987, she had reached 97 years of age.

Life for two girls who stayed at home

The postwar experiences of two other WAACs may be usefully compared and contrasted. While parallel in many ways, they both reveal an unexpected twist in the latter years of their lives.

On the one hand, there was Irish-born Jane Matilda Nevin who, having spent most of her life back in Ireland married to a farmer and raising a family of four, was to spend many later years of her life, not in Ireland – but as a widow living near a daughter in England.[7] On the other hand, there was a former WAAC colleague from the same Signal unit in Rouen, an English girl called Mary (Mollie) Crook, whose postwar years had been also spent as a homemaker in both the north of England and in Ireland, and who was to live out her last three decades in Dublin with husband, children and, eventually, many grandchildren. Yet, not unlike the two girls who went to Australia, the lives of these two 'stay-at-homes' can demonstrate the same traits of character to be found in most of those former GPO girls, which encouraged flexibility and willingness to tackle whatever new experiences were to come their way.

Matilda (Tillie) Nevin (1896–1982)

Tillie had been the sixth of eight children of a farmer in Ballymoney, County Antrim, who died at the relatively young age of 41, leaving Tillie's widowed mother to keep their farm going for the family until most of them they reached adulthood. However, having kept the place going successfully over the years, her decision to sell up the farm brought about an unforeseen setback to their finances. Unfortunately, she had invested the balance of her capital in railway shares and when the railway company later failed, money was scarce. One of Tillie's older brothers had already left for Canada by that time and when it was her turn to leave school it was important that she find herself a solid career with good prospects. She was a bright girl and her teacher advised her to obtain a position in the local post office where she received training in the operation of telegraph equipment using Morse code. Later transferred to the larger Carlow Exchange, she made a good friend of a Westmeath girl from Athlone, Marjorie Simmons, and when the call went out in 1918 for additional recruits to go to France, the two girls signed up to the QMAAC and served together at the large BEF base in Rouen until October 1919.

On returning home, the Post Office sent her back to Ballymoney, where she resumed life as before. Clearly talented in many other fields of activity and not afraid to tackle something new – she had been a member of a rowing club in prewar Carlow – she took up woodwork and upholstery in her spare time, creating small pieces of furniture – box stools and a sewing table which to this day are still recalled by her daughter.

She married a local farmer in March 1925 and they farmed in County Down for a three or four years before moving on to another outside Coleraine which had an Ice Age deposit of good building sand which they sold to local construction firms. The income helped maintain the farm during the depression of the 1930s and the couple was able to employ many local workers. They had twelve hand-milked cows and kept poultry. In addition to taking care of the farm and business accounts, Tillie – the ever-enterprising farmer's wife – made and sold her own butter, raised hens and sold poultry and eggs. Time was given to growing flowers and vegetables in her garden but she also baked twice a week, made jams and pickles, and made sure all their farmworkers were well fed, especially at harvest time.

Tillie would have remembered her army days in France in 1918, by which time the unsatisfactory course of the war had brought about a considerable deterioration in their army rations. Back then, the content and quality of the meals served up to the WAAC had grown increasingly scanty and grim. They were toiling night and day and putting in long and stressful hours of shift work. Health and nerves had suffered badly. The memory of those hard days must have remained sharp in her thoughts as she served up hearty stews, home-baked puddings and bread warm from the oven to the farmworkers she carefully looked after.

From the 1930s onwards, Tillie and her husband provided a home for her widowed mother in addition to raising their four children. Days were full of activity and – while the family farm income was enough to employ a maid to help with all the work – her creativity throughout this time included a great deal of sewing, darning and mending of clothes, not to mention home dressmaking for her two girls and herself, which was a quite normal routine for households at a time when shop 'ready-made' clothing was both scarce and expensive. A life of such unremitting activity to keep everything moving smoothly was in no way extraordinary in those interwar decades, and it can be shown that hundreds of thousands of households in England, Scotland and Wales were run in exactly the same manner, whether they were farming homes or not.

By 1944, displaying the same determined focus to make improvements to their lives, the household was once more on the move. The farm was sold and they moved to another farm in Ballysally on the other side of the River Bann between Colerain and Portstewart. Here, the couple continued to farm and kept poultry but only kept one 'house cow' for their own use. Life was convivial, with plenty of visits from friends and relatives, bridge parties and chat. By then they were growing barley, oats and seed potatoes although the main income came from fattening cattle brought up from the south-west of Ireland.

Having benefitted from the example of their parents and a mixture of third-level academic education, Tillie's four children, two boys and two girls, born between 1926 and 1941 would all go on to carve out fulfilling and interesting careers for themselves. It entailed three of them moving to England – but the family's close ties to country living and farming were not entirely lost. By the early 1950s her eldest son was running a fruit farm in Kent, and Tillie's second daughter, working as an analytical chemist in London, would later marry a Hertfordshire farmer. Meanwhile, the eldest daughter had married an English husband. The couple also lived in Hertfordshire where she worked as an infant schoolteacher. By 1966, the academic qualifications of Tillie's youngest son were to lead him much further afield when he left Ireland for Boston, Massachusetts, to engage in physics research. In due course, a career in stress management in New York would follow.

In their later years, Tillie and her husband decided to take it easy and retired to a bungalow in Portstewart, from where, in 1972, on the death of her husband, Tillie moved once more, displaying the ability to readily adapt to changed circumstances – a trait that can be found in the lives of so many who had joined the WAAC as young women. In order to be near one of her daughters, Tillie spent the final decades of her life – not at home in Ireland – but across the water in England, where she died in 1986, at the age of ninety.

Mary (Mollie) Crook[8]

In 1924, the press correspondent of Manchester's branch of the *OCA Gazette* ended her September's newsletter report with what she considered a novel and newsworthy item: 'On Sunday 12th August we had a WAAC visit at the hut, Adlington. Miss Mollie Crook (Signals, Rouen) who came over from Preston on her motor-cycle.'[9]

The 'hut' referred to was a weekend retreat for former 'comrades' in the countryside near the West Pennine Moors – a long-abandoned farm animal shelter that had begun life as an old railway carriage but by 1923 had been bought or rented for refurbishing by a few enterprising local ex-WAACs. (There was a similar OCA retreat being well used in Scotland at Loch Lomond).

After the war, Mollie Crook, a convent-educated, fluent French speaker whose elderly French relatives lived not far from where she lived in Lancashire, had gone back to her career in the Post Office in exactly the same way that Tillie had recommended her job on her return home to Ulster. The employment prospects for these girls were good; money had been saved and their gratuities for marriage and pension rights were all safe. They were fortunate.

Mollie Crook's arrival home in 1919 had presented her with very little to celebrate. She had to face up the prospect of a household fallen into utter disarray. The past four and a half years of war had brought about a serious decline of her father's once-thriving business which was run from his own shop premises in the centre of town. For decades, he had specialized in made-to-order hand-crafted saddles, harness and tack for local estate owners. Before the war, regular clients had prided themselves on stables full of well-bred steeds for the display of fine horsemanship on local hunting fields – but the battlefields of France had soon emptied those stables. The horses were gone and many of those family households' grieved-for sons and heirs would also never return from the war. By 1916, Mollie's two elder brothers, upon whom the success of the family saddling business was now reliant, had been called up for army service, too. They survived the conflict, but prospects were bleak. Both young men were soon married. One found work elsewhere but by 1919 the family's once-prosperous business had completely collapsed. Mollie's mother was bed-ridden from a heart attack, one of her elder sisters was seriously ailing from terminal tuberculosis, and her disheartened father was on the brink of bankruptcy. Surrounded by this very changed scene, Mollie and one other sister, a teacher, were now the household's sole breadwinners for the next three years. The family's prewar economic security never recovered and, by 1923, Mollie had lost her mother, her ailing sister and her home.

There was, nonetheless, a solid Post Office career, and the support of the old friends and colleagues from her army days who still kept in touch. A short-lived romance with an Australian soldier while serving in France had come to nothing – as had an offer to pursue a new career in musical comedy as a result of that Rouen unit's Christmas show, but Mollie's solidly secure position at work was providing a modicum of financial security. Her work in a Signal unit had given her an enduring interest in technology, and ownership of early crystal sets and headphones for wireless experiments at home became one of her hobbies. Moreover, having witnessed the use of women despatch riders behind the lines in France, she inveigled a brother-in-law to teach her the art of motorcycling. It held the offer of hitherto unknown vistas. Those first years of utter freedom of the roads were not to last for long, however.

One of the young servicemen she had met in Rouen had recently come back into her life. Marriage lay ahead in 1925 – and her husband's postwar career as a manager with an up-and-coming retail chain store brought a series of swift promotions. It was his firm's company policy to move their male staff to a new work location every three years or so. Wives, homes (houses were always rented) and families were expected to move too, and it was the entire responsibility of the men's spouses to organize that aspect of their lives.

Essentially living a nomadic lifestyle, the children soon became accustomed to being moved from school to school, wives became adept at using furniture removal services and the whole family had, in addition, to learn the skill of quickly familiarizing themselves with new towns and new neighbours. The ability to accept these challenges was paramount. Within a decade, Mollie's husband had been sent across the Irish Sea for a post in Dublin which, following several more short breaks elsewhere, brought the couple and their two children back to Ireland to settle for good. No further moves had to be endured.

Despite being always 'on the go', although perhaps in a more dramatic way than Tillie's shifting from farm to farm, Mollie's day-to-day lifestyle settled into a pattern similar to many of Tillie's domestic responsibilities. She had nonetheless continued to develop an interest in new technologies such as photography and set up her own darkroom to develop and print her own work. She then turned to amateur filming, first in black and white and very soon in colour. Frequent house moves increased her skills in home-decorating and adaptation of furnishings. Sewing and darning, cooking, baking and jam-making ran a parallel course with that of many other homemakers of that era. Like Tillie, she grew her own vegetables and flowers to which was sometimes added the keeping of a few hens for their eggs, although it was not on a commercial basis but only for home use. Always keen to try out some new technique or creative skill, she became adept in preserving fruit, and took up tatting (a complicated form of crochet) when in her mid-seventies.

Mollie's old WAAC comrades from Ireland and England continued to keep in touch over the decades in much the same way that her contacts with retired Post Office pals had held up well. It was not in any way an extraordinary home life for its time – although, like Tillie's busy days as a farmer's wife, it was very typical of many lifestyles that have received little attention in the past. She died quietly at home one afternoon in 1977, aged 83.

An overview of the compare and contrast scenarios

Mollie's and Tillie's lives display many of the core values common to Ireland and England. As young married women, they both had to adapt to the changing priorities and economic circumstances of their times. When set beside the experiences of the two ex-WAACs who travelled into the wilds of Australia to carve out far more uncertain futures for themselves and their husbands, it could be posited that all four postwar lives were typical of the times they lived in and not in any way extraordinarily dissimilar. All four were ready to tackle whatever lay ahead; they showed no fear of facing the unknown and never balked at a challenge. Had their confidence been boosted by their service days as WAACs? Or was it that they shared traits that epitomized what the women of the Roaring Twenties strove to achieve? One might hazard the opinion that they were indeed typical of many others of their time.

There was the ability to work hard, certainly. There was also courage and innovative thinking which were tempered by a great deal of patience and understanding because the memories of those war days and the knowledge of how things were in those very different times were to stay with them until to the end of their lives.

Chapter 12

Armistice Days in Dublin

'I never shared the happy belief that a "war to end war" had been won.'

Gwynne-Vaughan[1]

On 11 November 1924, four young Irishwomen carrying a wreath headed into the city centre of Dublin to attend a Great War Armistice Day ceremony.[2] One was wearing her WAAC uniform.[3] All were members of the QMAAC Old Comrades' Association. They had planned to meet outside Trinity College with their wreath at 10 a.m. so as to be in good time for that morning's ceremony, which was to be the unveiling of a Celtic cross at College Green to commemorate the war's fallen soldiers of the 16th Irish Division. When later recalling the experience for the *OCA Gazette*, they had been surprised to find that morning's ceremony had generated a dense and unexpected crowd – which is rumoured to have been 'between 50,000 and 100,000'. The crush of people had been so great that one of the girls afterwards complained that all she saw of the ceremony was 'the back of a policeman', while another 'got lost in the crowd' and then spent the rest of her time 'rescuing two children from being trampled on by bringing them to a St. John Ambulance Station'. Fortunately, their uniformed companion fared better: 'I managed to struggle on to get near to the Cross in order to take my place when called upon to place our wreath. We were seventh on the list.'

The event had been a deeply emotional occasion.

It was a day for us to remember. No one who has lived in Ireland during the happenings of the past few years could have imagined that such a heartening and impressive sight could have been witnessed in the capital of the Irish Free State. The Silence was solemn and unbroken. General Hickie unveiled the Cross and afterwards the crowds, in jubilant mood, were cheering for everybody and everything. The Cross has now been removed and is to find a permanent resting-place in Guillemont.

The Guillemont cemetery is just a few miles from the site of the Somme battlefield.

Next morning *The Irish Times* reported that 'hundreds of ex-servicemen, wearing their ribbons and medals [gathered] round the Celtic cross in addition to those who took part in the official parades' and it was noted that: 'after the Reveille had been sounded the National Anthem was sung publicly and lustily in the streets of Dublin for the first time for many years'. The editor was, of course, being provocative. The controversy over whether the use of the anthem in public should be entirely discontinued had not as yet been officially settled.[4]

The undercurrent of competing ideologies

For the next morning's newspaper readers, such incidents evidenced the continued existence of competing ideologies in the new Free State.[5] Pro- and anti-Treaty opinions were still strong. Southern Unionists still grappled with change and it is more than likely that these Dublin girls were reluctant to get involved in rancorous arguments over the rights and wrongs of the symbol of the poppy. They would have viewed their sale on Armistice Day as a way to assist the work of a charity – created first in France and popularized by Great War American veterans – which aimed to raise money to aid wounded survivors of all nationalities – their 'Old Comrades', men and women alike.

One of the responsibilities of the Association's branches across the world was to undertake the annual laying of a wreath on Armistice Day. There is no record to show if the four Dublin friends attended the ceremony the following year, 1925. It is possible that they had heard rumours of threatened street violence, as there had been a spate of 'poppy-snatching' in the city and may have decided it wiser not to attend.

Moved to Phoenix Park

By 1926, the annual event had moved to the Phoenix Park to avoid similar scenes. The Dublin friends once more attended and reported a 'huge crowd' gathered around the Wellington Monument, where a temporary structure – described as a 'Cenotaph' – was erected for the occasion. It was announced that morning, that the wooden cross that had stood in Guillemont to honour the Irish war dead had finally been replaced by a permanent stone cross since that summer. The wooden one could now come back to Dublin to be cherished by those who had served in the Great War. Described as 'a simple cross of Celtic design, it was very weather beaten and worn, having withstood battle and storm all these years'. Hugely nostalgic, it would be displayed during the Dublin ceremonies for many more years after this.

For the 1926 ceremony, space had been allocated for six ex-WAAC members, one of whom laid a wreath at the foot of the cross on behalf of former wartime colleagues – no doubt especially remembering their Irish WAAC casualties. Their report for that morning recorded: 'When the Last Post was sounded, the silence was as absolute as that round the Cenotaph in Whitehall.'

The same year, 1926, was also a special year for the Dublin-based girls because an Irish branch of the Old Comrades' Association had been inaugurated. Membership was open to ex-WAACs from all thirty-two counties with the aim of renewing and strengthening the bonds of wartime friendships.

Specific examples of the discreet practical assistance provided by the Corps' benevolent funds are hard to find. There was no publicity. One earlier instance of an emergency has been noted, however. It took the form of an SOS from London in 1923 to enquire if any Old Comrades living in Cork could offer help to a former servicewoman in that area. Likely enough, some ex-WAACs from down that direction would have quietly responded.

Another rare description of a case handled by their almost two-year-old branch was reported in 1928. It told how aid was swiftly rallied for an ex-WAAC, married to an 'ex-Serviceman [with] ... a family that was very badly off owing to the husband losing his work through ill-health'. The report that was circulated described how: 'The girl is twenty-six and has four children—the eldest is five and tubercular, and the youngest, twins one year old'. Food, clothes, 'help with rent' and 'a new spinal jacket' for the eldest child were all supplied by willing OCA members without delay.[6] Similar quiet support continued when other cases of hardship or ill-health came to their notice. Their branch met at regular intervals and contact was maintained with any of their Old Comrades who turned up as visitors or passed on news of army friends abroad.

In 1935, their branch report on the Phoenix Park's Armistice ceremony comments: 'The attendance was good. Even in these days great crowds always gather to keep the two minutes' silence.' In November 1936, 'the rain had come down in torrents and the march past had to be abandoned' and, in 1937, the construction of a new memorial park at Islandbridge was being 'delayed by a builders' strike'. Nonetheless, that year saw an innovative way of marking the day for the mourners who attended. A section of ground in the Phoenix Park adjacent to where the old Celtic cross stood had been divided up into plots for each county in Ireland. Those attending the ceremony could purchase a small cross which could be placed in their chosen county. At the end of the week all the crosses were collected, taken to France and burned, and the ashes scattered over the graves of the Irish dead. The crowds 'who came to remember their dead were as dense as ever [and] the band played Schubert's Ave Maria as wreaths were laid'.[7]

Change was in the wind, however. In spring 1938, the Irish branch was renamed the Eire or Free State branch (later simplified to 'Southern Ireland') and a new Northern Ireland branch was founded. Far from causing a split, close cooperation saw memberships increased. Old pals regularly travelled up and down between Dublin and Belfast for special occasions. When a member from Coleraine Post Office, Dorothea Tanner, was promoted to the exchange in Holywood, County Down, her Dublin friends recalled that her war service years were spent with Signal units in the Le Havre area and at St. Omer.[8] (It is very likely that she was one of those girls who stayed on duty in St. Omer during that March 1918 front line crisis.)

By 1938, Armistice Day attendees are shown to have been in sombre mood. 'There seemed to be more wreaths this year; perhaps the shadow of war which so lately hung over us bestirred us to help those who had survived and suffered from the horrors of the last war'.[9] Twelve months later, neighbouring Britain was embroiled in the grim reality of the Second World War and it would be good to pause for a moment to reflect that by 1939, six active members of Ireland's Old Comrades had come forward in response to the call for help and had promptly enrolled in the newly formed ATS No. 8 Clerical Company, which was to be attached to the regular army in event of an emergency. Like many other former servicewomen they had not forgotten the experience and knowledge they had gained in their early youth as WAACs and were ready to pass it on to newcomers to army life.

That year, Remembrance Day still went ahead in the Phoenix Park. Members of the diplomatic corps attended. Regimental standards were flown. But 'ex-servicemen did not march' and 'there'd been a complete absence of show and parade'.[10]

Irish National War Memorial Gardens, Islandbridge

In 1940 the two-minute silent tribute and low-key ceremony were held for the first time in the new National Memorial Park at Islandbridge. Funded by both the state and public subscriptions, the monument in its new setting – designed by Sir Edward Lutyens – was described by the women as 'beautiful, although simple in design'. Thousands of men and women gathered. Music for the ceremony began with Chopin's 'Funeral March'. Bugles sounded the 'Last Post' and two minutes' silence were observed.[11]

The hostilities of the Second World War ceased in 1945. Three years later, in 1948, the women of the Southern Ireland branch of what had been formerly the Association of Old Comrades were once more stirred to report on events at Memorial Park in Dublin. By then, with its membership middle-aged or older, their Association was now merged with some new 'comrades' known as the Auxiliary Territorial Service (ATS), because Irishwomen had been also drawn into that later conflict.

In 1948, watchers at the Remembrance Day ceremonies had noted: 'In spite of the inclement weather, on 7 November, about eighteen ex-ATS marched with ex-servicemen to the Memorial Park, Islandbridge, Dublin.'[12]

The attendees' thoughts on seeing those uniformed women that morning can be imagined. Thirty years earlier, in the hope of ending the slaughter of so many young people in that terrible war, they had left the safety of jobs as civil servants, governesses, cooks, teachers, waitresses and post office workers. As young women they had learned how to 'form fours' to march in uniform at parades in the same way that was now being displayed by these ATS girls, but their efforts to help bring about an end to 'the war to end all wars' in 1918 had ended in futility. As a result, many former WAACs actively pursued the cause of peace and tolerance, as did many others, throughout the uncertainties of the 1930s. Pacifism was popular. People had seen for themselves the true horrors of war and sacrifice of lives cut short and, as the century approached its mid-point, it would have been their heartfelt hope that the once-more-restored harmony could now remain for evermore – and for all. It was an aspiration that has never been completely fulfilled.

Applying the wider conclusion
It was suggested in the introduction to this study that its overall aim would not present readers with a definitive set of conclusions but, instead, raise a number of hitherto neglected topics that would benefit from further investigation. As they stand, the contents of each chapter can therefore speak for themselves. However, there may be questions that arise and, while answers can be indicated, it is hoped that a curiosity to learn more will remain.

Adequate acknowledgment that young women from all parts of Ireland, drawn from every class, creed and ability, had volunteered to serve in 1917 just as eagerly as girls from England, Scotland and Wales, became fated to remain an almost entirely unexplored and unspoken topic for decades. They were not alone in being forgotten. The crucial role of the few hundred WAAC/QMAAC women proficient in GPO telecommunication technology who worked closely with the Royal Engineers in the final years of the conflict has been also largely ignored within the far broader historiography of all war service women and their subsequent postwar lives. With today's easily accessible digitized sources now within the reach of all researchers, local and individual family historians and scholars, the promise of many more stories to uncover is an exciting prospect. New paths into the past await to be explored and enjoyed.

Appendix I

Table 1: The categories of work undertaken by the WAAC / QMAAC by 1918.

Category	Employment was further divided into either 'Mobile' or 'Immobile' service terms	Choice of Home only / or Overseas
'A'	Ordinary General clerks (including telephone clerks)	Both
	Supervising Forewomen Clerks	Both
	Shorthand typists	Both
'B'	General domestic workers	Both
	Cooks, waitresses, laundresses, pantry-maids, housemaids vegetable women, by-product women	Both
	Forewomen waitresses for Officers' Mess and Officer's Cadet Mess	Both
	Forewomen Cooks and Hostel Forewomen	Both
'C'	Qualified Driver Mechanics	Overseas only
	Forewomen (Qualified Driver Mechanics)	Overseas only
'D'	Storehouse women, packers, issuers, messengers, checkers, leading hands, general unskilled labour, sausage makers, chaff cutters	Both
	Forewomen unskilled	Both
	Assistant Forewomen unskilled	Both
'E'	Telephonists	Overseas only
	Telegraphists	Overseas only
	Forewomen Telephonists	Overseas only
	Forewomen Telegraphists	Overseas only
	Sorters and Post-women	Both
'F'	Printers, warehousewomen, binders and folders, shoemakers, bakers, tailors, gardeners, grooms, women riders	Both
	Forewomen (printer, gardener, groom, shoemaker, baker and tailor)	Both

Category	Employment was further divided into either 'Mobile' or 'Immobile' service terms	Choice of Home only / or Overseas
'G'	Technical Employment (Mechanical Section), with 9 sub-categories including acetylene welders / electricians/ magneto repairers/engine fitters/ machinists/ turners /fabric workers /colourists / photographers	Both
	Forewomen for these sections	Both

Covert section to add:

The Hush–WAAC	Bi-lingual recruits secretly attached to Army Intelligence, they remained a hidden and unheralded sector, engaged in top-secret cryptographic analysis. Forerunners to the Second World War army women in Bletchley Park.	Overseas

* 'Mobile' indicated postings to an Army installation anywhere; 'Immobile' indicated members who remained living at home and who worked for the military in their local area.

Source: Army Council Instruction No 652 of 1918 Regulations for the QMAAC, 1918, pp.33–39.

Table 2: Sample of WAAC /QMAAC Irish-born / known categories of Work and Postings.

Sample Total	Administrators		'A' Clerks		'B' Domestics		'E' Signals
	Home Service	Overseas	Home Service	Overseas	Home Service	Overseas	Only Overseas
	10	5	66	36	237	33	24
411	15		102		270		24
100%	3.6%		24.8 %		65.8 %		5.8 %

Sources: National Archives, The QMAAC Old Comrades' Association,& the BT Digital Archives.

Table 3: Identified arrival dates / Irish Signallers serving on the Western Front, 1917–1919.

Service No.	Name / Home and or work address in 1917	Work	Where served	Date Arrived
977	HENRY, Jean Pringle, Belfast address	Telephonist	Boulogne	16/6/17
1021	WELCH, Kathleen, Belfast address	Telephonist	Boulogne	17/6/17
1621	CLEARY, Florence Rachel, Dublin address	Telegraphist	Havre	22/7/17
1630	HANNA, Martha Anne, Dublin address but home/ born in Co. Armagh	Telegraphist	Havre	22/7/17
1634	JACKSON, Matilda, Dublin address, but home/ born in Co. Monaghan	Telegraphist	Havre	22/7/17
1640	MURPHY, Dora Mary Rose, Co. Cork address	Telegraphist	Harfleur	22/7/17
1643	NELSON, Selina Rose, Co. Limerick address	Telegraphist	Havre	22/7/17
1610	YOUNG, Harriet Jane, Co. Wicklow address but born in Co. Carlow	Telegraphist	Havre and Rouen	29/7/17
1612	AINSCOW, Minnie Elizabeth, Dublin address	Telephonist	Havre	29/7/17
1629	HAMMOND, Elinor Isobel, Dublin address	Asst. F/W Telegraphist	Havre	29/7/17
1559	LEACH, Deborah Beatrice, Dublin address	Asst. F/W Telegraphist	Rouen	30/7/17
1560	LEACH, Victoria Ethel, Dublin address, but born in Belfast (sister of Deborah Leach)	Asst. F/W Telegraphist	Rouen	30/7/17
1627	GOUGH, Julia, Co. Waterford address, but born in Belfast	Telegraphist	Rouen	30/7/17
1975	BLACK, Teresa Mary, Co. Donegal address	Telegraphist	Havre	8/8/17
2025	MURPHY, Kathleen Frances, born in Roscommon	Telegraphist	Rouen	12/8/17
2048	BAYNE, Agnes Rolleston, Co. Tyrone address	Telegraphist	Havre	18/8/17

Service No.	Name Home and or work address in 1917	Work	Where served	Date arrived
2054	MULLALLY, Florence M, Dublin address	Telegraphist	Havre	18/8/17
2058	TANNER, Dorothea, Co. Derry address	Telegraphist	Havre and St. Omer	18/8/17
2059	THISTLE, Anna Lydia, Co. Meath address	Telegraphist	Havre	18/8/17
45373	CARSON, Hanna, Elizabeth, Co. Armagh address but born in Co. Down	Telegraphist	Rouen and Wimeraux	26/7/18
45374	NEVIN, Jane Matilda, Co.Antrim address	Telegraphist	Rouen	26/7/18
45375	SIMMONS, Marjorie Kathleen, Co. Westmeath address but born in Co. Antrim	Telegraphist	Rouen and Wimeraux	26/7/18
48430	PAINE, Lily Victoria Anne, Dublin address	Telephonist	Calais	13/9/18
48431	LAIRD, Sara, Co. Derry address	Telegraphist	Boulogne	13/9/18

Source: National Archives, London. WO-398 QMAAC Army Service files.

Table 4: The mixed draft of signallers and general clerks despatched with PO
Telegraphist Supervisor Alice Clarke, on 17 August 1917.

Army Service No.	Name	Signals staff and General Clerks	Home and/or Workplace
2046	BARR, Mary Elizabeth	Telegraphist	Newbury, Berkshire
2047	BARRODALE, Ruth	Telegraphist	Stockport, Cheshire
2048	BAYNE, Agnes Rolleston	Telegraphist	Dungannon, Co. Tyrone
2049	BLACKEBY, Bessie Nora	Telegraphist	Hoddeston, Hampshire
2050	CLARKE, Alice Constance (F/w)	Telegraphist	Liverpool, Lancashire
2051	CLOUGH, Elizabeth, Marion	Telegraphist	Sowerby Bridge, Yorkshire
2052	CRAMPTON, Catherine Gladys	Telegraphist	Newark, Nottingham
2053	DOUBLE, Nellie Anna	Telegraphist	Walton-on-Naze, Essex
2054	MULLALLY, Florence M	Telegraphist	Dublin, Ireland
2055	SINCLAIR, Marion. (Act.Ast. F/w)	Telegraphist	Eccles, Lancashire
2056	SHEEN, Martres Kate	Telegraphist	Birmingham
2057	SMITH, Janet	Telegraphist	Bonnyrigg, Scotland
2058	TANNER, Dorothea	Telegraphist	Coleraine, Co. Derry
2059	THISTLE, Anna Lydia	Telegraphist	Kells, Co. Meath
2060	TURNER, Lizzie Buchanan	Telegraphist	Kirkaldy, Fife, Scotland
2061	WATT, Charlotte P	Telegraphist	Aberdeen, Scotland
2062	HORSINGTON, Helen (Ast. F/w)	Telephonist	Weston-super-Mare, Somerset
2063	HOWELL, Dorothy Mary	Telephonist	Bournemouth, Dorset

Army service no.	Name	Signals staff and general clerks	Home and/or workplace
2064	TAIT, Amy Caroline	Clerk	West Kirby, Cheshire
2065	THOMAS, Emmeline Victoria	Clerk	Bradford, Yorkshire
2066	WILLIAMS, Ruby Helen	Clerk	Chatham, Manchester
2067	SMITH, Lilian Maud	Clerk	Crosby, Liverpool
2068	PARDOE, Florence Wilfred	Clerk	Stoke-on-Trent, Staffordshire
2069	DAVIES, Edith May	Clerk	Liverpool, Lancashire
2070	MACLEOD, Hilda (Poss. F/w)	Unknown	Full army service records not found
2071	KNOWLES, Hilda Annie	Clerk	Broughton, Manchester
2072	WEIGHELL, Nora Emma	Clerk	Easingwold, Yorkshire
2073	WALSH, Emily	Clerk	Bradford, Yorkshire
2074	GAWNE, Eva Fayle	Clerk	Douglas, Isle of Man
TOTAL: 29 GIRLS Telephonists: 2 ; Telegraphists: 16; Clerks: 10; Unknown: 1 (no full service file)			

Source: *National Archives, London. WO-398 QMAAC Army Service Files.*

Table 5: The First Estimates: Base Areas and Equipment/Facilities changes. Extracted from Report of 27 February1917.

BASE & AREA	New Apparatus to be added to Wheatstone	Selected remarks from Report
BOULOGNE Military; Barracks; D.A.D.R.T. (Boulogne); D.A.D.R.T. (Bassin-Loubet); Supplies; Ordnance; Maritime; Commandant; Henriville; Pont-de-Briques; Supplies Outreau; D.A.D.R.T. Outreau; Meerut; Wimereux; A.A. Outreau; D.N.T.O.; Rue Martot	4 x Kleinschmidt and/or 4 x Kotyras / typewriters New Switchboards for telephonists	New building for increasing traffic and equipment to be moved
ETAPLES Dannes; Camiers; Etaples; French Civil; Hardelot Guns; Neuf-chatel; St-Cecile; Reinforcements Camp; Commandant; Le Touquet (Paris-Plage)	Extension imminent	Men could be retained to work the longer hours on Wheatstone The first 3 locations had Morse
GHQ and D.G.T	Kotyras to be installed	15 men telegraphists could be retained to assist the need for longer hours
ABBEVILLE Camps and Station		Premises to be extended
DIEPPE and Trépot		Planned Morse Office here not yet open
LE HAVRE Central + A.M.F.O; MT Depot; Quai d'Escale; Graville; Docks; Old Fort; Harfleur; François; Gare Maritime; and Sanvic;	Kotyras and Typewriters	Some Exchanges to be moved /and merged
ROUEN Central; 3rd Echelon and Camps	4 x Kotyras and 2 x Typewriters	Morse in use

Source: POST 31/99 File 3.

Table 6: Proposed PO women to staff all BEF Bases and new equipment or other changes in the Report of 27 February1917).

BASE & AREA	Telephonists	Telegraphists	Supervisors	New Apparatus to be added to Wheatstone	TOTAL	Selected remarks
BOULOGNE and thirteen other locations	65	38	2	Kleinschmidt x 4 and/or Kotyras x 4 / typewriters New Switchboards for telephonists Moves or new buildings	105	
ETAPLES and ten other locations	50	22	1		73	Men could be retained to work longer hours on Wheatstone
GHQ and one other location	21	66	1		88	15 men working longer hours OR Kotyras installed
ABBEVILLE and two other locations	20	85	1		106	Exchanges extended
DIEPPE and one other locations	9	15	1		25	Morse Office not yet open
LE HAVRE and ten other locations	52	55	1		108	Kotyras and Typewriters Exchanges moved /and merged

BASE & AREA	Telephonists	Telegraphists	Supervisors	New Apparatus to be added to Wheatstone	TOTAL	Selected remarks
ROUEN and two other locations Camps (Morse) and 3rd Echelon	21	55	1	Kotyras x 4 and Typewriters x 2	77	
TOTALS	238 Telephonists * included extra for relief etc	336 Telegraphists * included extra for relief etc	8		582	

Source: Compressed data extracted from the individual reports on each Base: POST 31/99/3/9.

NOTE: The full report contained a detailed written preliminary comments and chart for each individual base and the other exchanges / camps / subsidiary locations in their immediate areas. The option of providing a supervisor was usually shown in a bracket. The calculations supplied were later reduced to a total of 574 when the 8 supervisors were removed but later reinstated.

Appendix II

Alternative telegraph equipment for the BEF in France and post-war civilian exchanges in the UK.

	Make	Comment
1.	The Wheatstone	An early electrical telegraph system invented in the 1850s
2.	Wheatstone with Gel perforators and Creed receivers	The Wheatstone with Gel perforators and Creed receivers in French bases had the disadvantage that the equipment needed a mechanic on duty who was either 'an existing enlisted man or one sent from the UK'
3.	Duplex	A system of telegraphy for sending two messages over the same wire simultaneously
4.	Simplex	Simplex system sent just one message. The term 'vibrator' referred to the drive / control of a phonic wheel or motor
5.	The Baudot code	The Baudot code or International Teleprinter code was invented by Frenchman Emile Baudot in 1870. It was a binary code which used crosses and dots for teleprinter messages instead of Morse code and allowed an operator to encode $2^5 = 32$ characters efficiently. Each character was preceded and followed by a bit to announce its start and end
6.	Kleinschmidt/ Kotyra	In 1916, Edward Kleinschmidt filed a patent application for a typebar page printer. The American Kotyra keyboard perforators with three tapper keys for multiple tape perforation were already being used by the Post Office in London. Signals Director, Col. Ogilvie described them as: 'although cheaper to purchase' by comparison to Creed, they were 'otherwise not recommended'
7.	Teleprinters	A teleprinter (teletypewriter) is an electromechanical typewriter that can be used to send and receive typed messages through various communications channels, in both point-to-point and point-to-multipoint configurations

Sources: *POST 31/99 File 2 in addition to web references*
https://cs.stanford.edu/people/eroberts/courses/soco/projects/2008-09/colossus/baudot.html

Notes

Chapter 1: A British Army Corps of Women in Ireland?

1. Arthur Marwick, *Women at War 1914–1918* (London: 1977) p. 85.
2. Digitised National Archives, London ref: WO-398-238. Correspondence in Army Service No. 4569 Wynne C.E.
3. Demobilized' became a familiar term but was never used officially by the WAAC to describe a member's discharge. *Regulations for the Queen Mary's Army Auxiliary Corps 1918 (*London, Reprint 2009) p. 131.
4. *The Irish Times*, 21 September 1917.
5. *Statistics of the Military Effort of the British Empire during the Great War 1914–1918* (War Office, March, 1922, p. 204). See also Marwick, p. 169, and Jennifer Margaret Gould, *The Women's Corps: The establishment of women's military services in Britain.* (1988) p. 449; Dame Helen Gwynne-Vaughan, *Service with the Army* (1941) p. 70.
6. The detailed background and full history of the foundation of the WAAC (later QMAAC) has been well documented by many other historians – see bibliography.
7. Marwick, p. 83.
8. See bibliography for other works on women's war work which include mentions of the Women's Volunteer Reserve (WVR); the Home Service Corps; Women's Auxiliary Force; Women's Signallers Territorial Corps, and so on.
9. Lucy Noakes, *Women in the British Army: War and the gentle sex, 1907–1948* (2006) p. 62.
10. Eileen Reilly, 'Women and Voluntary War Work' in Adrian Gregory and Senia Paseta (Eds.) *Ireland and the Great War (*2002) cites these two bodies, p. 63 and p. 49.
11. Brigadier Shelford Bidwell, *The Women's Royal Army Corps (*London: 1977) p. 14.
12. War Studies *Lions led by Donkeys*, research project University of Birmingham, 'D'-'H' 6/16.
13. The BT Digital Archives: *POST 99/31/1/2* (www.bt.com/btdigitalarchives).
14. Gwynn-Vaughan, p. 42.
15. Army Council Instruction No. 537 for 1917; No.1069 for 1917; No.1111 of 1917; No.1412 of 117; 1874 of 1917; and No. 652 of 1918.
16. *Regulations for the Queen Mary's Army Auxiliary Corps 1918.* (London, Reprint 2009).
17. Fionnuala Walsh, 'The Impact of the Great War on Women in Ireland 1914–1919', PhD *thesis* (2016) raises this issue briefly, citing complaints over pay in the *Irish Citizen* in May 1917 and in the *Woman Worker* over 'harsh punishments' in 1918, p. 215.
18. Marwick, p. 86.
19. Lynda Dennant, 'Women at the Front during the First World War: the politics of class, gender and empire', PhD thesis (1998) p. 195, fn 107.

20. Charles Messenger, *Call to Arms. The British Army 1914–18.* (2005) p. 263.
21. Izzard, p. 179.
22. Roy Terry, *Women in Khaki* (1988) p. 45; and Kate Adie, *Fighting on the Home Front* (2014) p. 275.
23. Army Service Nos 711 Fitzpatrick, K; 794 Lowe.
24. The locations of these commands are referred to in various Army Service files; Edinburgh is cited in correspondence for Belfast-born Violet Murray, Army Service No. 42245, in 1918; York is in the Army Service file for Assistant Administrator Rawlinson in 1919.
25. Marjorie Hay, *On Wacctive Service* (1919) pp. 29–30.

Chapter 2: Setting Up Under the Irish Command

1. I. Grindlay, *Ripples from the Ranks* (London, 1918) p. 38.
2. Fionnuala Walsh's work cites BLPES, Markham papers, 4/5: The calculations are based on the number of application forms up to and including 19 July 1917, p. 215. She later alludes to statistics for April 1918, citing WM WWS Army 3.35.
3. St. Clair Frances Swanzy's Army record as Controller of Recruitment, WO/398/213.
4. *Alexandra College Magazine,* June issue, 1918, pp. 17–23.
5. Laura Kelly, *Irishwomen in Medicine 1880s–1920s* (2012) p. 203.
6. *Alexandra College Magazine*, December, 1917, p. 40; *The Irish Times*, 5 February 2018, p. 5.
7. Army Service No. 794 Lowe, F.E.
8. Army Service No. 977 Henry, J.P. and Army Service No. 1021 Welch, K.
9. UK WW1 Service Medal and Award Rolls 1914–1920.
10. *The Telephone and Telegraph Journal,* 1916–17, July 1917, p. 140.
11. Martin Easdown in the Folkestone and District Local History Society (2004) www.folkestonehistory.org.
12. Gertrude Eaton, edited by Marion Waddell, *With the Signallers in France* (2010) p. 6 and Army Service No. 42269 Eaton, G.
13. Army Service No. 1882 Allen, A.
14. Army Service Nos 42096, Moroney, H; 42098 Prendiville, N.
15. Army Service No. 38763 Guerin, G.
16. Army Service No. 1530 Corcoran, A.J.
17. Army Service No. 1160 Fowler, E., received promotion to AA.
18. *The Alexandra College Magazine*, December 1917, p. 40.
19. Army Service No. 38614, Blair, née Mullins.
20. *Alexandra College Magazine*, June 1918, p. 22.
21. Army Service No. 45699, Wynne, C.E.
22. *Regulations for QMAAC, 1918*, p. 40.
23. *The Lioness*, 1977 No. 2, p. 30, carried more details provided by a former Signaller.
24. These fur collars receive a mention in notes from one of the first Signallers to go to France. *The Telegraph and Telephone Journal*, Vol. 5, 1918–19, p. 16.
25. *The QMAAC Old Comrades' Association Gazette (OCA Gazette)* Vol. XV, No. 34, June 1935, p. 3, and Vol. XV, No. 35, October 1935, p. 3, each have a mention of the postwar work of two Dublin ladies as being a Miss Jean Montgomery and a Miss Kelly. They may have held rank as either Forewomen or as Assistant Administrators.
26. James Durney, *In a Time of War. Kildare 1914–1918* (2014) p. 21.

27. *The OCA Gazette,* Vol. VII., No. 9. March, 1926, p. 6.
28. Army Service No. 39420 O'Rorke, M.
29. Traced Army Service Nos 36723, 36724, 36725, 39518 to 39529 and 51859 and one other name but unknown service number.
30. Files for Army Service Nos. 39522 Kennedy, K and 39520 Whyte, K.
31. Fionnuala Walsh, pp. 219–220.
32. John Ferris, 'The British Army and Signals Intelligence in the Field During the First World War' in *Journal of Intelligence and National Security*, Vol. 3, issue 4 1988. Online source.

Chapter 3: Serving 'Overseas'
 1. Adie, p. 275.
 2. WO-95-85-5_04 (QMAAC War Diary, Etaples).
 3. Hay, p. 10.
 4. Hay, p. 34 and pp. 46–7.
 5. *Regulations for QMAAC, 1918*, p. 20.
 6. Army Service No. 1560, Assist. Forewoman Leach, wrote on behalf of her serving sister, 1559.
 7. http://inspirationalwomenofww1.blogspot.com, cites AA May Westwell and WRNS G/4985 Carr. See also WO/398/230 Army Service for Assist. Administrator, Westwell.
 8. Izzard, p. 179 and Terry, pp. 78–9.
 9. Army Service No. 457. One of her sisters subsequently married an army man in Newbridge.
10. *OCA Gazette,* June 1933, Vol. XV., No.11, p. 3.
11. B.E.F. QMAAC War Diary for Rouen: WO 95-85-7_17. See also Agnes Anderson, *"Johnnie" QMAAC*, 1920 p. 28, on the protocol of sealed instructions being opened on arrival.
12. *Telegraph and Telephone Journal*, Vol. 3, 1916–17, p. 138.
13. WO 95-85-7_005.
14. WO 95-85-7_011.
15. WO 95-85-7_013, WO 95-85-7_016 and WO 95-85-7_017. Members of the final contingent have been confirmed as being comprised solely of PO girls by army service files in WO-398.
16. Note that the full archived records of most, but not all, the ex GPO Supervisors who served as Forewomen were later lost in a London bombing raid in the Second World War.
17. Dennant, p. 171.
18. Izzard, pp. 169–70.
19. Dennant, p. 174.
20. Izzard, p. 171 and Messenger, p. 262.
21. Noakes, p. 80.
22. *Daily Mail*, 1918, cited in *OCA Gazette,* November 1925, Vol. XV., No. 39, pp. 3–4.
23. Anderson, pp. 70–1 refers to a diary entry for 17 February 1918.
24. Contributor used her married name in the *OCA Gazette,* October 1937, Vol. XVI., No. 10, p. 2.

25. Administrator Mary Holmes Laird's own account of her service can be found in the September, October and November 1937 issues of the *OCA Gazette*.
26. *Telegraph and Telephone Journal* Vol. 3 July 1917, p. 140, Nora Mitchell, Army Service No. 400, was among the first draft of telegraphists sent from London.
27. Army Service No. 1593, Steele, W.M.
28. *OCA Gazette*, May 1924, Vol. IV., No. 11, p. 4.
29. Army Service No. 1590, Silver, E.V.
30. Hay, pp. 44–5.
31. Hay, p. 171.
32. Army Service No. 2036 Crook, M. Reminiscences conveyed to the author.
33. Hay, pp. 170–4. Her account of the catering and food continues up to p. 176.
34. *OCA Gazette*, March 1926, Vol. VII., No. 9, p. 6
35. Eaton, p. 5.

Chapter 4: The Diversity of Work 'Overseas'

1. *OCA Gazette* August, 1927. Vol. VIII., No. 2. Editor's note: A poem by John Oxenham, published in 1917 (or early in 1918) described the girls working in France.
2. All were originally enrolled as rank and file 'workers'.
3. Army Service Nos 6174 Finny E.C., 38478; Fleury, and 6658 Fitzpatrick, J.E., all had an address in Dublin; 11189 Fowler, K.E., was from County Sligo; and 4312 Rawlinson, L.A., from Cork.
4. Army Service No. 4312 Rawlinson, L.A.
5. Dennant, pp. 81–2.
6. Hay, pp. 19–20.
7. *OCA Gazette*, January 1933. Vol. XV., No. 6, pp. 4–5. The writer was a former AA, Olive K Jordan.
8. Bidwell, p.18.
9. *Telegraph and Telephone Journal*, Vol. 5, 1918–19, p. 16. See also Anderson referring to hockey matches between signallers and camp men, p. 94.
10. Izzard, p. 165.
11. Grindlay, p. 36.
12. Imperial War Museum Oral Collection Ref 1995-07-25 interview of Army Service No. 1504 Beard, R.
13. Hay, p. 32. The accuracy and authenticity of her account continued to be enthusiastically endorsed by former members of the Corps for years in their own *QCA Gazette* even as late as March 1930.
14. Messenger, p. 256.
15. Hay, pp. 93–4.
16. Priestley, R.E., *Work of R.E. in the European War, 1914–1919. The Signals Service (France)* (London, 1921 Reprint, East Sussex: The Naval & Military Press, 2006) p. 250.
17. *Telegraph and Telephone Journal*, Vol. 3 1916–17, July 1917, p. 138.
18. *OCA Gazette*, January, 1933. Vol. XV., No. 6, pp. 4–5.
19. Hay, p. 66.
20. WO-95-85-8_06, St. Omer. See also: Bidwell, p. 261; Gwynne-Vaughan, p. 35.
21. 'The Hush-WAACs – The secret ladies of St Omer' at www.gchq.gov.uk/information/hush-waacs.
22. *History Ireland*, September/October 2017, Vol. 25, No. 5, p. 11.

23. John Ferris, 'The British Army and Signals Intelligence in the Field During the First World War' in *Journal of Intelligence and National Security*, Vol. 3, issue 4 1988. Online source: www.tandfonline.com/doi/abs/10.1080/02684528808431968

24. *The Irish Times*, 16 July 2016, p. 12.

25. WO-95-4046-4 War Diary, p. 16.

26. War Diary, p. 51 and p. 53: 'July 1, Hostile aircraft at 12.25 am and 4.20 am. All clear signalled at 1.50 am and 5.10 am. Also on July 31, 'Air raid during the night, no damage done'.

27. War Diary, p. 16.

28. Hay, p. 136.

29. Priestley, p. 249.

30. Izzard, p. 176.

31. Marwick, pp. 96–7, Terry, pp. 60–1 and Messenger, p. 263.

32. *OCA Gazette*, November, 1929, Vol. XI., No. 4, p. 5. The writer was a girl called B. Williams.

33. *OCA Gazette*, April 1938. Vol. XVII., No. 4, p. 2.

34. Stephen Ferguson, *The Post Office in Ireland* (Newbridge Ireland, Irish Academic Press, 2016) p. 310.

Chapter 5: What Was the Problem in Signals?

1. Alan Clinton, *Post Office Workers: A Trade Union and Social History* (London: 1984) p. 191.

2. Bidwell, pp. 25–6. See also Gwynne-Vaughan, p. 56. Dame Helen was Chief Controller of the WAAC in France at the time of the incident.

3. Priestley, pp. 59–61.

4. Brian N. Hall, *Communications and British Operations on the Western Front, 1914– 1918* (2017) p. 75. See also Ferguson, p. 266.

5. POST 30/4061B.

6. *Telegraph and Telephone Journal* Vol. 3I 1916–17, issue for October 1916, p. 7.

7. Priestley, .p. 58.

8. POST 30/4061B.

9. In January 1917 Brigadier-General J. Fowler was promoted to major-general.

10. War Studies – University of Birmingham

11. POST 31/99/1/2.

12. POST 31/99/2/22.

13. POST 31/99/1/2.

14. Both men dealt with the enrolment of male GPO operators for the army, 1915. See POST 30/4061B.

15. POST 31/99/2/2 to /2/39 cover the preliminary correspondence.

16. POST 31/99/3/5 to /3/27 cover the subsequent report and correspondence.

17. www.samhallas.co.uk/bt_museum/telegraph.htm explains this procedure.

18. Priestley, p. 14.

19. POST 31/99/2/4 typewritten letter from Ogilvie, dated 8 January1917.

20. Alan Clinton, *Post Office Workers: A Trade Union and Social History* (London: 1984) p. 242.

21. POST 31/99/2/7.

22. POST 31/99/2/18. The connection of a piece of electrical equipment to an overhead socket normally used for a light bulb was common practice in those days. For example, cables for electric Singer sewing machines for household use invariably came thus equipped in preference supplying a 'plug' for a wall socket.
23. POST 31/994/20, 21, 22, 26 and POST 31/99/7/4.
24. POST 31/99/2/4 and 2/5.
25. Marwick, p. 88.
26. As indicated in Terry, pp. 43–6.
27. Clinton, p. 75.
28. POST 31/99/3/28.
29. Later Sir (George) Evelyn Pemberton Murray (1880–1947) who served until 1934.
30. POST 31/99/3/29, letter dated 12 April 1917.
31. Army Service No. 457 for Castle, B confirms her first posting here on 21 May 1917. See also *OCA Gazette,* June 1933, Vol. XV., No. 11, p. 3.
32. Messenger, p.256. GHQ was in St. Omer up to March 1918.
33. Clinton, p. 75.
34. POST 31/99 4/9; POST 31/99/ 7/18 and POST 31/99/10/58.
35. POST 31/99/4/25.
36. POST 31/99/4 28.
37. POST 31/99/10/42.
38. POST 31/99/2/22 and 2/23.
39. POST 31/99/7/4 and 7/11.
40. POST 31/99/11/50.
41. POST 31/99/11/51.
42. Marwick, p. 83.
43. POST 31/99/11/57 See also Clinton pp. 471–4 for further information on the writer who was the GPO administrator, E. Raven , Esq., the Second Secretary, and PO spokesman later seeking moderate solutions to Union claims in 1927.
44. POST 31/9911/58.
45. Clinton, p. 244.
46. Clinton in his Appendix 22.
47. Clinton, p. 248.
48. Helen R. Glew, 'Women's Employment in the General Post Office, 1914–1939', PhD thesis, (2010) p. 212.
49. Clinton, p. 242.

Chapter 6: The Status of Signaller Forewomen
1. Grindlay, p. 57.
2. POST 31/99/4/27.
3. POST 31/99/12/2. See also Army Service No. 2050 Clarke, A.
4. *OCA Gazette,* November 1928, Vol. X., No 5, p.5.
5. POST 31/99/12/1.
6. POST 31/99 /10/5.
7. *OCA Gazette*, November 1928, Vol. X., p.5, on the occasion of her retirement.
8. Clinton, pp. 236–7.
9. POST 31/99/12/8 and 9.
10. POST 31/99/62 and 72.
11. POST 31/99/10/73.

12. POST 31/99/12/51.
13. POST 31/99/11/65.
14. POST 31/99/10/73.
15. POST 31/99/10/74.
16. POST 31/99/12/57.
17. POST 31/99/12/62.
18. POST 31/99/12/68.
19. POST 31/99/12/68.
20. POST 31/99/12/66 and 67.
21. POST 31/99/12/60 and 61.
22. Neither of these woman can be clearly identified owing to lost Amy Service Files.
23. POST 31/99/10/71 and UK WW1 Service Medal and Awards Rolls 1914–1920.
24. 1911 Census.
25. POST 31/99/12/51.
26. POST 31/99/12/77 to 81.
27. POST 31/99/12/76.
28. POST 31/99/12/74.
29. Colonel A. M. Ogilvie, C.B., Second Secretary of the Post Office and Director of Army Signals (Home Defence) *The Telegraph and Telephone*, Vol. 3, 1916–17, April 1917, p.87. Later awarded a KBE to become Col. Sir A.M. Ogilvie, KBE in *The Telegraph and Telephone* Vol. 6., January 1920, p.1.
30. Mary Izant remained single and died in Gloucestershire in 1951.
31. POST 31/99/9/14.
32. Terry, p. 43.
33. Army Service No. 39148 Hegarty, K.
34. *The Lionesse*, November 1962.

Chapter 7: Lighter Moments and Winds of Change

1. Marwick, p. 163.
2. *OCA Gazette*, August 1929, Vol. X1., No.1, p. 5.
3. Army Service No. 2040, Thornton, Clara. Grateful thanks to Tim Dale for the army photograph and for sharing details of Clara's postwar life.
4. Army Service No. 2037 Mycock, Lilian.
5. Grateful thanks to Peter Green for confirming the information on her postwar life.
6. Anderson, p. 97, describes a gold identity bracelet being presented to a Rouen Unit Administrator, Miss Christian Lorrimer. A similar one was given to signaller Crook, M., Army Service No. 2036.
7. Gwynne-Vaughan, p. 43.
8. Army Service No. 711, Fitzpatrick, K. She had served briefly in Boulogne in May 1917 before returning to the UK for a short period of sick leave before resuming duties.
9. Obituary of Mrs. H. E. Dalton, CBE, née Horniblow, *The Lionesse/OCA Gazette*, March–April 1950 issue.
10. Izzard, p. 179. See also WO-95-85-7.
11. Gwynne-Vaughan, p. 43.
12. https://web.archive.org/web/20190329153747/https://www.nsa.gov/Portals /70/documents/about/cryptologic-heritage/historical-figures-publications/

publications/pre-wwii/women-phone-operators-in-wwi-france.pdf Jill Frahm, 'Women Signallers in World War I France, pp. 9–10.

13. Elizabeth Cobbs, *The Hello Girls* (1917) p. 85. See also Samantha Philo-Gill, *The Women's Army Auxiliary Corps in France 1917–1921* (2017). The forthcoming published work of Brian N. Hall, Salford University, will add greatly to knowledge of AEF women in telecommunications.

14. Cobbs, p. 104.

15. Army Service No. 711, Fitzpatrick, K.

16. Izzard, p. 179.

17. Cobbs, p. 145.

18. Benson, S.P., *Counter Cultures: Saleswomen, Managers and Customers in American Department Stores 1890–1940* (University of Illinois Press:1986) p. 231, cited in Barbara Walsh, 'Chain Store Retailing in Ireland: A case study of F.W. Woolworth & Co. Ltd. 1914–2008, in *Journal of Historical Research in Marketing*, Vol. 6, No. 1, 2014, (Bingley, UK) pp. 98–115.

19. Army Service No. 2036 Crook, M. often repeated her personal experience of that night with the author.

20. *The Lioness*, 1977, No. 2, p. 30, 'about 2 am on the morning of November 11, a voice from GHQ Signals gave us word'.

21. Army Service No. 2036 Crook, M., her own reminiscences conveyed to author.

22. WO-95-4046-4 War Diary Vol. 28.

23. Cara Cullen, *The World Upturning: Elsie Henry's Wartime Diaries 1913–1919* (2013) p. 214.

24. John Dorney, Editor of the Irish Story website www.theirishstory.com and author of *Peace After the Final Battle: The Story of the Irish Revolution 1912–1924* (New Island Books, 2014) and *The Civil War in Dublin: The Fight for the Irish Capital, 1922–1924* (Irish Academic Press, (2017).

25. Peter Hart, *Mick, the real Michael Collins* (London: 2005) p. 203.

26. Extracted from an article by Elizabeth Sigh Johnston in the *East Fife Observer*, 5 December 1918. My thanks to the Cupar Library Duncan Institute for their assistance in sourcing this piece.

27. In 1967, Ada Gummersall, a former Hostel Forewoman in Boulogne and one of the earliest WAAC recruits to be posted to France in May 1917, reminisced in *The Lionesse*, February 1967, p. 4.

28. The non-stage name used as a UA was Christian Gray Lorrimer. Born in 1887 in Edinburgh, she is described in the 1911 Census as an actress visiting Chelsea, London. Employed by the D'Oyly Carte Opera Company from 1910 to 1916, there is a break in her stage career from 1917–1919 (her army service period) but she resumed her work in musical comedy with another company as 'Christine/Christian Lorimer' in 1920 to go on a tour of South Africa from 1920 to 1923. www.gsarchive. net/whowaswho/L/LorimerChristian.htm.

29. BBC Written Archive Centre, Reading and the Cathedral Collection of St Paul's Cathedral, London.

30. *OCA Gazette*, January 1921, No. 7, p. 3.

31. An address-book owned by Army Service No. 2036 Crook, M, used from December 1918 onwards contains the names and addresses of these participants, including Tom Purvis, with whom she kept in touch for at least two decades. My grateful thanks to Tim Dale for the photograph of these army colleagues.

32. Army Service No. 39520 Whyte, K. contains this relevant correspondence.
33. Borgonovo, John, *Spies, Informers and the "Anti-Sinn Féin Society", The Intelligence War in Cork City, 1920–1921* (Dublin: Irish Academic Press, 2007) p. 143.
34. *The Irish Times* digitized archives cite evidence contained in a cache of letters written by a British soldier serving as a private with the King's Shropshire Light Infantry regiment in Fermoy which reveal his assessment of their political leanings, subsequently confirmed by local historian Christy Roche. See www.irishtimes.com/culture/heritage/british-soldier-scandalised-by-1918-fermoy-1.2198908.
35. Borgonovo, p. 141.
36. Borgonovo, pp. 145–6.
37. Borgonovo, p. 101.
38. Borgonovo, p. 55 and p. 100. See also Mallow Local History: www.irelandxo.com.
39. Borgonovo, p. 100.
40. See also Borgonovo's earlier work: *Florence and Josephine O'Donoghue's War of Independence, "A Destiny That Shapes Our Ends"* (Dublin: Irish Academic Press, 2006).

Chapter 8: An Unsettling Atmosphere Gathers
1. This introduction to contributors in the first issue of *Good Housekeeping,* February 1922 was written by its male editor. *Good Housekeeping*, 95th Anniversary Celebration Issue, April 2017, p. 7.
2. The topic of mutiny among British foot-soldiers has been investigated by Peter Tatchell, https://leftfootforward.org/2014/08/ww1-the-hidden-story-of-soliders-mutinies- strikes-and-riots/.
3. Eaton, p. 103.
4. Eaton, p. 112.
5. Army Service No. 52883, McBeth, F. The Templemore Bombing School official title was the Irish Command School of Instruction for Officers & NCOs.
6. Army Service No. 52883 McBeth, F.
7. Army Service No. 1975, Black, T.M.
8. Army Service No. 42182 Kelly, E.
9. Army Service No. 1612 Ainscow, W.E.
10. Army Service No. 48430 Paine, L.V.A.
11. Army Service No. 2023 Jackson, F.M.
12. Army Service No. 2038 Robertson, M.F.
13. Army Service No. 1612 Ainscow, W.E.
14. Army Service No. 2054 Mullally, F.M. The other girls were 2048 Bayne, A., from Dungannon; 2058 Tanner, D., from Coleraine and 2059 Thistle, A., from Kells.
15. POST 31/99/21/25.
16. POST 31/99/21/27.
17. POST 31 99/19/4.
18. POST 31 99/19/12.
19. Army Service No. 2039 Thompson, E.
20. My grateful thanks to Stephen Cockbill and his wife for sharing the story of Ellen's postwar life.
21. Milnes quoted in *St.Martin's-le-Grand*, Vol., XXXIII., 1923, p. 87.

Chapter 9: The Roaring Twenties

1. Hattersley, p. vii.
2. Army Service No. 794 Lowe, F.E.
3. Army Service Nos 3931 Bradish, I; and 3932 Bradish, O.
4. Army Service No. 39471 Goode, B.
5. Army Service No. 2035 Nicole, A.
6. Army Service No. 2026 Mackenzie, M.S.
7. Army Service Nos 48430, Paine, S; 48431, Laird, S.; and 48432, Hilton, A.
8. *Irish Examiner*, 21 July 1919.
9. Gwynne-Vaughan, p. 70.
10. *OCA Gazette*, December 1920, No. 6, p. 1.
11. *OCA Gazette*, October 1921, Vol. II., No. 4, p. 1.
12. *OCA Gazette*, November 1925, Vol. VIII., p. 12.
13. Noakes, p. 87.
14. POST 31/99/7/17 had set out preliminary terms on 28 March 2017.
15. Borgonova, p. 151.
16. Clinton, p. 279 and p. 281.
17. Clinton, p. 282–3.
18. Post Office staff journal, *St. Martin's-le-Grand*, Vol., XXVII., 1917, p. 249.
19. Clinton, pp. 282–3.
20. Army Service No. 36124 Reid, B., and grateful thanks to Genny Norris for sharing her late father's account of the life of her great-aunt, Bessie Reid.
21. Army Service No. 2109 Hall G, *OCA Gazette*, Vol. XIV., No. 8, March 1932, p. 5. The notice was signed by Rebecca Beard, Army Service No. 1504, the Morse operator referred to in Chapter 4 Gertrude had served in Rouen with several Irish colleagues.
22. Nora Milnes, BSc., 'The Economic Position of Women' in *St.Martin's-le-Grand*, Vol., XXIII., 1923, pp. 86–7.
23. *OCA Gazette*, January 1921 No. 7, p. 1.
24. *OCA Gazette*, August 1920, No. 2, p. 3.
25. *OCA Gazette*, February 1921, No. 8, p. 4.
26. *OCA Gazette*, March 1923, Vol. IV., No. 9, p. 7.
27. *OCA Gazette*, April 1923, Vol. IV., No. 10, p. 7.
28. *OCA Gazette*, February 1928, Vol. III., No. 8, p. 2.

Chapter 10: Call of the Wild: The Assisted Passage Scheme

1. I. Grindlay, p. 46.
2. *OCA Gazette*, July 1920, No 1, p. 2.
3. *OCA Gazette*, April 1923 Vol. III., No. 10, p. 1.
4. *OCA Gazette*, December 1920, No. 6, p. 2.
5. Noakes, p. 90.
6. *The Church of Ireland Gazette*, 27 July 1917, p. 531.
7. Army Service No. 32818 Delaney, C.A. (her official first name Cecily rarely used when serving).
8. Army Service No. 36460 Flynn, E., holds a query raised over the date of a sailing ticket issued for April. The Army Service file for her sister Annie has not survived.
9. The Purser's list for RMS *Empress* of Britain which left Liverpool on 24 March 1921 cites their two names as both having OS 'permits'.

10. Mary Moynihan's letter from her address in Saskatchewan is spread over two issues of the *OCA Gazette:* July 1928, Vol. IX., No. 1, p. 6 and August 1928, Vol. IX., No. 2, p. 6.

11. *OCA Gazette*, September 1928, Vol. IX., No. 3, p. 4. That writer lived in Bulwark, Alberta. Married name, Theodora L. Witherby.

12. Army Service No. 49231 Cunningham, M; Army Service No. 18667 Cunningham, S.; and Army Service No. (missing file) for Cunningham, B.

13. Fionnuala Walsh, p. 311.

14. *OCA Gazette*, December 1920, No. 6, p. 6.

15. Army Service No. 46093 Benson, E.

16. Army Service No. 1695 Minns, D. in *OCA Gazette*, December, 1920, p. 2.

17. *OCA Gazette*, November, 1925, Vol. VIII.,, No. 5, p. 12.

18. *OCA Gazette*, March 1930 Vol. XI., No. 8, p. 4. Extracted from 'Opportunities for well-educated women in Canada', by A.C. Franklin.

19. Barbara Walsh, *Roman Catholic Nuns in England and Wales 1800–1937* (2002).

20. Fionnuala Walsh, p. 311–12.

21. *OCA Gazette,* October 1931, Vol. XVI., No. 3, p. 4.

22. Army Service No 39027, Blain, G.

Chapter 11: Life 'Down Under' or Adventures at Home?

1. J. Rich, poem sent to *OCA Gazette*, April 1923, Vol. III., No. 10, p. 8.

2. Army Service No. 1630 Hanna, M.A and Army Service No. 2043 Dennett, W.

3. Grateful thanks to Martha Hanna's daughter Betty Tyzzer and grand-nephew William Hart for generously sharing photographs and detailed accounts of her life in Ireland and Australia.

4. Army Service No. 2043 Dennett, W. My grateful thanks goes also to Winifred Dennett's son-in-law Jack Flett and grandson Douglas for their great kindness in sharing photographs and many details of Winifred's life in Australia.

5. Army Service No. 1630 Hanna, M.A.

6. According to Winifred's family history, the plots were too small to be viable.

7. Army Service No. 453740 Nevin J.M. Grateful thanks for the generous assistance of her daughter Mary and grandson Ian Hart who have shared an account of her life and photographs

8. Army Service No. 2036 Crook, M.

9. *OCA Gazette*, September 1923, Vol. IV., No. 3, p. 4.

Chapter 12: Armistice Days in Dublin

1. Gwynne-Vaughan, p. 76.

2. The author has drawn on her article for *History Ireland*, November/December, 2018 issue, for this chapter.

3. *OCA Gazette*, December 1924, Vol. V., No. 6, p. 2.

4. *History Ireland*, Spring 1996, Vol. 4.

5. *History Ireland*, Spring issue No. 1, 1999.

6. *OCA Gazette*, January 1928, Vol. VIII., No. 7, p. 7.

7. *OCA Gazette*, December 1937, Vol. XVI. No. 12.

8. *OCA Gazette*, February 1939, Vol. XVIII., No. 2, p. 3.

9. *OCA Gazette,* January 1939, Vol. XVIII., No. 1, pp. 5–6.

10. *OCA Gazette*, October, November, December 1939, Vol. XVIII., No. 10, p. 4.

11. *OCA Gazette*, January–February 1942, p. 2.

12. *QMAAC & ATS Comrade Association Gazette*, November-December, 1948, p. 23.

Bibliography

Primary Sources

BT Heritage and Archives, London
Cathedral Collection of St Paul's Cathedral, London
Imperial War Museum, London
Library Archives of Alexandra College, Dublin
National Army Museum Archives, London
QMAAC Army Service Files, 1917–1920. National Archives, London
QMAAC War Diaries 1917–1919. National Archives, London
WRAC Association Archives, Winchester (Research access to WRAC members'
    digitized *OCA Gazettes* and subsequent issues is available on request)

Periodicals

Alexandra College Magazine, December 1917
The Anglo Celt, 10 October 1918
Daily Mail, 1918
East Fife Observer, January 1919
Good Housekeeping, February 1922, first issue
History Ireland, 1996, 1999, 2017
The Irish Times, 1917, 1924, 2016
QMAAC Old Comrades' Gazette, 1920–1942 (incorporated into *QMAAC &
    ATS Comrades Gazette* 1950)
The Lioness, 1951–1970
St. Martin's-le-Grand Post Office Journals, 1916–1923 (GPO London)
Telegraph and Telephone Journals, 1916–1923 (London GPO North C)

Books and journal articles

Adie, Kate, *Fighting on the Home Front* (Hodder, London, 2014)
Anderson, Agnes, *"Johnnie" Q.M.A.A.C* (Heath Cranton, London, 1920)
Benson, S. P., *Counter Cultures: Saleswomen, Managers and Customers in American
    Department Stores 1890–1940* (University of Illinois Press, Illinois, 1986)
Bidwell, Brigadier Shelford, *The Women's Royal Army Corps* (Leo Cooper Ltd.,
    London, 1977)
Borgonovo, John, *Spies, Informers and the "Anti-Sinn Féin Society": The
    Intelligence War in Cork City, 1920–1921* (Irish Academic Press, Dublin, 2007)

Clinton, Alan, *Post Office Workers: A Trade Union and Social History* (Allen and Unwin, London, 1984)

Cobbs, Elizabeth, *The Hello Girls* (Harvard University Press, Harvard, Massachusetts, and London, 2017)

Cullen, Cara, *The World Upturning: Elsie Henry's Wartime Diaries 1913–1919*, (Merrion Press, Dublin and Portland Or., 2013)

Dorney, John, *Peace After the Final Battle: The Story of the Irish Revolution 1912–1924*, (New Island Books, Dublin, 2014)

Dorney, John, *The Civil War in Dublin: The Fight for the Irish Capital, 1922–1924*, (Irish Academic Press, Dublin and Portland, Oregon, *2017*). *Also as* editor of the Irish Story website www.theirishstory.com

Durney, James, *In a Time of War. Kildare 1914–1918* (Merrion Press, Sallins, 2014)

Ferguson, Stephen, *The Post Office in Ireland* (Irish Academic Press, Newbridge, 2016)

Ferris, John, 'The British Army and Signals Intelligence in the Field During the First World War' in *Journal of Intelligence and National Security* Volume 3, issue 4 (New York, 1988)

Grindlay, I, *Ripples from the Ranks* (Erskine Macdonald, Ltd., London, 1918)

Gwynne-Vaughan, Dame Helen, *Service with the Army* (London, New York and Melbourne, 1941)

Hall, Brian N., *Communications and British Operations on the Western Front, 1914–1918*, (Cambridge University Press, Cambridge, 2017)

Hattersley, Roy, *Borrowed Time: The Story of Britain Between the Wars* (Little Brown, London, 2007)

Hay, Marjorie, *On Wacctive Service* (The Plymouth Press, Whitfield and Newman Ltd., Plymouth, 1919)

Izzard, Molly, *A Heroine in Her Time: The Life of Dame Helen Gwynne-Vaughan, 1879–1967* (Macmillan, London, 1969)

Kelly, Laura, *Irishwomen in Medicine 1880s–1920s* (Manchester University Press, Manchester, 2012)

Marwick, Arthur, *Woman at War 1914–1918* (Fontana Paperbacks, London, 1977)

Messenger, Charles, *Call to Arms. The British Army 1914–18* (Cassell, London, 2005)

Naughton, Lindie, *Lady Icarus* (Ashfield Press, Dublin, 2004)

Newman, Vivien, *We Also Served: The Forgotten Women of the First World War* (Pen and Sword Books, Barnsley, 2014)

Noakes, Lucy, *Women in the British Army: War and the Gentle Sex, 1907–1948* (Routledge, London, 2006)

Philo-Gill, Samantha, *The Women's Army Auxiliary Corps in France 1917–1921* (Pen and Sword Books, Barnsley, 2017)

Priestley, R. E., *Work of R.E in the European War, 1914–1919. The Signals Service (France)* (London, 1919 and reprint by The Naval and Military Press East Sussex, 2006)

Reilly, Eileen, 'Women and Voluntary War Work' in Adrian Gregory and Senia Paseta (Eds.) *Ireland and the Great War* (Manchester and New York, 2002)

Terry, Roy, *Women in Khaki* (Columbus Books, London, 1988)

Walsh, Barbara, *Roman Catholic Nuns in England and Wales 1800–1937* (Irish Academic Press, Dublin and Portland, Oregon, 2002)

War Office, *Statistics of the Military Effort of the British Empire during the Great War 1914–1918* (War Office, London, March 1922)

Unpublished theses

Glew, Helen R., 'Women's Employment in the General Post Office, 1914–1939', PhD thesis, University of London, Institute of Historical Research, 2010

Gould, Jennifer Margaret, 'The Women's Corps: The establishment of women's military services in Britain', PhD thesis, University College, London, 1988

Dennant, Lynda, 'Women at the Front during the First World War: the politics of class, gender and empire'. PhD thesis, University of Warwick, 1998

Walsh, Fionnuala, 'The Impact of the Great War on Women in Ireland 1914–1919', PhD thesis, Trinity College, Dublin, 2016

Internet sources

Ferris, John, at www.tandfonline.com/doi/abs/10.1080/02684528808431968

Frahm, Jill, 'Women Signallers in World War I France' at www.nsa.gov/Portals/70/documents

The Irish Story at www.theirishstory.com

War Studies, *Lions led by Donkeys*, research project University of Birmingham, at www.birmingham.ac.uk/research/activity/warstudies/research/projects/lionsdonkeys/index.aspx

www.gchq.gov.uk/information/hush-waacs

www.petertatchellfoundation.org/ww1-the-hidden-story-of-soldiers-mutinies-strikes-riots/

Index